ACKNOWLEDGMENT

DNV GL - Business Assurance would like to acknowledge the invaluable contributions and support of the people who helped produce Practical Leadership for Sustainable Business: Health and Safety Management:

Project Steering Team

The project team was advised and directed by a three-person team of Senior Managers from DNV GL - Business Assurance. These gentlemen served as the Project Steering Team.

Mark Line – Business Development Director, DNV GL - Business Assurance

Richard Stolk – Director of Division Asia & Australia DNV GL - Business Assurance

Mauricio Venturin – Director of Division Americas, DNV GL - Business Assurance

External Review Team

DNV GL engaged a team of industry professionals to serve as the External Review Team for the book. These people gave their time and expertise to review materials and provide feedback to ensure that the knowledge presented in the book was consistent with current, leading edge thinking and that the approach was engaging and attractive to the reader. DNV GL is grateful for their assistance and contributions.

Mark Clark - Corporate Director EHS, Republic Steel

Kathy DeVries - Principal for KDV Performance Solutions, LLC

Dr. Ronald G. Dotson EdD - Associate Professor, Eastern Kentucky University, Occupational Safety and Health Programs Coordinator

Bryan Makinen - Director of Environmental Health & Safety/Risk Management & Insurance for Eastern Kentucky University

Malcolm Ian Staves - Group Health and Safety Director, L'Oreal and Chairman of Conference Board of European Health and Safety Council

Contributing Authors

Practical Leadership for Sustainable Business: Safety and Health Management represents the collected experience and expertise of several professionals. Various authors contributed to the content and layout of the book. The project team would like to express our appreciation to the following persons:

Chapter	Authors
The Sustainable Organization	Bryan Makinen - Director of Environmental Health & Safety/Risk Management & Insurance for Eastern Kentucky University, USA
The Role of Leadership	Chris Urwin – Associate Director UK, DNV GL
Basic Concepts of Safety and Health Management Systems	Eric Roos - Principal Consultant DNV GL, Indonesia
Building an Improvement Culture	Thomas Valtier - Business Development Manager and Global Service Responsible for ISRS DNV GL – Business Assurance, France
Risk Management	Cheryl Stahl – Principal Consultant DNV GL, USA
Stakeholder Engagement	Dave Knight – Director, USA & Canada Sustainability, DNV GL - Business Assurance
Behavior Based Safety	Larry Walker - Principal Trainer & Consultant on behalf of DNV GL - Business Assurance, USA
Sustainable Supply Chain Management	Thomas Andresen Gosselin – Divisional Sustainability Manager for the Americas, DNV GL – Business Assurance, USA

Chapter	Authors
Task Competencies, Analysis and Training	Kees Morsman - Director of Training & Assessment Services, DNV GL - Business Assurance, USA
Change Management	Mark Fisher – Associate Director, Manchester Advisory Services, DNV GL - Oil and Gas, UK
Planned Inspections	Bill Lacy – Independent Contractor on behalf of DNV GL - Business Assurance, USA
Emergency Preparedness and Response	Jerry Baird – Principal Consultant/Auditor DNV GL - Business Assurance, USA
Learning From Events	Larry Walker - Principal Trainer & Consultant on behalf of DNV GL - Business Assurance, USA
Reviewing Performance	Ismael Camacho - Vice-President Step Change Innovations Corporation, USA
Closing the Circle - Achieving Sustainability	Michael Van Alphen – Principal Auditor and Trainer, DNV GL - Business Assurance, The Netherlands René de Vries – Senior Consultant, Assurance Services, DNV GL - Business Assurance, The Netherlands

PRACTICAL LEADERSHIP FOR SUSTAINABLE BUSINESS
Table of Contents

Chapter	Title	Page
1	The Sustainable Organization	12
2	The Role of Leadership	27
3	Basic Concepts of Safety and Health Management Systems	46
4	Building an Improvement Culture	71
5	Risk Management	90
6	Stakeholder Engagement	116
7	Behavior Based Safety	142
8	Sustainable Supply Chain Management	160
9	Task Competencies, Analysis and Training	179
10	Change Management	211
11	Planned Inspections	242
12	Emergency Preparedness and Response	264
13	Learning from Events	282
14	Reviewing Performance	307
15	Closing the Circle: Achieving Sustainability	322
16	The Future	340

Meet Lisa & Carlos

Lisa
Health and Safety Manager

Lisa is a dedicated professional who has the best interests of her company and its stakeholders at heart.

Lisa's primary concerns at work are centered on protecting the health and safety of 350 employees. She understands her role as primary advisor to management and tries to equip and support line management in the proper implementation of health and safety programs.

Her specific objectives are:
- To ensure that health and safety programs are implemented appropriately,
- To ensure compliance to all regulatory and internal requirements,
- To train and inspire line managers to accept health and safety, and
- To be an effective advisor to leadership on the continual improvement of health and safety performance.

Away from work, Lisa's role is as a wife and mother of two young children. She enjoys camping and hiking and usually spends her leisure time with her family in the great outdoors. Lisa earned the honor of captain of her university rowing team and led her crew to a first place finish in the national championships.

Carlos
Line Production Supervisor

Carlos was promoted to a supervisory position after a few years as an operator on the floor. He is a very conscientious leader and wants to contribute to the success of the company as well as develop his own career.

At work, Carlos is concerned about:
- Meeting his department's production and quality targets,
- Engaging and building relationships with his workers,
- Controlling costs,
- Finding innovative ways to improve his department's performance, and
- Keeping his seventeen direct reports healthy and safe at work and at home.

Carlos enjoys playing soccer with his friends and watching baseball on the weekends. He is working to restore a classic automobile. He is very energetic and that energy transfers over to his job.

Carlos is open to any help he can get. He knows he needs critique to improve.

Meet Henry

Henry
Vice President of Operations

Henry manages operations for twelve production facilities with a total employee population of approximately 3,300. His primary concern is ensuring the commercial success of the company, but, because he came from a site operations background, he is keenly aware of the responsibility of leaders to provide for the health and safety of all employees.

Henry has just finished leading a three-day meeting of all plant site managers as they developed an operational plan for the coming fiscal year. In addition to the group's focus on expanding production and market share, there were sessions devoted to quality improvement and health and safety. All the topics on the agenda were arranged under the banner of sustainability and a new mantra, "Building a Sustainable Future."

Henry understands the vital role health and safety programs play in sustainable business performance and their impact on production and economic success. He challenged his team to the following related objectives:

- Step out and put the words in the health and safety policy statement into action.
- Demonstrate by your individual actions your belief and commitment to improving health and safety performance.
- Educate your employees on how to carry out their health and safety responsibilities.
- Move your health and safety focus to leading indicators and activities that drive continual improvement.

Henry is considering retirement in a couple years. In his spare time, he plays golf and serves on the board of directors for his alma mater. Henry and his wife have three grown children and are concerned about leaving a better world for them.

Because of his pending retirement, Henry is also looking for a potential successor.

Joe
Plant General Manager

Joe has been with the company for over twenty-two years, starting as an operator and serving as a supervisor, maintenance manager, and plant operations manager. He has been the general manager for four years.

Joe attended the meeting led by his boss, Henry. He understands and believes in the direction his company is taking under the banner of sustainability. He also understands the vital role health and safety activities play in achieving the company's objectives. He is now in the process of designing a means of communicating the sustainability effort to his employees and engaging them in the process of driving success.

He has several concerns around which he has to manage:

- Production
- Cost control
- Efficiency
- Stakeholder demands and perception
- Protection of the environment
- Health and safety performance

Joe and his wife are "empty-nesters," having raised four children of whom he is justifiably proud. He enjoys gardening in his spare time and has served as president of the local orchid society. He is also involved in civic and community activities, currently serving as a city councilman.

Joe is committed to the effort. He just needs to know how to do it.

Meet Joe

WHAT IS THIS BOOK ABOUT?

Who Are We and Why Do We Care?

The people you have just met could be any of you; typical human beings who work hard for a living, have challenging responsibilities in running commercial operations, and are deeply committed to doing their jobs well. They want essentially the same things from life as you do. They want to earn a good living and enjoy everything life has to offer. They want to be respected by their community, including those with whom they work. They want health and happiness, family and friends. Finally, they want to leave the world in a better place than they found it.

Every day, you, Henry, Joe, Lisa, and Carlos, go to work knowing what the job requires, but also understanding that each day brings new, unanticipated challenges with which you must deal. Now comes the challenge of sustainability.

You have heard of your organization's commitment to sustainability or sustainable business development. You have seen various bits of information in e-mails and publications about sustainability. You have heard your leadership use the terms in meetings. What you haven't completely understood is exactly what the terms sustainability and sustainable business development mean and how the organization's related efforts will affect your job. Because your colleagues have similar questions, a meeting is arranged for the purpose of more fully explaining the initiative.

Although the topic of sustainability seems to be a bit complex, the explanation is rather practical and easy to understand. Your organization has developed a simple model demonstrating that the sustainability initiative is comprised of three specific concerns:

- Environmental Concerns – resource efficiency, product stewardship, life-cycle management, emissions and waste reduction, clean air and water, etc.
- Economic Concerns – innovation, risk management, margin improvement, growth, job creation, shareholder return, capital efficiency, etc.
- Social Concerns – diversity, human rights, community outreach, labor relations, business ethics, regulatory compliance, health and safety, etc.

How Do We Do It?

The presentation makes it abundantly clear that everyone in the organization has responsibilities relating to these concerns. Leadership also reinforces its commitment that these responsibilities will be translated into practical actions, clearly defined for each person, and that adequate training will be provided to enable each person to carry out those actions effectively.

Although you are concerned about the whole of sustainability, you realize that to try to address all three concerns and their related components at once would be a rather difficult, if not impossible, effort.

Your organization's leadership has invested in a comprehensive, third-party assessment of the current status of sustainability-related programs and activities. The assessment has revealed significant strengths in many areas, but has also helped the organization to prioritize efforts in other areas where deficiencies were noted. One such area is health and safety.

Health and Safety

You and your colleagues have always believed strongly in health and safety and are committed to doing your best to drive those efforts. No one is going to argue that health and safety efforts are a bad idea; however, translating your efforts into practical actions can be problematic.

Our Purpose

The purpose of this book is two-fold:

- To show how well-managed health and safety contribute to an organization's sustainability efforts.
- To provide practical knowledge, tools, and techniques to enable you to drive continual improvement in your organization's health and safety performance.

Simply put, the purpose is to support your continual improvement process for the health and safety of your organization and of your stakeholders.

The authors have chosen to include a story line in the book. We have created four fictional characters, whom you have already met, and who will be telling their story of struggle for continual health and safety improvement. We believe most, if not all of you, will be able to relate to these characters, their specific concerns and perspectives, and their satisfaction when efforts pay off.

We hope you find that this is a useful handbook for continual improvement of your organization's health and safety performance. You will find personal planning pages at the end of each chapter, including questions to prompt your critical thinking about the subject in the respective chapter and an action plan format. Reading this book can help you; however, it is what you do with what you learn that can really produce results and drive sustainability in your health and safety program. It is our hope that you will take advantage of the planning pages to develop your way forward and contribute to that sustainability.

THE ULTIMATE OBJECTIVE
Safeguarding Life, Property, and the Environment

Henry, the VP of Operations, has just completed a rather intensive annual planning session with his twelve plant managers. Although there were many topics of discussion, they were all organized around the Building a Safe and Sustainable Future banner.

Henry announced a strategic initiative to improve performance in several areas and strongly stressed his personal desire to see diligent efforts made toward improving health and safety performance.

Joe was one of the participants in Henry's meeting and came away with a renewed commitment to ensure health and safety in his own plant. He resolves not to wait for further direction from corporate, but to start working with his own staff to drive improvement. A few days following the meeting, Joe arranges a meeting with key leaders in his own operation.

Joe opens the meeting with an overview of the results of the plant manager's meeting, the Building a Safe and Sustainable Future initiative, and then expresses his own opinion that health and safety performance is a good place to start.

The comments from most managers are in support of Joe's agenda. A couple want to redirect the conversation to the improvement of market share and profit margin, but Joe is successful in demonstrating how improved health and safety performance can also have a positive effect on financial results.

Lisa, the Health and Safety Manager, smiles inwardly as she listens to the conversation. After a few minutes, Joe asks her for her input.

"As you might expect, I fully support Joe's initiative, and I think if we do this right, our efforts will make for a healthier plant in all aspects."

Although front-line supervisors were not included in Joe's meeting, Carlos, a supervisor, hears some things through the grapevine that both encourage him and raise some questions. He runs into Joe one morning as they were entering the plant and asks for some of the manager's time. "I have a few minutes right now," Joe says. "Want to get a cup of coffee?"

"Sure," Carlos answers, "I only have a couple minutes myself, but I would like to talk with you about the initiative to improve health and safety performance. It is something about which we all feel strongly."

"So do I, Carlos. We all have to develop a vision, set some goals and objectives, and design a plan to achieve them. You and your people will play an important role. Tell you what; we really don't have time to go into detail right now. How about if you and I have lunch together and discuss it? Noon in my office okay with you?"

"I'll be there."

Joe invites Lisa to join them for the meeting. Together, they go over the results of the discussions in the manager's meeting and ask Carlos for his input.

"I like what I have heard and I want to be a part of it. Tell me, how do we do it?" Lisa tells Carlos there will be a meeting soon to present the plan to all employees and that there is an effort to organize training for everyone to ensure they are equipped to carry out the plan.

"Until then," Lisa says, "here is a book I found that will provide you some valuable information and some tools. The upcoming training will cover the details, but this will be a good start."

"Thanks, Lisa!"

"No. Thank you, Carlos," says Joe. "I think you will be a key person in this effort. In fact, I want you on my planning team. Okay?"

"I'm willing. Just let me know when! Meanwhile, I'm going to read this book."

As Carlos leaves the office, Joe and Lisa look at each other and smile. They both know the future is going to be a little rocky, but they also know they are off to a good start.

THE SUSTAINABLE ORGANIZATION

Chapter 1

THE SUSTAINABLE ORGANIZATION

> **CHAPTER OBJECTIVES**
> 1. To introduce the concept of sustainability or sustainable business development.
> 2. To illustrate how health and safety concerns fit within an overall approach of sustainability.
> 3. To demonstrate how effectively managed health and safety systems contribute to the health of the organization.

SOME LEADERS ARE SKEPTICAL

Don is the sales and marketing manager for Joe's operation. His primary concerns are capturing more market shares and expanding revenue from existing customers. His annual performance bonus is calculated, at least in part, on improved financial results. He is concerned that new initiatives, like this sustainability thing, will require significant financial investment and could negatively impact profit. One morning, Don stops by Joe's office and asks for a minute of his time.

"Joe, can I have a couple minutes?"

"Come on in. I have to finish this e-mail, but I'll be with you in just a bit."

When Joe's e-mail is finished, he turns his attention to Don.

"What can I do for you?"

"I just want to ask you about this sustainability initiative we have heard about. What's going on with it? Is this the next program?"

"No, Don. Sustainability will become the way we do business. It is not a program that will go away. Our leadership believes—and I agree—that it is the way we are going to thrive and survive in the future. Why? Do you have some concerns about it?"

"Well, I don't really know a lot about it, so I'm not sure how I feel."

"I understand that. A lot of our people feel that way. I am going to take our monthly management meeting next week to cover it in some detail. I think you will feel much more comfortable after that."

"I'll reserve judgment until then, but my initial reaction was that this is just another management program that will require a lot of resources and probably be replaced by something else in a year or two. It's happened before."

"Yes, it has. However, I really don't think sustainability can ever go away. Not if we are going to even be here in a few years. Look, Don, I understand your concerns. I even asked myself if this initiative could actually improve our overall performance or if it was just something we had to do regardless. I am convinced it can improve the health of our business. Tell you what; let me give you a copy of some information I found on the business case for sustainability. Its focus is health and safety, but it gives a good overall description of the potential results when sustainability is done right. We are going to also focus on health and safety improvement in the short term. I think you will be pleased with how improved health and safety performance can contribute to improved financial performance."

"Okay, I'll take a look at it and keep an open mind."

"Thanks, Don. If you have any questions along the way, please ask."

"Will do. Thanks for your time."

What is Sustainability?

There are many different terms used by organizations to describe sustainability. Among others, the terms sustainable business development, corporate social responsibility, responsible entrepreneurship, creating shared value, and corporate citizenship are commonly used. They all tend to mean similar things. They refer to how organizations respond to and seize opportunities related to people, planet, and profit.

There are three spheres or dimensions of sustainability illustrated in Figure 1.1.

Sustainability is not a thing. It is a way. Sustainable business development is the process by which organizations "meet the needs of the present without compromising the ability of future generations to meet their own needs"

(Bruntland Commission, 1987)

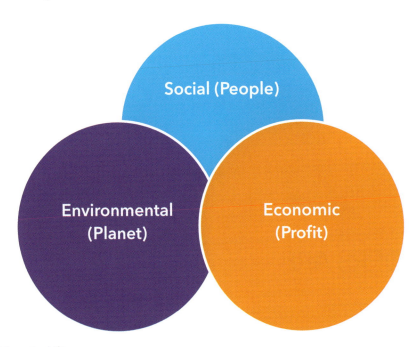

Figure 1.1 Dimensions of Sustainability

Each of these dimensions consists of related areas of concern. In general, they include:

Environmental Dimension – resource efficiency, product stewardship, waste management, responsible energy management, pollution prevention, life-cycle management, etc.

Economic Dimension – innovation, risk management, growth, margin improvement, cost savings, profit, shareholder return, etc.

Social Dimension – human rights, labor relations, human resource retention, equal opportunity, outreach, health and safety, etc.

"Those companies that wait to be forced into action or who see it solely in terms of reputation management or CSR (corporate social responsibility), will do too little too late and may not even survive."

Paul Polman
Chief Executive, Unilever

"Companies with an eye on their triple bottom line outperform their less fastidious peers on the stock market."

The Economist

"Corporate citizenship is simply the way we do business. Why? Because there is business value in doing so and there are unwelcome costs in taking a narrow, blinkered approach."

Sir Mark Moody-Stuart
Chairman, Anglo American

A more recent definition of sustainability is found in the ISO26000, 2010 standard.

"Sustainable development is about integrating the goals of a high quality of life, health and prosperity with social justice and maintaining the earth's capacity to support life in all its diversity."

ISO also refers to sustainability as "the ability to maintain or develop performance in the long term." It can be thought of as the way business survives.

Why Sustainability?

There is a clear link between business performance and sustainability and organizations that have sustainability initiatives tend to perform better.

Sustainable business performance expands the judgment of success beyond investors and managers to include all those who are affected by the business, including the stakeholders. It is no longer enough for organizations to think only about profit – stakeholders are demanding a broader approach that includes the social and environmental impacts of the business as well as its economic results.

The organization that understands and effectively manages the synergistic relationship of social, environmental, and economic concerns not only improves its "triple bottom line" today, but also significantly improves the potential for that performance to continue long into the future.

Global Megatrends

The world is changing and being shaped by a collection of so-called megatrends. A megatrend is a phenomenon that will significantly impact the way the world operates and how individuals live their lives. The most commonly recognized megatrends are pictured in Figure 1.2.

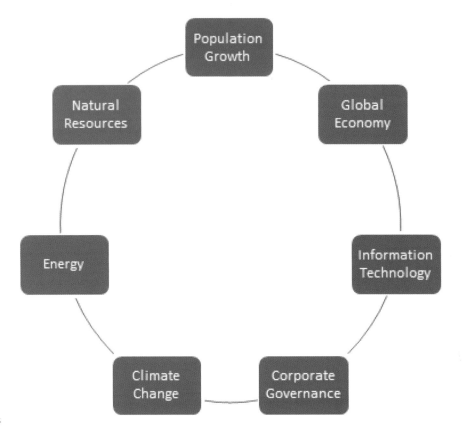

Figure 1.2 Megatrends

These trends are inextricably linked and their impacts on business, individually and collectively, must be incorporated into any organization's strategic planning. These trends will bring increasing risk, uncertainty, and challenges that must be managed.

These challenges will be in the form of:
- Price increases and volatility
- New and stricter regulations (and related costs of compliance)
- Changing consumer demands for products and services
- Resource constraints that affect production
- Stakeholder demands for increased due diligence in the management of resources

However, these trends also bring business opportunity. That opportunity may come in the form of:
- More efficient use of resources resulting in savings to operating costs.
- Increased attention and respect from the market place, resulting in increased sales and market share.
- Improved innovation, resulting in development of new revenue streams and more efficient processes.

Focus on Safety and Health: a Megatrend

The move to sustainability is helping to focus attention internationally on health and safety performance. Several safety-focused sustainability movements are on the rise and are gaining attention in standards writing industries such as the American Society of Safety Engineers (ASSE), American Industrial Hygiene Association (AIHA), and the Institution of Occupational Safety and Health (IOSH). These are a few of the organizations in the United States interested in creating and maintaining a dialogue relative to health and safety in sustainability. These three organizations have collaborated in the creation of the Center for Safety & Health Sustainability (CSHS) in an attempt to have a voice in the international conversation on sustainability and corporate social responsibility (Seabrook). On an international level, the United Nations Safe Planet campaign, a part of the sustainability initiative, is promoting dialogue regarding risks of hazardous chemicals and wastes. International organizations such as Xerox, Global Foundries, and Kimberly Clark have incorporated health and safety as a significant part of their sustainability initiatives. A review of corporate websites in industries from construction to food, space exploration, and manufacturing across the globe reveals that the vast majority of organizations have high-profile sustainability initiatives and that they have incorporated health and safety as key ingredients in those initiatives.

Many countries around the world are taking similar initiatives, often as a consequence of government initiatives or due to economical agreements or pressure from global customers.

The purpose of this chapter is to help you understand how effective health and safety management links to business concerns and how it can be leveraged for sustainable business performance.

Safety and Health in Your Organization

Is your organization sustainable? What does it take to become sustainable in today's marketplace? Are health and safety concerns integrated into the sustainable mission of your organization? How can a local site be a sustainable leader in the overall organization?

Health and safety concerns affect every organization economically. Corporate profitability is a necessity that local management and health and safety professionals cannot ignore. In fact, we can use this to our advantage when leveraging for our voices to be heard at the executive level. All organizations are part of an ever-growing global marketplace. To survive, organizations must continuously re-evaluate their operations in order to compete with and stand out among peers. Familiar certifications, such as ISO 14001 (environmental), ISO/TS-16949 (quality) and OHSAS 18001 (safety), are becoming necessary requirements for securing business. This is evidenced where health and safety key performance indicators are becoming requirements of large contractors in business sectors such as:

- Federal, state and local government
- Tier I, Tier II, and Tier III automotive suppliers
- International parts and raw materials suppliers
- Technology corporations

The ability of organizations to do business in today's marketplace depends, at least in part, on their health and safety performance. Organizations that cannot demonstrate a systematic and comprehensive health and safety effort will be at a distinct disadvantage.

The increasing acceptance of the Occupational Health and Safety Assessment Series (OHSAS18001) as an international safety standard is driving organizations to invest in a more proactive approach in order to demonstrate due diligence to the marketplace.

Developing regulatory schemes give more attention to an organization's health and safety management system than to physical conditions and lagging indicators.

Successful organizations have realized that all stakeholders need to buy into the overall sustainability initiative. It is time for health and safety to take its rightful place in this discussion and become commonplace in sustainability conversations.

In the not too distant past, health and safety were discussed in the boardroom primarily in terms of lagging indicators (frequency rates) and mandates to health and safety professionals to do something to improve performance. Today, we can see more discussion among senior leadership of leading indicators for health and safety and the incorporation of health and safety into strategic planning. Senior leadership in prudent organizations is becoming more aware of its role in establishing a proper organizational culture and a robust health and safety management system. Health and safety initiatives are becoming recognized as contributing to positive economic performance rather than as merely cost centers. Sustainability initiatives are at least partially responsible for driving this phenomenon.

Organizations that have health and safety as part of their core mission can reap benefits beyond lower incident rates. These include:

- Enhancement of the company image
- Reduced cost of loss
- Improved morale and worker retention
- Increase external legitimacy
- Creation of competitive advantage opportunities

Our friends Henry, Joe, Lisa, and Carlos are all committed to protecting the health and safety of their organization's stakeholders. However, they also realize that health and safety efforts have to be balanced with the commercial concerns of the organization. Including health and safety as an equal partner in the sustainability initiative means that health and safety have a place at the strategic planning table. The synergies of the various sustainability components and the dynamics of their interaction can be carefully considered, resulting in more robust, accurate, and effective planning.

There is a cost for health and safety, but as the old automobile mechanic said about changing the oil filter in your car, "You can pay me now or you can pay me later." He was making the point that it might be prudent to invest in an oil and filter change for your automobile now in order to avoid major repair costs to your engine later. There are many organizations that have made budget decisions for health and safety based solely on initial cost without understanding or appreciating the risks involved. Unfortunately, many of them have paid a much heftier price later.

How Does This Affect My Job?

Sustainability and the related health and safety focus sounds great. Why do I need to know this and what am I being asked to do?

A 2012 study conducted by the Aberdeen Group revealed that EH&S (Environment, Health, and Safety) professionals shoulder the responsibility for the "sustainability strategy" in their respective organizations (see Figure 1.3) (Ismail, 2012).

the health and safety of employees. In prudent organizations, that responsibility lies with line management while the EH&S staff serve as internal consultants to equip and support line management to carry out their health and safety responsibilities. Examples of such requirements for senior leadership can be found in The Role of Leadership chapter.

Effective, health and safety activities must be integrated into line management. This means that each individual in an organization, from the CEO to the hourly worker, has a role to play in health and safety.

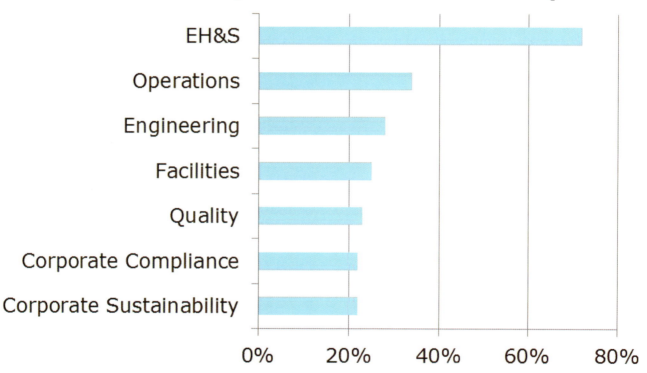

Source: Environmental, Health and Safety: Going Beyond Compliance, by N. Ismail, 2012, Aberdeen Group.

Figure 1.3 Aberdeen Group Study

While it may be true that EH&S professionals are key persons to implementation of a sustainability strategy, it is unwise to consider them as having sole responsibility. As with any initiative that has the potential to significantly impact the whole of a business, all stakeholders should participate in its development, implementation, and continual improvement. Likewise, it is unwise to assume that the EH&S staff has the sole responsibility for

Requirements for their participation should be developed in writing, communicated effectively, supported with training, and monitored as part of personal performance.

New Risk Reality

Risk management in any corporation is a complex array of reviewing threats and protecting a company from fortuitous loss. The chapter on Risk Management provides guidance on effective means of implementing a robust risk management process in your organization. The world of risk in which businesses live is complex, multi-faceted, and ever changing. It incorporates a broad world of risk; however, in keeping with the purpose and objective of this book, we will focus on health and safety risks.

There are several components of the new risk reality that any business must consider.

New Exposures

New health and safety exposures are being created every day. The chapter on Change Management provides some valuable insight into how these new exposures can be effectively managed.

1. There are hundreds of new chemical substances produced every year, intentionally through research and development, or unintentionally through unmanaged experimentation in the workplace. The potential harmful effects of these substances may or may not be known.

2. New technologies, developed with the best of intentions and introduced to the workplace, can bring unintended consequences and new health and safety challenges.

3. New employees are hired into businesses every day. They bring their own safety attitudes, experiences, values, and beliefs with them. When these characteristics are not in harmony with the culture of the organization, new risks are introduced.

4. Management policies can have unintended consequences for the working force. Over the last few decades, the world has seen a move to non-smoking workplaces. While a non-smoking workplace may be a very worthwhile achievement, the initial efforts to achieve it may result in health and safety exposures such as nervousness, withdrawal symptoms, hiding to smoke, irritability, eyes and minds not on task, etc.

New Liabilities

Employers are being increasingly held responsible for the consequences of incidents. While civil penalties such as fines and citations have been routinely used to get management's attention, there is a definite move to employ criminal penalties, especially in situations where willful violations occur. Canadian Crimal Code Section 217.1, holds both hourly employees and management criminally liable for willful violations of health and safety requirements. The reality is that organizations can no longer escape responsibility.

New Stakeholder Attention

Employees, as well as the general public, have more knowledge of health and safety exposures and are more aware of the employer's responsibilities to control them. Shareholders, concerned about the image of the organizations in which they invest, demand due diligence in the management of health and safety issues and understand the negative impact that incidents can have on their return on investment.

New Communication Technology

In the world in which our ancestors managed risk, communication technology was such that it took days or even weeks before news of serious incidents reached the general public. Today, it may take literally seconds. The vast majority of employees carry mobile phones and most of those phones have camera capability. News organizations employ helicopters to quickly reach incident scenes. Instead of interviewing witnesses and publishing their comments in the next day's paper, live broadcasts enable reporters to disseminate information, accurate or not, in real time. This is part of the new risk reality that all organizations must manage.

Using Health and Safety Strategy to Improve Business

Continual improvement is essential in sustaining and growing an organization. Remaining stagnant will eventually put most companies out of business.

> "If we want everything to remain as it is, it will be necessary for everything to change."
>
> *Prince Giuseppe Tomasi de Lampedusa, The Leopard.*

If an organization wishes to be viable and survive, it must do things in addition to, instead of, or better than they have done in the past.

As leaders in your organization, you and your health and safety efforts can have a direct impact on the bottom line. One way to positively impact the profitability of a company is to evaluate and control injuries and illnesses both on and off the job.

Injuries and illnesses, whether they occur on or off the job, have a significant cost implication. According to the National Safety Council in the United States, injuries cost approximately $753.0 billion dollars in 2011 ("Injury Facts," 2013 Edition). Of this figure, approximately 25% was attributed to work-related causes, 27% to off-the-job causes, and the remaining to motor vehicle and public non-motor vehicle causes. Assuming the 25% figure for work-related causes is correct, this means American business lost around $188 billion dollars due to incidents in 2011. Many companies either directly (through healthcare benefits, workers' compensation programs, etc.) or indirectly (through lost time, training expenses, etc.) assume the financial burden for injuries both on and off the job. Various factors help determine the actual, direct costs of incidents to business, including laws in different countries; however, research tells us incident costs around the world are significant, no matter the jurisdiction in which an organization operates.

For example, the Health and Safety Executive (HSE) in the United Kingdom estimates the costs of work-related illnesses for the UK in the 2010-2011 time period to be approximately £8.4 billion while injuries and fatalities added another £5.4 billion. The Australian National Accounts office estimates the total cost of work-related injuries and illnesses for 2005-2006 to be approximately $32 billion Australian dollars. Developing strategies to manage and mitigate risks associated with these injuries and illnesses will facilitate cost savings and have an improvement on our most important asset, our human capital.

Not only can investment in health and safety initiatives cut the costs of incidents, but there can also be simultaneous benefits in quality, efficiency, and profit.

Morale and, subsequently, quality and quantity of work improves because employees perceive the organization cares and is a good place to work.

Recruiting of future talent is enhanced because the community at large perceives the same thing.

A paper manufacturing operation found that, by using task analysis in their health and safety process, they not only identified and more effectively controlled H&S exposures, but also actually improved the efficiency of operating procedures.

A senior manager of a food production company stated that they found health and safety tools and techniques to be very effective for improving quality as well.

An organization producing a consumer product found that it took the profit from the entire operation to pay for the incidents in just one sales region. By improving health and safety performance, they simultaneously improved financial results.

An operating unit of a particular organization is located in a small town (approximately 500 inhabitants). Due to poor health and safety performance, the operation once found it difficult to recruit, especially when there was one other major employer in town who had a better reputation for health and safety. Over a period of five years, the organization invested significantly in health and safety activities, demonstrated marked performance improvement, and solved many of their recruitment problems. They are now the preferred place to work.

Forget for a moment the financial aspects of incidental loss. At the end of the day, protecting the health and safety of our people is just the right thing to do. It's part of being a good corporate citizen and a critical part of sustainable business development.

More information regarding the cost of incidental loss and its impact on business performance can be found in the chapter Basic Concepts of Management Systems.

Taking Your Organization's Sustainability Temperature

How well does your organization practice its sustainability commitment? There are some questions that all organizations should ask themselves.

Are we looking after our people so that they have the resources they need to do their jobs well, a high level of job satisfaction, and protection from illness and injury?

Are we protecting our reputation by managing our risks properly?

Are we organized in a way that allocates management responsibility for all aspects of our sustainability initiative?

Do we communicate effectively both internally and externally so that all stakeholders are aware of our health and safety investments?

Are we able to adapt and innovate in response to the ever-changing risk reality?

Are we listening to our stakeholders and responding appropriately?

Do we make resource and budget decisions for health and safety based solely on initial cost or do we practice a high level of risk competence and make financial decisions based on established risk criteria and using a robust cost/benefit process?

A comprehensive sustainability assessment with a strong focus on health and safety can be an effective thermometer. Not only can it tell the organization where it stands in comparison to best practices, but it can also provide a roadmap for continual improvement.

Skepticism Partially Alleviated

Just before Joe's next management meeting, Don asks for a quick discussion.

"Joe, I wanted to let you know that I read the material you gave me on the business case for sustainability. Very interesting."

"Glad to hear it! What did you think about its validity?"

"Well, I had always considered health and safety investment to be a necessary evil to keep regulators off our backs. I mean, I understand the moral and ethical obligation to protect our employees from harm, but I didn't always see how what we were spending on health and safety really was effective. I guess I look at it a little differently now."

"Okay. Can you see how improvement in health and safety performance can contribute to our bottom line?"

"In theory, yes. But I will have to be convinced. I mean, the scope of sustainability is vast and well beyond health and safety. The entire effort will require significant investment and add to our budget commitments. I'm not sure of the cost/benefit proposition. What will this do to our profitability?"

"Let's continue this discussion in the larger group, okay?"

Joe presents essentially the same information to his management team as Don read. He then opens the floor to a general discussion. While some managers are just as skeptical as Don, after the opportunity to discuss specific costs of incidental loss, their skepticism is somewhat relieved. Joe presents a chart that indexes the cost of loss in their specific operation to profit margin. The profit margin for the previous fiscal year is approximately 6% and not bad for their industry. The calculated direct and indirect costs of incidental loss are approximately $180,000. The chart illustrates that, in order to recover the

$180,000 loss, while operating at a 6% profit margin, the organization will have to manufacture and sell approximately $3M worth of product. The managers then calculate that this represents approximately one month's production.

Don is impressed and a bit dismayed.

"This means that my department had to sell $3M worth of product just to pay for our annual losses due to poor health and safety performance. That's significant."

A production manager says, "It also means that we had to work a full month before we started making money. That's also significant."

After a little more discussion, the management team starts coming around.

Lisa speaks up.

"I would like to impress on all of you that health and safety isn't really a cost center. Our efforts can drive improved financial performance."

By the end of the meeting, Joe has been successful in convincing the team that health and safety initiatives were at least worth a try. He asks various team members to take leadership roles and promises to keep the team engaged in every activity, including strategic planning and budget considerations.

With skepticism somewhat relieved, Joe feels he has the support of his team and sets about driving the initiative.

Key Point Summary

Sustainability is not a thing; it is a way. Sustainable business development is the process by which organizations "meet the needs of the present without compromising the ability of future generations to meet their own needs."

Sustainability consists of three dimensions: economic, environmental, and social.

This book focuses on the health and safety aspect of the social dimension. However, we can make a strong case that efforts to improve health and safety systems are proven to contribute to success in all three dimensions.

Aside from its responsibilities to the community, an organization has the responsibility to produce a financial return for its shareholders. Health and safety efforts can contribute to improved financial performance.

Any prudent organization must be able to describe its sustainability efforts, including health and safety, and measure them appropriately.

Personal Planning

Does my organization have a sustainability or sustainable business development initiative?

Do I understand that initiative and how it affects my job?

Where can I find information on our initiative?

How do our health and safety initiatives contribute to business performance?

What should I do to be a more effective contributor/leader to our sustainability initiative or our health and safety program?

Action Plan

Steps	Target Date	Completion Date	Notes

Y – Model for Action Planning

Present Situation

Desired Situation

Need for Change

Present Situation

Stop Responsibility Target Date

THE ROLE OF LEADERSHIP

Chapter 2

THE ROLE OF LEADERSHIP

CHAPTER OBJECTIVES

1. To illustrate the vital role leadership at all levels plays in the effective implementation of a sustainable health and safety strategy.
2. To define leadership and the characteristics of effective leaders.
3. To emphasize the importance of leadership in the dimension of change.
4. To present time-tested principles of leadership that can help any leader improve their performance.
5. To present practical actions leaders can take to demonstrate their personal commitment and engagement in health and safety activities.

Joe Learns from Past Mistakes

Joe is a leader in his organization, but he is also human and has made a few mistakes along the way. A couple years back, Joe led an effort to implement a comprehensive workplace inspection process in his plant. There were inspections being done, but they were mostly unorganized and ineffective. Joe attended a health and safety conference where he heard a speaker outline an effective inspection process and he determined it was appropriate for his company. On returning to work, Joe outlined his plan to the leadership team and directed a smaller team, including the health and safety manager at the time, a supervisor, and the maintenance manager, to design and implement the new initiative.

After several months, it became apparent that the effort was not working out as expected. In fact, there was significant resistance and non-compliance. Joe and his team sat down and discussed what was going wrong. The discussions themselves were not very fruitful, but through them Joe began to perceive some issues that concerned him. After some reflection, Joe realized that they had gone about the project all wrong. Whatever problems there were could be traced to inadequate leadership and poor preparation.

Joe arranged to have dinner with his trusted friend, Carter, who also managed a plant in a similar industry. He wanted to enlist the help of his friend to identify specific issues and develop improvement strategies.

After some informal conversation, Joe asks, "Carter, I need your expertise and experience on something. Do you mind a bit of serious discussion?"

"Not at all. I'm just glad you think I can help."

Joe describes his problem and Carter listens attentively. When Joe finishes, Carter speaks up. "I experienced similar circumstances in the past, so you are not alone. I read a book a while back that really helped me learn from those experiences and I think it would help you. The author is John Kotter, a professor at Harvard. He identified eight steps for leading change in an organization. Can I ask you some questions?"

"Sure."

"Whose idea was this initiative?"

"Well, I heard some things at a conference and brought it back to my leadership team."

"So it was your idea to implement the program?"

"Yes."

"Did you get the leadership team engaged to the point where they actually endorsed the idea?"

"Well, I think they accepted it. I didn't hear any objections. Wait a minute! I see what you are getting at! As plant manager, they probably perceived I was forcing this on them and they might have been reluctant to question it."

"That's possible. What was their level of enthusiasm and urgency?"

"Looking back, I have to be honest and say I really don't know. I mean, they left the meeting with some direction, but possibly no ownership and motivation to follow through."

"Without that, their efforts may have been half-hearted," suggested Carter.

"True. What else?"

"Did you and the team define the vision for the project? Were you able to say what success would look like?"

"Not really. I assumed success would be that the inspections would be done."

"Okay. Was there a project plan with definite milestones that could be measured?

"That was the first objective I gave the implementation team. I can see now that was another mistake. The plan should have had input from all stakeholders and should have been agreed beforehand."

"One more question, Joe. Did you engage the people who would have to do the inspections in the development and implementation process?

"No! And that is something I would usually do! I guess I was so motivated to get this done, I forgot to consider its impact on other people. I can definitely see where some things went wrong. I guess we should start all over."

"Maybe, maybe not. In any case, I think what I learned from Professor Kotter's work could help you. I have a document that includes a summary of his work as well as some other helpful advice in the form of leadership principles that I can send you. Take a look at it and let me know."

"I will certainly do that. Thanks, Carter! This has been very helpful! Dinner is on me!"

Joe decides to pass on the information Carter shared with him.

What is leadership?

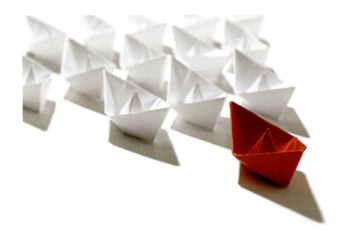

The original version of this material was written more than thirty years ago. In the past three decades, there have been enormous changes to the business environment we all share. Today's business context is characterized by continual and accelerating change, increased competition from a global marketplace, continual introductions of new technology, major shifts in the labor market associated with outsourcing and job mobility, and growing numbers of stakeholders with increasing expectations. These and other changes have resulted in significant changes in the health and safety concerns all organizations must manage. The new risk reality, as discussed earlier in this book, demands that organizations break from tradition and find new ways to meet their health and safety challenges. This requires real leadership.

Managing risk is important. Leading change in how the organization deals with its risks is critical. Sustainable business development is not possible unless the organization continually looks for new ways to deal with its new risk reality.

It is clear that standing still is not an option for organizations today. Organizations must change to survive. To beat the competition, organizations must be excellent at driving change. Driving change requires leadership.

Leadership is the process wherein a leader engages with and mobilizes others to drive change in an organization.

Before exploring further what leadership is, it is helpful to point out what it is not. Contrary to popular belief, leadership is not a mysterious activity of a chosen few senior executives. It has nothing to do with having "charisma" or other exotic personality traits.

In fact, leaders may be found at all levels of an organization. They may be managers, supervisors, or front line workers. They may be found in the private, public, or voluntary sectors or in the community. As we will explore in this chapter, leaders are defined more by their passion and ability to make a difference than by their position in an organization.

Health and safety leadership is no different. These leaders are found at all levels of an organization. In fact, in an ideal organizational culture, every member, from CEO to the operator at the working face, accepts their responsibility to lead health and safety efforts.

"If we want everything to remain as it is, it will be necessary for everything to change."

Prince Giuseppe Tomasi de Lampedusa, The Leopard.

Characteristics of Admired Leaders

The characteristics people look for in their leaders have changed very little. Research indicates that the following characteristics are important for leaders: a leader should be intelligent, fair minded, broad minded, supportive, straightforward, dependable, cooperative, determined, imaginative, ambitious, courageous, caring, mature, loyal, self controlled and independent. However, in a repeated survey with 75,000 respondents over 20 years, only four characteristics repeatedly scored over 50%. These characteristics were:

- Honesty
- Forward Looking
- Competent
- Inspiring

These four characteristics are the foundations for the credibility of any leader. People want leaders who are credible. Above all else, we must believe in our leaders because if you don't believe in the messenger, you won't believe the message.

What does this mean for one who accepts responsibility as a health and safety leader?

Honesty – The leader is perceived as having integrity because he or she tells the truth, even when it is difficult to hear. They recognize and reward when such attention is earned, but also confront when necessary. They consistently enforce health and safety requirements and don't make exceptions or play favorites. It has been said that the good leader is one who accepts more of the blame than they should when things go wrong and less of the credit than they should when things go right.

Forward Looking – The effective health and safety leader understands that what the organization is doing to manage its health and safety exposures today will not be sufficient tomorrow. In light of the new risk reality, they are able to establish and clearly articulate a vision for the future. They are not satisfied with good enough. They ask the question, "What about tomorrow?" They are about driving sustainability in health and safety matters.

Competent – The leader is perceived as having developed the requisite knowledge and skills to be effective in their roles. Most organizational leaders did not achieve their levels of responsibility because of their knowledge of health and safety. If they are to perform effectively in that arena, they must be equipped to do so. All leaders should have at least a basic understanding of the concepts, tools, and techniques that characterize effective health and safety systems.

Inspiring – The leader demonstrates passion for the cause and seeks to create that passion in others. "Together, we can do this!"

Leadership vs. Management

It is important here to clarify the differences between management and leadership.

Leadership is different from management. Leadership and management are two different but complimentary activities with their own characteristics. Leadership is not better than management or a substitute for it; in fact both are essential in all organizations.
Management is about coping with complexity. Leadership, by contrast, is about coping with change. As the pace of change increases in today's business world, many organizations find themselves over-managed and under-led.

Management is concerned with developing, implementing, and controlling practices and procedures to manage the complex business processes found in modern organizations. Good management provides order and consistency in the workplace. It ensures that business processes are executed efficiently to deliver good quality products and services. Organizations without good management will become inefficient and chaotic in ways that may threaten their survival.

Leadership, on the other hand, is concerned with recognizing the changing context in which the organization operates, identifying a new direction, engaging with people, and mobilizing them to achieve the desired change. In today's world, it doesn't always follow that doing something 5% better than last year is a formula for success. Leadership is required to drive the major changes often necessary to survive and compete. Leadership isn't satisfied with the status quo. Leadership continually challenges the systems and approaches that exist in the organization on the basis of the belief that what works today will not be sufficient for tomorrow. Leadership is about sustainability.

It doesn't necessarily follow that people who are good at managing are also good at leading. Some people have the capacity to be excellent managers but are not strong leaders. Smart organizations try to develop people who can both manage and lead. All of us can improve our leadership skills, as we will explore later in this chapter.

"Management is doing things right. Leadership is doing the right things."

Peter Drucker

Leading Change

John Kotter is a Professor at Harvard Business School and is recognized worldwide as an expert on leadership and change. Kotter has studied successful and unsuccessful change efforts at hundreds of companies and proposes the following eight-stage process for leading change in any organization.

1. Establish a Sense of Urgency

Stakeholders must be aware of and accept the need for change. Compared to the other stages of change, this may sound easy. It is not. According to the research, 50% of change efforts fail at this stage.

This is often very challenging because the forces to maintain traditional practices are very strong. Change challenges our comfort zone. It requires us to learn and practice new ways of working. Most people resist change unless and until they perceive the change provides a benefit to them personally. If we are to be successful, we must be able to demonstrate the benefits of planned change to all stakeholders. "What's in it for me?" is a common question that must be answered.

2. Form a Powerful Guiding Coalition

The leading group must have enough power in the organization to lead the change effort. It is often said that change efforts fail without the commitment of the senior manager. Research indicates, however, most other senior managers must also buy in to the change. This group should work together well as a team.

3. Create a Vision

Create a meaningful direction and strategy to help direct the change effort. The vision should be something the stakeholders can relate to personally and align with their own needs. Leaders must be able to articulate the vision clearly. It should be possible to state the vision in less than five minutes and get a reaction of understanding and interest. In failed change programs, one will find plenty of plans but no vision. Vision comes first.

4. Communicate the Vision

Leaders must use every channel available to communicate the new vision and strategies. Speeches, meetings, newsletters, and emails are not enough. To be effective, leaders must include their change messages into their hourly activities and integrate them into daily business processes. They must teach the new behaviors by leading by example and "walk the talk." In the chapter Building an Improvement Culture, you will find interesting information on how leadership actions drive organizational culture.

5. Empower Others to Act on the Vision

Leaders must remove any obstacles to change, like systems or structures that reinforce old practices. Often an employee understands the new vision and wants to make it happen, but an elephant appears to be blocking the path. The elephant may be a too narrow job description or an inappropriate compensation scheme that makes people choose between the new vision and their own self-interest. These obstacles have to be identified and removed. Leaders often encourage risk taking and non-traditional ideas and activities to achieve the vision. It is easy to tell others, "You are empowered!" However, it can be difficult to provide the mechanisms and vision to convince them, motivate them to action, and make empowerment easy.

6. Plan and Create Short Term Wins

Leaders plan to create measurable performance improvements. When these are achieved, the personnel involved must be recognized and rewarded. Such recognition should not be reserved for completion of the change, but should be applied when clearly defined milestones are achieved. Celebration of small victories can be strong motivators to continue pursuit of the ultimate goal. Clearly recognizable victories within the first few months of a change effort will help convince doubters that it is worth all the effort.

7. Consolidate Improvements and Produce Still More Change

Successful application of the first six steps above will build the credibility of leadership and drive further changes to systems and structures. Leaders look for the opportunity to add new recruits to their cause. To change the organizational culture may take quite some time. Leaders must be careful not to declare victory too early and risk watching behaviors slip back into traditional practices.

> "Leaders don't create followers. Leaders create other leaders."
>
> *Tom Peters*

8. Institutionalize the New Approach

Leaders should be able to articulate the connections between the new behaviors and resulting improved performance to ensure people truly understand the linkage. They must develop the means to ensure leadership development and succession planning to ensure all the good work is not undone. Organizations only truly change when new behaviors become "the way we do things around here" and are cemented into social norms and shared values.

Leadership Activities

Earlier we saw that successful leaders share certain characteristics including being honest, forward looking, competent, and inspiring. In this section, we develop further the activities required of successful leaders.

1. Agreed Purpose and Values

The purpose of leadership is to create change. Therefore setting the direction of that change is fundamental to leadership. What is critical about the purpose, however, is that it can be used to effectively align the interests of important stakeholders and encourage them to coordinated action. A fundamental role of the leader is aligning people. The leader must communicate the new direction to all-important parties in such a way that they understand it, buy into it, and become committed to achieving it. To creating commitment to the new direction, the leader must then motivate and inspire the team to achieve the purpose.

The leader should establish processes to define the values and behaviors for their organization, which might include:

- How we behave with each other
- How we regard our customers and other stakeholders
- Encouraging creativity and innovation
- Recognizing good performance
- Building trust in the organization
- The importance of maintaining professional integrity
- Empowering individuals
- Team working
- Effective communications

2. Goal Setting

Leaders have a forward looking perspective and set measurable goals committing their organization to realizable levels of performance over the next period. They should focus on high priority areas and critical processes. Goals should be SMART (Specific, Measurable, Attainable, Realistic and Time-bounded). Goals should include measures of outcomes (lagging indicators) and inputs (leading indicators). Examples of health and safety goals include occupational illness and injury rates (lagging) and quality and number of safety tours and inspections conducted (leading). These health and safety measures are discussed in detail in the chapter on Reviewing Performance.

3. Leading by Example

Demonstrating personal commitment to the change by "walking the talk" is critical to success. The leader must be an enthusiastic role model for change and show that his/her own behavior has changed if he/she wishes others to do the same. The change may be associated with some sacrifice in stopping long established practices. The leader must demonstrate he/she is prepared to make this sacrifice if he/she wishes others to do the same. If the leader fails to do this, it will be a quick death for the change program. The Principle of Leadership Example is critical here.

Examples of Practical Leadership

100% personal compliance with all organizational performance standards – use of personal protective equipment, completion of mandatory training.

Management tours – leaders conducting formal walk through the workplace, engaging employees in conversation about health and safety issues, discussing topical concerns and improvements.

Participation in incident investigations – leaders becoming personally involved in the process and showing their commitment to continual improvement.

Participation in group meetings – giving presentations, taking part in health and safety discussions and raising important issues up through the organization for action where necessary.

Giving recognition for good performance – through informal communication and formal letters, awards and presentations.

Ensure improvement actions are followed up and closed out.

4. Recognition and Feedback

Leaders should use positive recognition as a primary means of increasing motivation and reinforcing the new desired behaviors. Research shows that the positive recognition is one of very few statistically significant activities that directly improves organizational performance. Positive recognition directly meets every individual's need to be valued and esteemed by others. Recognition also contributes to individuals building their own self-respect and self-confidence. Good leaders should be good coaches. Coaching is effective in explaining and encouraging the desired changes and to correct any unwanted behaviors. Feedback should always be respectful and constructive.

5. Team Building

Many of us can remember being part of a high performing team when the team performance was somehow greater than the sum of the individuals. High performing teams enjoy synergistic effects by playing to the strengths of all team members and compensating for their weaknesses. Leaders need strong team building to improve team effectiveness. This is done in a number of ways. Fostering high trust relationships between team members improves communication and collaboration. It encourages diversity and differences of opinion as an engine of creative conflict, supports an environment of respect and solidarity where all team members are valued, and encourages team members to constructively challenge the team and each other to eliminate untested ideas.

6. Stakeholder Engagement

Stakeholders are any individuals or groups that have an interest or influence over the operation of the organization. The primary stakeholders in most organizations are the owners / shareholders, employees, managers, customers, and suppliers. For most organizations, the customer remains a key stakeholder to satisfy. However, globalization, climate change, increasing regulation, terrorism, 24-hour media, and increasing importance of corporate social responsibility mean that the numbers and expectations of stakeholders are increasing. One of the central tasks of today's leaders is to engage with these stakeholders and try to align their expectations where possible with those of the organization. The chapter on Stakeholder Engagement deals with this in detail.

Principles for Effective Safety and Health Leadership

Most disciplines have certain fundamental truths or principles that guide the workers' actions, and health and safety systems are no different.

While many principles have special value during the implementation of any program or project, the following have been selected as those that have proven to be of special value in the implementation of a health and safety system. Most of them have ongoing value as a leader strives for never-ending improvement.

1. The Principle of Reaction to Change

People accept change more readily when it is presented in relatively small amounts. Where possible, changes to health and safety systems should be made in incremental steps. Resistance is reduced and success in small changes can be a motivator to pursue the next change.

2. The Principle of Behavior Reinforcement

Behavior with negative effects tends to decrease or stop; behavior with positive effects tends to continue or increase. Gaining conformance with health and safety requirements has traditionally relied heavily on disciplinary actions for those who do not conform. There will always be a need for such actions. They have the effect of diminishing undesired behaviors. At the end of the day, employees at all levels must be held accountable for their actions. However, this traditional approach, when used as the only means of gaining conformance, has the undesired consequence of contributing to a blame-fixing, fault-finding culture in which the individual is always identified as somehow deficient, while leadership and the management system are absolved of any responsibility. As discussed elsewhere in this book, most often, substandard acts or at-risk behaviors (rules and procedural violations) are not intentional on the part of individuals. They are the result of weaknesses in the management system or culture. In such instances, disciplinary actions are not only inappropriate, but are also ineffective and result in negative impacts on organizational culture. It is also important to recognize that, if the individual perceives positive effects from a substandard or at-risk behavior, this increases the chance they will continue that behavior. For example, if a mobile equipment operator speeds, doesn't take time to fasten the seatbelt, or skips the pre-use inspection on the vehicle and gets a truck loaded quicker, they may be congratulated by a supervisor for getting the job done. That positive recognition results in the operator continuing the substandard behavior believing he or she is doing what the supervisor, and thereby the organization, wants. If the same substandard behavior results in the operator having more time for a break or getting to leave work early, that is also positive reinforcement of an improper behavior. Leaders must be careful to reinforce proper or desired behaviors.

There is much to be gained from positive reinforcement of proper behaviors. Most people are doing things right, but are never recognized for doing so. Some managers have the attitude that, since their people get paid to do things right, there is no need for additional recognition. The only time they have any dialogue with individuals is when there is a problem. This contributes to a deficient organizational culture. The effective leader appreciates the efforts of his or her team and routinely reinforces the things they do well. Individuals who set the example for proper health and safety performance need to be recognized. Otherwise, they can easily come to perceive that their actions are not appreciated and do not matter.

3. The Principle of Mutual Interest

Programs, projects, and ideas are best sold when they bridge the wants and desires of both parties. This is easy to talk about, but quite difficult to actually achieve. Earlier in this chapter, we discussed the issue of creating a sense of urgency and the need to let all stakeholders know the benefits of proposed changes. Stakeholders must perceive there is a benefit to them personally or they will naturally be skeptical of management-driven change.

For example, imagine an organization wishes to expand its management of change (MOC) process to include assessment of administrative or organizational changes and their potential impact on health and safety issues. Persons who are responsible for completing MOC requirements will likely see this as requiring more paperwork and effort on their part. The organization must be able to clearly explain exactly what is to be gained by the initiative. Statistical and anecdotal data must be sufficient to convince stakeholders of the need for the initiative.

4. The Principle of the Point of Action

Management efforts are most effective when they focus at the point where the work is actually done. Health and safety efforts cannot simply consist of manuals, directives, procedures, risk registers, etc. The value and impact of these components must be explicit in the minds and behaviors of people at the working face. Organizational culture must support the consistent application of work controls.

5. The Principle of Leadership Example

People tend to emulate their leaders. Can inadequate leadership be a basic or root cause of incidents? Evidence says yes. If ineffective leaders do not comply with health and safety requirements themselves, workers on the floor quite rightly question whether they could do the same. If ineffective leaders do not take ownership of health and safety problems—that is, confront at-risk behaviors or fail to follow-up—then the message is clear: these things are not important.

6. The Principle of Basic Causes

Solutions to problems are more effective when they treat the basic or root causes. No one disputes this. The problem with practical application is that identifying and dealing with basic causes is much more difficult than dealing with symptoms. It is much easier to stop the process with the person who violated a rule or procedure and discipline or retrain them or stop the process with the inadequate guard and repair or replace it rather than dig deeper and find the underlying problem. Often, the underlying problem reflects on leadership and/or the management system so investigators are more comfortable dealing with the symptoms. This principle is discussed in more detail in the chapter Basic Concepts of Safety and Health Management Systems.

7. The Principle of the Critical/Vital Few

The majority (80%) of any group of effects is produced by a relatively few (20%) number of causes. This is often referred to as the Pareto Principle. How does this economic principle apply to health and safety concerns? There are almost innumerable health and safety risks that may affect an organization. Are all of these risks critical? Are some of them so insignificant, the organization may choose to accept or tolerate them with no plan of action? This is the underlying principle for risk assessment as discussed elsewhere in this book. Given limited resources for health and safety investment, the organization must apply cost-benefit assessments and focus its efforts on those exposures that really matter: the 20% that have the potential to produce 80% of loss.

8. The Principle of the Key Advocate

It is easier to persuade a group of people when at least one person within their own circle believes in the proposal well enough to champion the cause. As quoted earlier in this chapter, Tom Peters said, "Leaders don't create followers. Leaders create other leaders." This should be our goal – to create the next generation of leaders. That's sustainable business development.

9. The Principle of Minimum Commitment

It is easier to gain approval and commitment for a portion of a system than the entire project or program. Small wins can generate interest and enthusiasm for the next step. Leaders celebrate those small wins.

10. The Principle of System Integration

The better new activities are integrated into existing systems, the higher the chance of acceptance and success. Some organizations reach a point of over-burdening that eventually collapses a system.

Each new health and safety initiative should be approached with the following question in mind: is there something already in existence, a reporting system, a form, a data base, a procedure, etc., that can be modified or leveraged to accommodate our need?

For example, some organizations have different incident investigation reporting forms for injuries, illnesses, property damage, environmental incidents, contractor incidents, vehicle incidents, etc. It is possible to design one form that can accommodate all incidents regardless of their character or origin.

In addition, it is quite possible and desirable to have one preventive and corrective action follow-up system that can accommodate input from inspections, risk assessments, employee input, behavior observation programs, and other sources. Why have different systems for different programs?

11. The Principle of Involvement

Meaningful involvement increases motivation and support. Stakeholder engagement and ownership is critical to the success of health and safety efforts. Employees who are given the opportunity to participate in the development or revision of rules, procedures, policies, etc., understand the need for these controls, are more motivated to comply, and can explain them to their peers. The key word in the principle is meaningful. Unless stakeholders can see tangible results of their efforts, they may see the request for their input as a mere attempt at appeasement.

12. The Principle of Multiple Causes

Accidents and other problems are seldom, if ever, the result of a single cause. It is improper to ask, "What was the cause of this incident?" The proper question is, "What were the causes?" When an investigator looks for the cause, it is all too easy to identify the substandard act, practice, or condition, then fix it and move on. As discussed elsewhere in this book, this results in the likely repetition of similar incidents. When all causes are identified and effectively addressed, the likelihood of repetition is significantly reduced.

Tool Kit: Leadership Actions Checklist

The following is a checklist in the form of questions that can be used to guide an individual to examine their own leadership efforts as they relate to health and safety.

Leadership Actions Checklist

1. Does senior leadership participate in a joint health and safety committee with representatives of the workforce?
2. Does the joint health and safety committee serve as a primary resource for ideas for continual improvement?
3. Do senior leaders endorse health and safety initiatives by:
    a. Regular communications with all employees on health and safety subjects and progress on goals and targets? Examples:
        i. E-Mails, memos, written announcements, and employee newsletter articles.
        ii. Notice board postings.
        iii. Actively participating in team meetings where health and safety issues are discussed.
        iv. Leading plant-wide meetings where health and safety are part of the agenda.
    b. Conducting personal health and safety tours including physical inspection of high-risk areas, direct discussions with the workforce, and checks of progress on corrective and preventive actions?
    c. Including health and safety as a significant part of the agenda of all leadership meetings? Examples:
        i. Opening all meetings with a safety moment where participants are invited to share a health or safety-related experience or advice.
        ii. Actively discussing progress on health and safety initiatives and plans for continual improvement rather than simply reporting incident statistics and problems.
4. Is senior leadership visibly active in health and safety issues in the community? In the organization as a whole? In the industry? Examples:
    a. Serving on boards or task forces that deal with health and safety issues outside their specific operation.
    b. Maintaining active membership in health and safety-related organizations, such as the American Society of Safety Engineers.
    c. Making presentations on health and safety-related topics to schools, civic groups, or other interested parties.
5. Do senior leaders demonstrate care and concern for workers by:
    a. Maintaining regular contact with workers who may be off work due to injury or illness, whether or not such injury or illness is work-related?
    b. Actively participating in incident investigations where appropriate?
    c. Actively monitoring progress on health and safety initiatives and corrective and preventive actions?
    d. Maintaining personal contact with workers, including discussion of health and safety issues?
6. Do all organization leaders consistently follow rules and requirements?
7. Are all organization leaders willing to confront substandard or at-risk behaviors?
8. Do middle-level leaders participate in similar activities as those identified for senior leaders?

9. Are front-line leaders responsible for:
   a. Conducting effective team meetings with their work-groups that include health and safety topics?
   b. Leading workplace inspections, identifying health and safety exposures, developing and carrying out corrective and preventive actions?
   c. Enforcing rules and procedures?
   d. Actively participating in incident investigations?
10. Do front-line leaders demonstrate care and concern for their work-groups by:
    a. Continually coaching individuals for improvement?
    b. Keeping the workforce informed of progress on health and safety initiatives and corrective and preventive actions?
    c. Consistently and fairly enforcing rules and procedures?

There are natural leaders in all organizations that do not necessarily carry titles. They are members of the workforce who, through their experience, expertise, and personal attributes, have earned the respect of their colleagues.

Has the organizational culture matured to the point where these persons recognize and accept their responsibilities to positively lead health and safety initiatives and compliance with requirements? Do they demonstrate care and concern for their fellow workers by:

1. Being willing to confront and help correct substandard or at-risk behaviors?
2. Reminding coworkers about health and safety requirements?
3. Setting the example by consistently following rules and procedures?
4. Voluntarily serving on teams for the purpose of addressing health and safety concerns or implementing new initiatives?

All leaders should be constantly working to create a health and safety consciousness within their organization that ultimately motivates all employees to recognize and accept their roles as leaders.

Tool Kit: Safety and Health Leadership Behaviors

The following is an expanded list of specific behaviors that demonstrate care and concern for people:

- Listens to safety-related complaints, reports of hazards, concerns, etc. and deals with them appropriately.
- Keeps people informed of progress on remedial actions.
- Communicates rationale for alternative solutions or responses.
- Doesn't view complaints or issues as personal attacks.
- Takes advantage of opportunities to learn new approaches, tools, and techniques for managing safety.
- Keeps up-to-date on existing and pending regulatory issues relating to responsibilities.
- Ensures all employees have access to current safety training and information.
- Constantly seeks ways to improve safety performance.
- Challenges the status quo.
- Open to new ideas.
- Unafraid to challenge the system.
- Understands that well-managed change is critical to safety and health performance.
- Accepts responsibility for the safety of all stakeholders.
- Accepts that safety is an equal responsibility to production, quality, budget management, etc.
- Demonstrates emotional intelligence; the ability to relate to people, empathize, and demonstrate concern.
- Approaches safety-related issues with the same degree of passion and enthusiasm as business-related issues.
- Willing to speak to individuals and groups about both positive and negative safety issues.
- Creates the vision of a workplace that is perceived by all stakeholders to be safe.
- Continually challenges all stakeholders to pursue improved safety and health performance.
- Defines the means by which safety and health improvement is possible.
- Unwilling to compromise on safety standards and expectations.
- Consistently enforces rules and procedures.
- Personally follows rules and procedures consistently.
- Honest. Possesses integrity.
- Positively recognizes those who consistently comply with safety requirements or who give extra effort to performance.
- Doesn't rely on tangible incentives (bonuses, trinkets, awards, etc.) as primary recognition methods.
- Possesses a personal safety culture that is positive and optimistic.
- Constantly works to improve personal communication skills.
- First, a listener; then, a speaker.
- Provides honest feedback.
- Understands and uses leading-edge thinking, systems, and tools to improve performance.
- Understands and draws on the body of knowledge that exists for safety and health leadership.
- Understands the criticality of measuring leading indicators as the primary indicators for continual improvement.

Key Point Summary

- There are four primary characteristics of admired leaders: honesty, forward-looking, competency, and inspiring.

- There are differences between management and leadership. Management is about coping with complexity. Leadership is about coping with change.

- According to John Kotter at Harvard Business School, leading change involves eight phases:
    1. Establish a sense of urgency,
    2. Form a powerful guiding coalition,
    3. Create a vision,
    4. Communicate the vision,
    5. Empower others to act on the vision,
    6. Plan and create short-term wins,
    7. Consolidate improvements and produce still more change, and
    8. Institutionalize the new approach.

- A competent leader:
    a. Drives agreement on purpose and values,
    b. Is proficient at goal-setting,
    c. Leads by example,
    d. Provides positive recognition and feedback,
    e. Builds teams, and
    f. Engages stakeholders.

- There are basic principles that can guide leadership behaviors.

Personal Planning

1. How well do I match up with the primary characteristics of an effective leader?
2. What should I do to improve the organization's perception of my leadership abilities?
3. How well do I deal with change?
4. How well do I practice the principles of leadership and what should I do to improve?

Principle	Personal Assessment	Steps to Improvement
Principle of Reaction to Change		
Principle of Behavior Reinforcement		
Principle of Mutual Interest		
Principle of Point of Action		
Principle of Leadership Example		
Principle of Basic Causes		
Principle of the Critical/Vital Few		
Principle of the Key Advocate		
Principle of Minimum Commitment		
Principle of System Integration		
Principle of Involvement		
Principle of Multiple Causes		

Y – Model for Action Planning

Present Situation

Desired Situation

Need for Change

Present Situation

Stop　　　　　　　　　Responsibility　　　　　　　　　Target Date

BASIC CONCEPTS OF SAFETY AND HEALTH MANAGEMENT SYSTEMS

Chapter 3

BASIC CONCEPTS OF SAFETY & HEALTH MANAGEMENT SYSTEMS

CHAPTER OBJECTIVES

The objectives of this chapter are:

1. To show how losses occur in an organization, how many there tend to be, their cost, and why they occur.
2. To provide advice on the design of an effective management system that addresses the reduction of organizational losses and, by implication,
3. Increase the chances of organizational success.
4. To show how management systems can drive their own sustainability.

Henry Wants to Set *"The Big Picture"*

Henry, Vice President of Operations, has had a nagging feeling for a long time. Although things generally run smoothly in the organization, he feels the vast majority of employees still have not grasped the basic theory and foundation for why undesired events still occur, and how this poor understanding ultimately affects the organization in terms of its ability to successfully sustain itself over the long term.

In other words, if employees and contractors cannot link the causes of loss and their effects on the organization:

- Then the existing management system is really only "luck-based" and not competency-based,
- Proper learning from events, both positive and negative, cannot realistically occur, and
- Good and/or improving HSE loss indexes cannot be sustained, and if these cannot be sustained, it will affect business continuity.

Because of this, Henry has requested his team, specifically Joe and Lisa and other key personnel from their departments, to develop a concise training package to increase personnel competency to understand how and why losses occur, and how they can affect the viability and sustainability of the business.

To kick it off, Henry approaches Lisa one day. "Lisa…as you know, I've been concerned for a long time that we, as an organization, really don't have a basic understanding of how a management systems approach can help us better deal with our incidents and accidents. Can we get together, perhaps with Joe and several of your key people, to do something about this?"

"Sure, Henry. I also feel we need to develop some basic training or knowledge regarding this issue. I have some ideas for how we can put this together already."

"Good, Lisa. It's time we focused more on basic knowledge and why we do what we do, rather than just doing it for no reason. I know you have been trying to lead us in a more positive direction and I apologize that I haven't brought this up earlier. We really need to face the fact that the boundaries of our accountability are moving fast.

I see a trend towards more sustainable management and that means not only do we need to reduce accidents, but we also need to implement a system-wide approach that links the various parts of our business with the greater environment at large and our stakeholders out there. Hey, better late than never, right?"

"Okay…let me contact Joe and get his input. In addition, I'll put some initial materials together that I know represents the latest thinking in management systems, sustainability, and what you want to achieve. I think if we deal with laying out some basic definitions, explain why a management system is so important to sustain the business, reduce losses, maximize our success, and link these concepts together logically, we'll make some major headway into creating the sustainability culture we've been hoping for."

"Great! In the meantime, I'm going to email you some supporting information on best practices in this area, too. Let me know if I can do anything else for you."

Introduction

Those who believe that most undesired events happen simply as a result of carelessness or negligence miss a golden opportunity each time an accident or incident happens. When they don't see the true basic reasons as to why the event occurred, they fail to gain valuable information about how to prevent it from happening again. All too often, employee error is seen as the problem, and therefore becomes the problem. This leads to several problems:

1. It encourages leaders to lay blame, to fault find rather than fact find.
2. It encourages behaviors to cover up such events due to fear of discipline, reprisal, victimization, etc.
3. It diverts attention from one of the main causes of the problem - an inadequate management system.
4. And, it leads to an organizational culture that, over the long term, cannot be sustained and denies the organization the success it deserves.

There is a logical cause-effect relationship and/or sequence inherent in organizations that can lead them to experience undesired events. In addition, there is a proper and successful way to address these issues by implementing a management systems approach. By taking this approach, the concept of sustainability or sustainable management can and should be built into the process.

Definitions

To understand the sequence of events that can lead to a loss, it is essential to understand what one is trying to prevent, control, and/or implement.

An accident may be defined as an event that results in unintended harm or damage. This may include anything in the work or external environment. It could be the result of a contact with a source of energy (kinetic, chemical, thermal, acoustical, mechanical, electrical, radiation, etc.) or a substance above the threshold limit of any animate or inanimate object. In terms of people, contact may result in a cut, burn, abrasion, fracture, etc. or in an alteration of or interference with a normal body function (cancer, asbestos, repetitive motion injury, etc.). In terms of damage, it could be fire, breakage, distortion, etc. There are three important aspects of this definition.

1. It is not limited to injury, but includes harm to anything in the work and/or external environment.
2. This definition does not confuse injury with accident. They are not the same. Injuries and illnesses result from accidents, but accidents are not limited to injuries or illnesses.
3. If the event results in property damage or loss and no injury, it is still an accident. Often, of course, accidents result in harm to people, property, and process. However, there are many more damage accidents than injury accidents. Not only is damage expensive, but damaged tools, machinery, and equipment also often lead to further accidents.

Many organizations use the term accident routinely, but most people do not know precisely what the term means. The information in the paragraphs above should be shared with all stakeholders.

Most organizations today are moving away from the term accident and toward exclusive use of the term incident. There are two primary reasons for this move.

1. The term accident sometimes carries with it the implication that the event could not have been prevented. It was an accident. It just happened and we don't or can't know why. This reinforces a fatalistic view of health and safety that inhibits the process of finding and fixing the causes and potential causes. We want to avoid that implication.
2. Accident historically and culturally often is understood to refer only to personal injury events. As discussed above, accidents result in a myriad of types of loss. We want to expand our understanding of loss so that all types of loss come under the umbrella of our risk management and health and safety systems.

The term incident is defined as "an event that could or does result in unintended harm or damage." This definition includes actual losses of all types and no-loss or near-miss events. We will consistently use the term incident throughout this book.

Certain no-loss events are referred to as high potential so that the same special attention is paid to them as to serious loss-producing events. This definition of incident includes accidents, near-accidents, security breaches, production or quality losses or near-losses, etc.

Like the traditional term accident, incidents in the health and safety arena are the result of contact with a source of energy or substance above the threshold limit of the body or structure. The human body has tolerance levels or injury thresholds for each form of energy or substance. Generally, the harmful effects of a single contact, such as a cut, fracture, sprain, amputation, chemical burn, etc., are regarded as injuries. The harmful effects of repeated contacts, such as repetitive motion injuries, cancer, liver damage, hearing loss, stress, etc., are regarded as illnesses (it should be recognized that illnesses can also result from a single contact).

The critical point that must be made is that both have a common factor: contact with an energy source or substance above the local or whole-body threshold. Ultimately, both have the same controls: the prevention of the contact or its reduction to a level where no harm is done. Both involve the same steps: identification of exposures, evaluation of the severity and probability of occurrence, and the development of appropriate controls. This is not to minimize the specialized knowledge required to deal with occupational health problems. An effective management system must be comprehensive enough to deal with all incident events, whether the result is injury, illness, property damage, and/or a near-miss.

A management system is a framework of controls for managing key business processes, organizational risks, and driving continual improvement.

An effective management system ensures people and processes are aligned to meet organizational objectives over both the short and long term and are sustainable. Management systems are composed of procedures and practices with clear performance requirements describing who does what, when, and/or how often. Taken together, the controls of the management system define "the way we work around here."

A management system is simply a systematic way to manage. It is a powerful tool that managers can use to cope with the complexity of their organization and drive it in their chosen direction.

Sustainable management can be defined as the application of sustainable practices in the categories of businesses, society, the environment, and other relevant areas by managing them in a way that will benefit current generations and future generations.

Management Systems Why Do We Need Them?

As indicated in the above definition, the primary purposes of a management system are:

1. To ensure the effective operation of key business processes,
2. To enable effective risk management,
3. To drive continual improvement.

Ensure the effective operation of key business processes.

An organization's key business processes are the sales, operations, logistics, and support processes necessary for the organization to create and deliver its products and/or services. The management system is the tool to manage and sustain these processes. Effective management systems will ensure best practice processes—including sustainability practices—are in place to deliver the organization's objectives.

Effective risk management.

Managing organizational risks concerns the systematic recognition, evaluation, control, and monitoring of health, safety, environmental, quality, and business risks. Effective risk management is a primary responsibility of management; and, in complex, high-risk organizations, a management systems approach is the only viable means of sustainable control.

Driving continual improvement. In competitive environments where the expectations of customers, regulators, the community, and other relevant stakeholders are increasing, continual improvement is essential for organizational sustainability. Management systems are an effective means of institutionalizing organizational change, ensuring systematic organizational learning, and ensuring organizational continuity, i.e., sustainability.

Management Systems Help to Maintain Consistency

When managers change, the system remains to provide continuity through the transition. Management systems also provide structured paths for improved communication, accomplishment of goals, development of human resources, improvement of business processes, etc.

We know that good health, safety, environmental, quality, and overall business performance doesn't just happen. It has to be managed. We also know that what we put into our management process (inputs) largely determines our business performance (outputs). Historical data proves that business performance leaders are those who work on the right things, in the right ways, at the right times. A systematic approach is essential to making that happen.

"People work in the system. Management creates the system."

Dr. W. Edwards Deming

Ideally, organizations should try to integrate their health, safety, quality, environmental, and other business activities into one overall management system.

The management system ensures the systematic and sustainable practice of identifying hazards, threats, and opportunities, evaluating the associated risks, making decisions on appropriate controls, implementing the controls, and establishing monitoring systems for these processes. Finally, to close the loop, management review processes guide and drive the organization to achieve continual improvement and, by implication, a sustainable business.

Developing Management Systems

All organizations differ in terms of their purpose, risks, size, complexity, maturity, and stakeholder expectations. These and other factors must be considered when developing the management system for an organization.

As already indicated, a management system is a series of interconnected activities to assure the effective and sustainable operation of an organization's business processes. It therefore follows that organizations with complex business processes will require more comprehensive management systems to ensure risks are properly identified and managed. Organizations with less complex business processes require smaller, less prescriptive management systems. Inappropriate decisions concerning management systems will result in too few or too many processes, procedures, programs, etc.

Management Systems for Managing Risk

Managing risk is a vital part of the management system and the organization's approach to implementing their management system. This should require that any activity being planned or being performed begin with a risk recognition process, which leads to risk evaluation using an appropriate method, determination of the risk controls required, and monitoring of the risk and the risk management system itself. This process is described in detail in the Risk Management chapter.

A management systems approach requires that we adopt and adapt to "process thinking." A simple, sustainable way to view this process is shown in Figure 3.1.

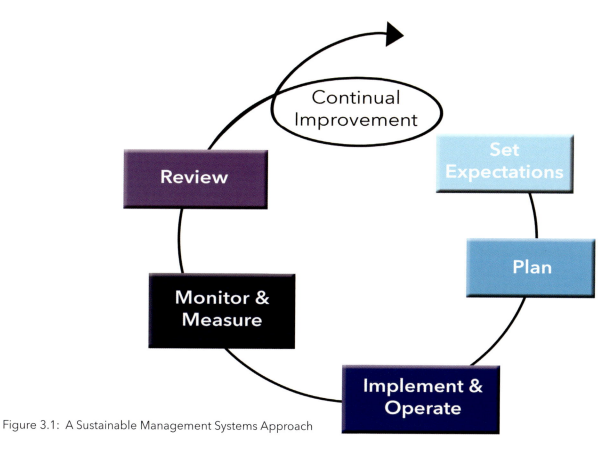

Figure 3.1: A Sustainable Management Systems Approach

This process is also summarized in the Managing Risk model shown in Figure 3.2, which is consistent with the information in the Risk Management chapter.

Figure 3.2: Managing Risk

Developing Sustainable Management Systems to Control Losses and Maximize Opportunities

When asked how and why losses occur in an organization, it is often difficult to pinpoint an accurate answer to the question. However, by understanding that the management system itself is a major contributor to our problems, we can also quickly start to solve and overcome our problems in a more systematic way.

Loss Causation

An organization requires a systematic approach to understanding how its losses occur if it is ever going to make the required improvements to reduce such losses.

Loss Causation, as shown by the model in Figure 3.3 is practical, user-friendly, and contains the necessary key points that enable the user to understand and retain the critical few facts important to the control of the vast majority of accidents, losses, and other management problems. It is consistent with what HSEQ and business leaders throughout the world are saying about event and loss causation. The model can also be seen from a positive, upside perspective; after all, if there are causes of loss, there are also causes for success.

Viewing from left to right, the Loss Causation model describes a cause-and-effect relationship in the management system that ultimately results in loss. Read from right to left, this same model becomes a powerful problem-solving tool for the organization, often used for analyzing and learning from events, as discussed in detail later in the chapter Learning from Events.

"If You have one business, you'll need one management system to run it."

Unknown

Figure 3.3: The Loss Causation Model

Loss: Unintended Harm or Damage

The result of an incident is loss. The most obvious losses are visible harm to people, property damage, environment, and quality. Implied and important related losses are performance interruption and profit reduction. Losses, therefore, involve harm or damage to anything in the occupational or external environment. Because of its ease of recognition, much of our discussion will relate to on-the-job injury, illness, property damage, environmental, and quality losses.

Once the sequence has occurred, the type and degree of loss are somewhat a matter of chance. The effect may range from insignificant to catastrophic, from a scratch or dent to multiple fatalities or loss of a plant. The type and degree of loss depend partly on fortuitous circumstances and partly on the actions taken to minimize loss. For example, actions to minimize loss at this stage of the sequence may include:
- prompt and proper first aid and medical care,
- prompt repair of damaged equipment and facilities,
- efficient implementation of emergency action plans,
- quick response to customer complaints,
- effective product recall, and
- effective spill/environmental cleanup operations.

Nothing is more important or more tragic than the human aspects of loss: injury, pain, sorrow, anguish, loss of body parts or functions, occupational illness, disability, or death. Effective management techniques employ methods to minimize these and to use both humane aspects and economic aspects to motivate control of the accidents that lead to the losses.

When looking at the Loss block of the Loss Causation model, an organization with the proper tools should be able to answer two basic questions:
1. How many losses do we have and what type are they?
2. How much do they cost?

How Many Losses Do We Have and What Type Are They?

The first to answer this question was a landmark study conducted by Frank E. Bird, Jr., in 1969, of over 1,750,000 accidents reported by 297 companies in 21 different industrial groups.

This, in conjunction with 4,000 hours of confidential interviews by trained supervisors, revealed a very interesting ratio of serious injuries to minor injuries, property damage accidents, and near misses. See Figure 3.4.

These studies clearly indicate how unwise it is to direct our major effort at the relatively few events resulting in serious or disabling injury when there are so many significant opportunities that provide a much larger basis for more effective management and control of all losses, including environmental and quality losses.

Additionally, they clearly show that the ratio pattern, over time and multiple industries, largely repeats itself. In terms of shape, organizations have incident ratio pyramids. It should be noted as well that, over time, these pyramids should be continually improved, i.e., reduced in size and base. A suitable, adequate, and effective management system, sustained over time, should deliver such results.

Figure 3.4: Accident Ratio Study (1969)

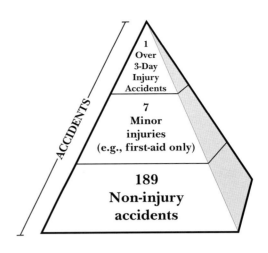

Figure 3.5: UK - HSE Executive Ratio Study (1993)

How Much Do They Cost?

Our first concern in a suitable, adequate, and effective management system is the protection of our people from pain and suffering. However, effective management techniques employ methods to both minimize these and to use humane and economic aspects to motivate control of events that lead to losses.

Whether or not people are injured, such events do cost money—and lots of it. Injury or illness costs are a relatively small part of the total costs. Figure 3.6 summarizes a study conducted in the USA.

The Costs of Accidents at Work

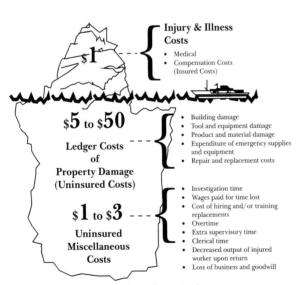

Figure 3.6: Accident Costs Iceberg

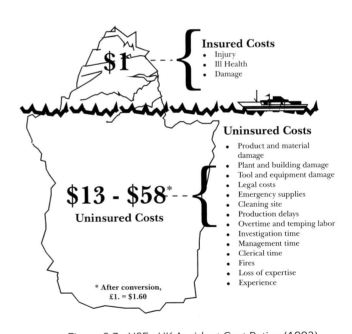

Figure 3.7: HSE - UK Accident Cost Ratios (1993)

The Health and Safety Executive in the United Kingdom reported similar findings in 1993 (Figure 3.7). The study analyzed a wide cross section of industry including a construction site, a creamery, a transport company, a North Sea oil platform, and a National Health Services hospital. As with the previous study, a direct comparison was made between insured and uninsured costs. For every $1 of insured costs i.e.—injury, health, and damage—additional uninsured costs of $8–$36 were absorbed.

Both studies indicate that the true costs of loss are far more than most managers realize. By controlling those incidents that either have demonstrated substantial losses by way of injury to people, damage, loss of process, etc. or that hold the potential to do so, an organization can improve the profit margin. After all, accident costs come straight off the bottom line.

Perhaps even more impressive is the actual effect losses can have on an organization's profit and sustainability. See Figure 3.8.

Yearly Event ORGANIZATIONAL PROFIT MARGIN	ORGANIZATIONAL PROFIT MARGIN			
	1%	2%	4%	5%
$10,000-	1,000,000	500,000	250,000	200,000
25,000-	2,500,000	1,250,000	625,000	500,000
50,000-	5,000,000	2,500,000	1,250,000	1,000,000
100,000-	10,000,000	5,000,000	2,500,000	2,000,000
200,000-	20,000,000	10,000,000	5,000,000	4,000,000
500,000-	50,000,000	25,000,000	12,500,000	10,000,000
1,000,000-	100,000,000	50,000,000	25,000,000	20,000,000
SALES REQUIRED TO COVER LOSSES				
This table shows the dollars of sales required to pay for different amounts of costs for accident losses; i.e., if an organization's profit margin is 5%, it would have to make sales of $500,000 to pay for $25,000 worth of losses. With a 1% margin, $10,000,000 of sales would be necessary to pay for $100,000 of the costs involved with accidents. Clearly this has serious ramifications for overall profitability, shareholder value, continuity, sustainability, etc.				

Figure 3.8: Table of Profit Margins and Sales Required to Cover Losses

Incident: An Event

This is the event that precedes the loss – normally a contact that could or does cause the harm and/or damage to anything in the working or external environment. When potential causes of accidents are permitted to exist, the way is open for a contact with a source of energy or substance above the threshold limit of the body or structure. As an example, a flying or moving object involves kinetic energy, which transfers to the body or structure it hits or contacts. If the amount of energy transferred is beyond the threshold limit, it causes personal harm or property damage. This is true not only of kinetic energy, but also electrical energy, acoustic energy, thermal energy, radiant energy, chemical energy, etc.

Thinking of the incident in terms of a contact with a harmful amount of energy or substance helps to plan for a means of control. Measures that prevent, alter, or absorb the energy can be taken to minimize the harm or damage at the time and point of contact. Personal protective equipment and protective barriers are common examples. A hard hat, for instance, does not prevent contact by a falling object, but it could absorb and/or deflect some of the energy and prevent or minimize injury. Other control measures at the contact stage may include substitution of a less harmful chemical or a less volatile solvent; reduction of the amount of energy released, such as keeping the shower water below the scalding level or putting governors on engines to limit their speed; modifying a hazardous surface by rounding off sharp edges or padding the point of contact; and reinforcing the object (column, truck bed, floor) or body (muscles) so that it has a higher threshold limit.

When substandard conditions are permitted to exist (such as unguarded machine tools) or substandard acts are allowed (such as cleaning with gasoline), there is always the potential for contacts and energy exchanges which can lead to harm and/or damage.

Finally, we must also recognize that many losses do not occur from contacts, but from other events that do not always fit the traditional definitions we have used in the model, such as experiencing a lack of proper contact at the proper time.

Many of these relate to quality and are not commonly associated with traditional safety and environmental contacts. However, application of the loss causation model still applies even if there is no contact. Although not exhaustive, here is a list of many commonly encountered health, safety, environmental and quality contact events:

- Abnormal operations
- Product, process nonconformities
- Customer/stakeholder complaints
- Environmental release
- Struck against (running or bumping into)
- Struck by (hit by moving object)
- Fall to lower level (either the body falls or the object falls and hits the body)
- Fall on same level (slip and fall, tip over)
- Caught in (pinch and nip points)
- Caught on (snagged, hung)
- Caught between (crushed or amputated)
- Contact with (any harmful energy or substance; includes ignition, explosions, emissions, etc.)
- Overstress/overexertion/overload.

Immediate Causes: Substandard Acts/Practices and Conditions

The immediate causes of incidents are the circumstances that immediately precede the contact. They usually can be seen or sensed. Frequently they are called hazards, active factors, or symptoms.

Management systems thinking tends to use the terms of substandard acts/practices and substandard conditions (deviations from an accepted standard or practice). This line of thinking has distinct advantages:

1. It relates practices and conditions to a performance standard or requirement— a basis for measurement, evaluation, and correction.
2. It somewhat minimizes the blame-fixing stigma of the term unsafe act.

It broadens the scope of interest from health and safety to control of all losses, encompassing health, safety, environmental, quality, production, and cost control. Some people advocate substituting the word error (e.g., management error, operational error, maintenance error, engineering error) to identify management responsibility. The term error, however, is often misunderstood as blame. Blame leads to defensive behavior and management problems get disguised rather than solved. Also, an increasing number of business leaders confirm the results from research in quality control that as many as 85% of the mistakes (substandard/unsafe acts) that people make are the result of factors over which only management has control. This significant finding gives a completely new direction of control to the long-held perception that 85-95% of accidents result from the unsafe acts or faults of people.

This new direction of thinking encourages the progressive manager to think in terms of how the management system influences human behavior rather than just on the unsafe acts of people. Thus, the term substandard seems more in-tune, more acceptable, more useful, and more professional.

Examples of substandard acts/practices and conditions may be seen in Figures 3.9 and 3.10:

Immediate Causes: Substandard Acts/Practices

- Operating equipment without authority
- Failure to warn
- Failure to secure
- Operating at improper speed
- Failure to communicate/coordinate
- Failure to check/monitor
- Using defective equipment
- Using equipment improperly
- Failure to use PPE properly
- Improper demeanor, attitude, and/or appearance
- Improper loading
- Improper placement
- Improper lifting
- Improper position for task
- Servicing equipment in operation
- Failure to identify hazards/risks
- Under influence of alcohol and/or other drugs
- Failure to follow procedures/work instructions
- Failure to analyze, react, and/or correct
- Unethical actions

Figure 3.9: Examples of Substandard Acts / Practices

Immediate Causes: Substandard Conditions

- Inadequate guards or barriers
- Inadequate or improper protective equipment
- Defective tools, equipment, and/or materials
- Congestion or restricted action
- Inadequate warning systems
- Fire and explosion hazards
- Poor housekeeping/disorder
- Inadequate instructions or procedures
- Inadequate information/data indicators
- Noise exposures
- Presence of harmful materials
- Inadequate support/assistance/resources
- Inadequate quality, safety, health, and environmental exposures
- Inadequate design preparation, and/or planning

Figure 3.10: Examples of Substandard Conditions

It is essential to consider these practices and conditions only as immediate causes or symptoms and to do a thorough job of diagnosing the basic causes behind the symptoms. If you treat only the symptoms, they will occur again and again. You need to ask the essential question, "Why?"

- Why did that substandard act or practice occur?
- Why did that substandard condition exist?
- Why did our management system permit that practice or condition?

If your investigation is thorough, the answers will point the way to more effective management control. To solve business performance problems, you must get at the basic, real, or root causes.

Basic Causes: Personal and Job/System Factors

Basic causes are the diseases or real causes behind the symptoms; they are the reasons why the substandard acts and conditions occurred and the factors that, when identified, permit meaningful management control. Often, these are referred to as root causes, latent factors, real causes or underlying causes. While immediate causes (the symptoms; the substandard acts/practices and conditions) are usually quite apparent, it takes a bit of probing to get at basic causes and to gain control of them. Basic causes help explain why people perform substandard practices. Logically, a person is not likely to follow an unknown procedure.

Likewise, the operator of complex equipment will not operate it efficiently and safely without the chance to develop skill through guided practice. It is equally logical that poor quality of work and substantial waste will result from placing a person with faulty eyesight on a job where good vision is critical for proper performance. Similarly, a person who is never told the importance of a job is unlikely to be motivated to a high degree of pride in his or her work.

Basic causes also help explain why substandard conditions exist. Equipment and materials that are inadequate or hazardous will be purchased if there are not adequate standards, and if compliance with standards is not managed. Substandard structures and work process layouts will be designed and built if there are not adequate standards and compliance for design and construction. Equipment will wear out and produce a substandard product, create waste and/or break down and cause accidents if that equipment is not properly selected, properly used, and properly maintained.

Just as it is helpful to consider two major categories of immediate causes (substandard acts/practices and substandard conditions), so is it helpful to think of basic causes in two major categories:

1.   Personal Factors (Figure 3.11), and
2.   Job/System Factors (Figure 3.12).

Basic causes are the origins of substandard acts/practices and conditions. However, they are not the beginning of the cause and effect sequence. What starts the sequence, ending in loss, is lack of management control.

Basic Causes: Personal Factors

1. **Inadequate Physical / Physiological Capability**
    1.1. inappropriate height, weight, size, strength, reach, etc.
    1.2. restricted range of body movement
    1.3. limited ability to sustain body positions
    1.4. substance sensitivities or allergies
    1.5. sensitivities to sensory extremes (temperature, sound, etc.)
    1.6. vision deficiency
    1.7. hearing deficiency
    1.8. other sensory deficiency (touch, taste, smell, balance)
    1.9. respiratory incapacity
    1.10. other permanent physical disabilities
    1.11. temporary disabilities

2. **Inadequate Mental/Psychological Capability**
    2.1. fears and phobias
    2.2. emotional disturbance
    2.3. mental illness
    2.4. intelligence level
    2.5. inability to comprehend
    2.6. poor judgment
    2.7. poor coordination
    2.8. slow reaction time
    2.9. memory failure
    2.10. low learning aptitude
    2.11. low mechanical aptitude

3. **Physical or Physiological Stress**
    3.1. injury or illness
    3.2. fatigue due to task load or duration
    3.3. fatigue due to lack of rest
    3.4. fatigue due to sensory overload
    3.5. exposure to health hazards
    3.6. exposure to temperature extremes
    3.7. oxygen deficiency
    3.8. atmospheric pressure variation
    3.9. constrained movement
    3.10. blood sugar deficiency
    3.11. drugs

4. **Mental or Psychological Stress**
    4.1. emotional overload
    4.2. fatigue due to mental task load or speed
    4.3. extreme judgment/decision demanded
    4.4. routine, monotony, demand for uneventful vigilance
    4.5. extreme concentration/perception demands
    4.6. "meaningless" or "degrading" activities
    4.7. confusing directions
    4.8. conflicting demands
    4.9. preoccupation with problems
    4.10. mental illness
    4.11. frustration

5. **Lack of Knowledge**
    5.1. lack of experience
    5.2. inadequate orientation
    5.3. inadequate initial training
    5.4. inadequate updated training
    5.5. misunderstood directions
    5.6. lack of situational awareness

6. **Lack of Skill**
    6.1. inadequate initial instruction
    6.2. inadequate practice
    6.3. infrequent performance
    6.4. lack of coaching
    6.5. inadequate review instruction
    6.6. improper instructor qualification
    6.7. inadequate training systems

7. **Improper Motivation**
    7.1. improper performance is rewarded (tolerated)
    7.2. proper performance is punished
    7.3. lack of incentives
    7.4. excessive frustration
    7.5. inappropriate aggression
    7.6. improper attempt to save time or effort
    7.7. inadequate reinforcement of proper
    7.8. improper attempt to gain attention
    7.9. inappropriate peer pressure
    7.10. improper supervisory example
    7.11. inadequate performance feedback
    7.12. improper attempt to avoid discomfort
    7.13. inadequate production incentives
    7.14. inadequate process of organizational change

Figure 3.11: Examples of Personal Factors

Basic Causes: Job / System Factors

1. Inadequate Leadership and/or Supervision
1.1. unclear or conflicting reporting relationships
1.2. unclear or conflicting assignment of responsibility
1.3. improper or insufficient delegation
1.4. giving inadequate policy, procedure, practices, and/or guidelines
1.5. giving conflicting objectives, goals, and/or standards
1.6. inadequate work planning or programming
1.7. inadequate instructions, orientation and/or training
1.8. providing inadequate reference documents, directives and guidance publications
1.9. inadequate identification and evaluation of loss exposures
1.10. lack of supervisory/management job knowledge
1.11. inadequate matching of individual qualifications and job/task requirements
1.12. inadequate performance measurements and evaluation
1.13. inadequate or incorrect performance feedback

2. Inadequate Project Management and Engineering
2.1. inadequate assessment of loss exposures
2.2. inadequate consideration of human factors/ergonomics
2.3. inadequate standards, specifications, and/or design criteria
2.4. inadequate monitoring of construction
2.5. inadequate assessment of operational readiness
2.6. inadequate monitoring of initial operation
2.7. inadequate evaluation of changes

3. Inadequate Purchasing and Contractor Management
3.1. inadequate specifications on requisitions
3.2. inadequate research on materials/equipment
3.3. inadequate specifications to vendors
3.4. inadequate mode or route of shipment
3.5. inadequate receiving inspection and acceptance
3.6. inadequate communication of safety and health data
3.7. improper handling of materials
3.8. improper storage of materials
3.9. improper transporting of materials
3.10. inadequate identification of hazardous items
3.11. improper salvage and/or waste disposal

4. Inadequate Maintenance, Inspection, and Controls
4.1. inadequate preventive
   ...assessment of needs
   ...adjustment / assembly
   ...lubrication and servicing
   ...cleaning or resurfacing
4.2. inadequate reparative
   ...communication of needs
   ...examination of units
   ...scheduling of work
   ...part substitution organizations

5. Inadequate Product, Tools, and Equipment
5.1. inadequate assessment of needs and risks
5.2. inadequate human factors/ergonomics considerations
5.3. inadequate standards or specifications
5.4. inadequate availability
5.5. inadequate adjustment/repair/maintenance
5.6. inadequate salvage and reclamation
5.7. inadequate removal and replacement of unsuitable items

6. Inadequate Work Standards / Compliance Requirements
- 6.1. inadequate development of standards inventory and evaluation of exposures and needs
  - ...coordination with process design
  - ...employee involvement
  - ...inconsistent standards/procedures/rules
- 6.2. inadequate communication of standards
  - ...publication
  - ...distribution
  - ...translation to appropriate languages
  - ...reinforcing with signs, color codes and job aids
- 6.3. inadequate maintenance of standards
  - ...tracking of work flow
  - ...updating
  - ...monitoring use of standards/ procedures/rules

7. Excessive Wear and Tear
- 7.1. inadequate planning of use
- 7.2. improper extension of service life
- 7.3. inadequate inspection and/or monitoring
- 7.4. improper loading or rate of use
- 7.5. inadequate maintenance
- 7.6. use by unqualified or untrained people
- 7.7. use for wrong purpose

8. Inadequate Communications
- 8.1. Inadequate horizontal communication between peers
- 8.2. Inadequate verbal communication between supervisor and person
- 8.3. Inadequate communication between different
- 8.4. Inadequate communication between work groups
- 8.5. Inadequate communication between shifts
- 8.6. Inadequate communication methods
- 8.7. No communication method available
- 8.8. Incorrect instructions

Figure 3.12: Examples of Job / System Factors

Lack of Control: Inadequate System, Requirements (Standards), and/or Compliance

Control is one of the four essential management functions: plan, organize, lead/direct, and control. These functions relate to any manager's work, regardless of level, title, and/or managed activity.

The person who manages, professionally knows the management system and performance requirements, plans and organizes work to meet the standards, leads people to attain the standards, measures performance of self and others, evaluates results and needs, and commends and constructively corrects performance. This is management control. Without it, the sequence of events begins and triggers the continuing causal factors that ultimately lead to loss. Without an adequate management system, the incident cause and effect sequence is started and, unless corrected in time, leads to losses, and the system cannot sustain itself over time.

There are three common reasons for lack of control:
- inadequate system,
- inadequate standards, and
- inadequate compliance with standards.

Inadequate System

Remember the basic management system model we saw in figure 3.1? A management system may be inadequate and, ultimately, unsustainable because of too few and/or improper system activities. While the necessary activities vary with an organization's scope, nature, type, and risk potential, significant research and the experience of successful systems in many different companies and countries show that there are common processes for building a management system.

These typical activities are shown in Figure 3.13 with the management system model/continual improvement loop that was noted earlier in the book.

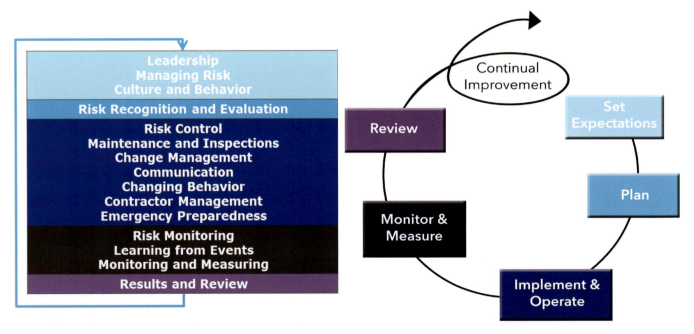

Figure 3.13: Main Activities within a Management System

Inadequate Requirements (Standards)

A common cause of confusion and failure is requirements that are not specific enough, not clear enough and/or not high enough. Proper requirements let people know what is expected of them and permit meaningful measurement of how well they perform in relation to those requirements. Simply put, management system requirements should specify:

- WHO does WHAT
- WHEN or
- HOW OFTEN?

Adequate performance requirements are essential for achieving adequate control. Requirements that do not include all three of these components are more wishful thinking than they are meaningful.

Additionally, when determining, writing, and implementing performance requirements, these questions should also be considered and answered:

- What is the deliverable?
- Why is it important?
- What reviews are required?
- Do they contribute to sustainability where relevant?

Organization should have specific, clear, challenging, and demanding requirements for all management system processes and for all major work activities identified. Below are some sample performance requirements from several processes in a management system.

- The Site Senior Manager will include HSEQ issues and concerns as a significant part (at least 25%) of the agenda at all monthly general management coordination meetings.
- The HSEQ performance of each member of management will be evaluated annually by the manager's immediate supervisor.
- Annual HSEQ performance objectives will be established by each member of management during the fourth quarter. These objectives will be oriented to management system development and improvements in overall business performance, including quality.
- All Senior Managers will lead at least one HSEQ promotional campaign annually in order to promote safe behavior stand culture.
- All new members of management will be given an HSEQ Management System orientation during the first week of work assignment by their immediate supervisor.
- All Sales Managers will survey, evaluate, and report customer satisfaction data quarterly to Senior Management for further review.
- Shift supervisors will conduct planned general inspections not less than every two months, with a customized area checklist.
- Shift supervisors will conduct behavioral observations, along with an employee feedback session, not less than once per month, using their Critical Behaviors List.
- Warehouse Supervisors will conduct quality control (QA/QC) inspections of their critical stock items for damage, expiry dates, etc., every two weeks using a standard checklist. Any findings resulting from these QA/QC inspections are to be followed up by the Warehouse Supervisor with Purchasing Department personnel within 10 days.

Inadequate Compliance with Requirements (Standards)

Lack of compliance with existing requirements is a common reason for lack of management control. In fact, many managers/leaders feel that this is the single greatest reason for failure to control loss, although studies have shown that failure is more often associated with inadequate performance requirements, not compliance.

Effective ways of gaining and continually improving the compliance to performance requirements include the following activities:

- Communication of performance requirements
- Training
- Promotion
- Observation
- Coaching
- Review and update, as necessary, of requirements
- Reinforcement of performance
- Re-education on oversights
- Progressive discipline

Establishing Management Control

Developing a sustainable management system for proactive, effective health and safety management means moving from lack of control to management control. Management control is established by:

- Developing a suitable, adequate, and effective management system
- Developing suitable, adequate, and effective performance requirements
- Ensuring compliance with performance requirements through measurement of performance, evaluation of strengths and opportunities, and coaching to improve performance in individuals.

When these are achieved, loss causation is transformed into loss control or management control.

Correcting these three common reasons for lack of control is a critical management/leadership responsibility. Furthermore:

- Developing a suitable, adequate, and effective management system and standards is a leadership function, aided by supervisors.
- Maintaining compliance with standards is a supervisory function, aided by leaders.

Figure 3.14 shows this basic process.

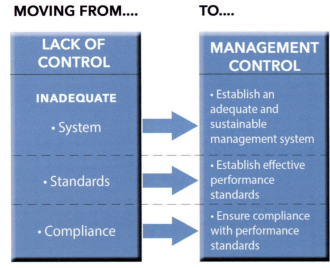

Figure 3.14: Establishing Management Control

Plan – Do – Check – Act (PDCA)

The PDCA process, long advocated as a management control system in the quality arena, is a perfectly appropriate health and safety management system.

Plan

The organization must first determine the elements of a health and safety management system appropriate for their specific exposures.

There is a body of knowledge for managing safety. It is comprised of many different elements and, although there is general agreement on what these elements are, they are expressed in a variety of different ways by various organizations. The following are examples from internationally accepted standards for safety management.

First, from the International Safety Rating System (ISRS) 6th Edition, a proprietary product of DNV GL, there are twenty elements that comprise this body of knowledge, specifically for health and safety:

- Leadership and Administration
- Leadership Training
- Planned Inspections
- Task Analysis and Procedures
- Accident/Incident Investigation
- Task Observation
- Emergency Preparedness
- Rules and Work Permits
- Accident/Incident Analysis
- Knowledge and Skills Training
- Personal Protective Equipment
- Occupational Health and Industrial Hygiene
- System Evaluation
- Engineering and Change Management
- Personal Communications
- Group Communications
- General Promotions
- Hiring and Placement
- Materials and Services Management
- Off-the-Job Safety

Another DNV GL product, isrs7, expresses this body of knowledge from the perspective of an integrated system that includes safety, health, environment, quality, and business related risk management elements. They are:
- Leadership
- Planning and Administration
- Risk Evaluation
- Human Resources
- Compliance Assurance
- Project Management
- Training and Competence
- Communications and Promotions
- Risk Control
- Asset Management
- Contractor Management and Purchasing
- Emergency Preparedness
- Learning from Events
- Risk Monitoring
- Results and Review

The Occupational Health and Safety Assessment Series (OHSAS) 18001 is an internationally recognized standard for safety management systems certification. The OHSAS elements are:

4.1 General Requirements
4.2 Occupational Health and Safety Policy
4.3.1 Planning for Hazard Identification, Risk Assessment and Risk Control
4.3.2 Legal and Other Requirements
4.3.3 Objectives
4.3.4 OH&S Management Programs
4.4.1 Structure and Responsibility
4.4.2 Training, Awareness and Competence
4.4.3 Consultation and Communication
4.4.4 Documentation
4.4.5 Document and Data Control
4.4.6 Operational Control
4.4.7 Emergency Preparedness and Response
4.5.1 Performance Measurement and Monitoring
4.5.2 Accidents, Incidents, Non-Conformances and Corrective and Preventive Actions
4.5.3 Records and Records Management
4.5.4 Audits
4.6 Management Review

Finally, the American National Standards Institute has developed a standard for safety management systems (ANSI Z10) which includes five major elements:

- Management Leadership and Employee Participation
- Planning
- Implementation and Operation
- Evaluation and Corrective Action
- Management Review

The essential content of these instruments is the same. These resources can aid the organization to identify the elements appropriate for its health and safety management system. That system must be customized to the specific needs and exposures of the organization.

Do
The organization must write specific and appropriate system requirements (who, does what, when or how often). These requirements may need to be different for various locations and operations within the same organization depending on factors such as management structure and work schedules. Examples of appropriate requirements are provided earlier in this chapter.

Check
The organization must develop and routinely apply means of measuring the effectiveness of the health and safety management system. Please refer to the chapter on Reviewing Performance for detailed information on effective means of such measurements.

Act
Organizational leadership must regularly review the findings of the measurement systems and make decisions to correct or enhance the system. They must answer the question, "What's next?" This forward thinking makes the health and safety system sustainable.

ISO 14001:2004 and OHSAS 18001:2007

Figure 3.15 demonstrates how Plan, DO, Check, Act (PDCA) relates to the elements of the OHSAS18001 standard.

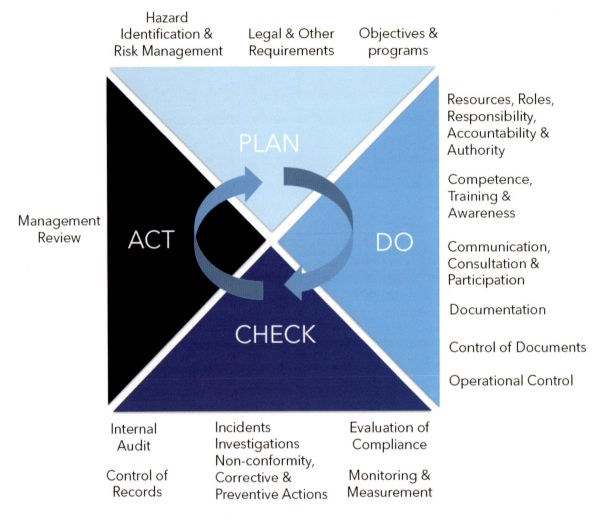

Figure 3.15: PDCA Applied to Health and Safety

Lisa Delivers!

Lisa is a dedicated professional who has proved to be an asset to the organization in her safety and health role. Recently, however, she has taken a deeper interest in issues related to sustainability and, because of this, wants to expand her role accordingly.

After her discussion with Henry, Lisa got together with Joe and was able to plan and develop a new employee/contractor training package addressing the following topics and objectives:

- To ensure that the workforce has a better understanding of what a management systems approach is and its benefits,

- To show how the organization's management system must also be sustainable so there is continuity to the business,

- To show how a risk-based approach must be integrated into the overall management system, and

- To train and inspire all levels of management to accept and adopt relevant sustainable management practices in their areas or departments.

Over the past three months, Lisa has piloted this training to overall high approval and participant ratings. Each participant has also been given some direct ownership of the concepts taught and is required to plan and implement a project that puts "theory into practice."

Some of the proposed and approved projects to date include:

1. Martin Thomas' work group is preparing a paper for a sustainability conference in Europe. Their project will discuss initiatives taken at the plant that correlate how "good safety records" lead to a more sustainable business.

2. The Purchasing Department is surveying suppliers at the local and state level who can supply more recycled and recyclable materials to the organization. Once an "Approved Supplier" list is created, the organization will use this in their revised tendering and purchasing processes.

3. Operations Planning is looking at ways to reduce overall energy usage, in addition to being more energy efficient. A team has drawn up proposals to retrofit existing buildings using LEED principles, establish policies and procedures for replacement of all lighting with LED-type fixtures, and the Legal Department is assisting them in reviewing the existing legal frameworks from both a compliance and a tax incentive/subsidy perspective to maximize these benefits.

4. The Human Resources Department is preparing both a short course in sustainability principles and practices for the middle school level to be used by the local school districts and providing qualified personnel from the organization to serve as instructors.

5. Joe has convinced senior management to start purchasing hybrid automobiles for the company car fleet and to, ultimately, replace all the older conventional models.

6. The Board of Directors has recently approved a partnership with VERDANT.com, an Online movement that uses social media to promote greener habits by allowing participants to accept or create Green Challenges – specific acts to reduce their CO_2 emissions as part of a collective effort to combat climate change.

7. The HSE Department is launching an "Off-the-Job Sustainability" program. This program is behavior-based and taps into the following logic:

> For a person to be responsible for his/her actions is also a part of managing, which, in turn, is part of managing sustainably. To be able to manage oneself sustainably, there are many factors to consider, because to be able to manage oneself, a person needs to be able to see what they are doing unsustainably and how to become sustainable.

The HSE Department has produced posters and presentations using the following themes and behaviors for their focused campaigns:

1. Using plastic bags at a supermarket is unsustainable because it creates pollutants. Using reusable biodegradable bags can resolve the problem.
2. Deciding to buy local food to make the community stronger through community sustainable management is more emotionally, environmentally, and physically rewarding.

Key Point Summary

1. We can define a management system as "a framework of controls for managing key processes, organizational risks, and driving continual improvement."
2. Sustainable management can be defined as "the application of sustainable practices in the categories of businesses, society, the environment, and other relevant areas by managing them in a way that will benefit current generations and future generations."
3. Taking a "management systems approach" provides consistency and continuity to an organization and provides the structure for it to achieve its purpose and goals, as well as to make continual improvements.
4. Ideally, all management systems should integrate risk-based thinking and approaches. This was seen in the Managing Risk model presented, which included Risk Recognition, Risk Evaluation, Risk Control, and Risk Monitoring.
5. Risk Control is represented by an approach known as the "4-T's," which includes strategies for Terminating, Treating, Tolerating, and/or Transferring risks.
6. The Loss Causation model provides a simple and structured approach to understanding how an inadequate management system contributes to loss causation and can threaten the sustainability of the organization. The model consists of five blocks covering Lack of Control, Basic Causes, Immediate Causes, Incident, and Loss. Ultimately, a management system can be considered as a series of performance requirements established to prevent and minimize losses, maximize opportunities, and which should be established based on a thorough understanding of the causes of loss in an organization.
7. The number of incidents can be represented by the various Ratio Studies presented. The first, classical study done in 1969 showed a 1 – 10 – 30 – 600 ratio of serious/major injury to minor injuries to property damage to near-misses, respectively.
8. The costs of incidents are represented by the Costs Icebergs presented. Typically, an organization can experience anywhere from 5 – 50 dollars (or other unit of currency) of uninsured property damage costs for every 1 dollar spent on injury and illness costs, plus an additional 1 – 3 dollars of uninsured miscellaneous costs.
9. Performance requirements must be clearly defined by the organization and include three factors: what work is to be done, who is to do it, and when or how often it is to be done.
10. Implementation of management performance requirements is strengthened when the following questions are adequately addressed for each requirement:
    - What is the deliverable?
    - Why is it important?
    - What reviews are required?
    - Do they contribute to sustainability where relevant?

Personal Planning

- Can I explain, in general terms, my organization's safety and health management system?
- Can I identify the elements of the system?
- Do I know how the system is measured?
- Do I know what management system requirements apply to me and my job?
- How does my organization define accident and incident?
- Which term do we use?
- Do we understand what types of events are included in the terms?
- What can I do to help my colleagues and the people who report to me understand our system and its requirements?

Y – Model for Action Planning

Present Situation

Desired Situation

Need for Change

Present Situation

Stop Responsibility Target Date

BUILDING AN IMPROVEMENT CULTURE

Chapter 4

BUILDING AN IMPROVEMENT CULTURE

> **CHAPTER OBJECTIVES**
> 1. To define organizational culture and its various components.
> 2. To illustrate how organizational culture drives development and implementation of health and safety systems.
> 3. To identify the characteristics of a positive organizational culture, especially as they relate to health and safety performance.
> 4. To provide practical tools for an organization to assess its culture.

Carlos – A Valuable Resource

Joe has developed an interest in conducting a comprehensive survey to identify strengths and opportunities in his organization's culture. He has worked with Human Resources to acquire the services of a reputable consultant to conduct the survey, which is scheduled for next month. One day, as Joe is walking through the plant and chatting with people on the floor, he decides to conduct a little informal survey of his own.

Carlos and one of his operators are taking a break, so Joe engages them in a conversation. "Hi, guys! Mind if I join you for a few minutes?"

"Not at all, boss!" says the operator Kim. One of the workers says. "Have a seat. Can I get you a water?"

"Thanks, that would be good. Am I interrupting anything?"

"No. We were just talking about last night's game."

"I couldn't stay up to watch it all. Besides, I don't think it was a very good one."

"You're right. Not very exciting."

Joe asks, "Care if I change the subject for a few minutes?"

"Sure. What's up?"

"I would really like to get some idea of what our people think of our health and safety program. Do they think it works? What is good about it? What can be improved? That kind of thing."

Carlos speaks up, but the operator seems a bit shy. "I think they are pleased, for the most part. I don't hear a lot of conversation about it, but participation in our safety meetings is pretty good and near-miss reporting has improved a bit. What about you, Kim?"

"Well," Kim, the operator, adds, hesitantly, "I think it's fine. I mean, we haven't had any serious incidents in a while and people seem to care about each other."

Joe pushes a bit for more information. "Let me be specific. Do people feel they get good health and safety training?"

Carlos responds first, "Yeah, I think they are okay with it. I do hear a little grumbling when we have to do annual refresher training on compliance issues. A lot of people think it is too much."

"Kim?" Joe asks.

"Sometimes, I think we overdo it a little. I mean, we go over the same things all the time. It gets boring."

"I am sure that can happen. Maybe we should look for ways to fix that. Okay, how about the people's perception of leadership?"

At that point, Kim, the operator, seems a little uncomfortable and excuses herself to return to work.

"Carlos, what do you think?"

"I think our employees know the organization cares about their wellbeing, but sometimes they get mixed messages that cause some doubts."

"Like what?"

"Well, the organization's health and safety policy statement is very good. There are a lot of communications about things that are being done to improve. Health and safety have a high profile and there are many obvious efforts. Sometimes, though, people can't understand why certain things aren't fixed or why their suggestions are ignored. Those negatives sometimes outweigh the positives."

"How about their perception of our incident reporting and investigation system?"

"Most of the time, I think they see the good that comes out of them, but there are times when they perceive that the investigation just results in someone getting punished. I have discovered one or two significant events that should have been reported, but weren't because the people involved thought they would get in trouble."

"Carlos, thanks for the insight. I am really looking forward to the results of the culture survey. That should give us some key areas to work on for the next few months."

Five weeks later, Joe and his team sit down with the results of the culture survey. While the information Carlos provided proves to be very insightful, there are really no other major concerns that come to light. The team develops an improvement strategy and timetable. Later, Joe requests to meet with Carlos at a convenient time to present the findings and plans to him. Carlos responds,

"Okay, how can I help?" Joe hands him the following information and suggests they talk after Carlos had a chance to read it.

Introduction

As a component of sustainable business development, improving Safety and Health performance is a major concern of all organizations. As Safety and Health performance is closely related to organizational culture, this chapter aims to help organizational leadership understand how to assess and improve organizational culture and specifically their respective roles in driving that improvement.

What is Organizational Culture?

There is no single definition of organizational culture.

Collins English Dictionary defines organizational culture as "the customs, rituals, and values shared by the members of an organization that have to be accepted by new members."

Definitions of culture derived from the field of sociology tend to focus on the common roles, statuses, norms, and values shared by a group of people.

Business Dictionary.com defines organizational culture as "the values and behaviors that contribute to the unique social and psychological environment of an organization."

The definition continues. Organizational culture includes an organization's expectations, experiences, philosophy, and values that hold it together, and is expressed in its self-image, inner workings, interactions with the outside world, and future expectations. It is based on shared attitudes, beliefs, customs, and written and unwritten rules that have been developed over time and are considered valid. Also called corporate culture, it's shown in:

(1) the ways the organization conducts its business, treats its employees, customers, and the wider community,

(2) the extent to which freedom is allowed in decision making, developing new ideas, and personal expression,

(3) how power and information flow through its hierarchy, and

(4) how committed employees are towards collective objectives."
Are we all working toward the same objectives?

It may be oversimplification, but the most practical definition of organizational culture is the way the organization and its members think and act.

While the term safety culture is commonly used, it is the belief of the authors that this term tends to separate safety from other aspects, characteristics, or concerns of the organization, which is not necessarily a proper concept. Safety should be seen as an integral part of the whole of the organization; therefore, we prefer to use the term organizational culture.
The way the organization and its members think and act about safety and health is a vital component of its culture. If the values and behaviors around safety and health are based on sound, proven principles and driven by a proper understanding of how safety and health management systems should work, the organization is set up for success. If not, the organization's efforts at safety performance improvement may well be inconsistent, frustrating, or even harmful.

The following definitions of the Safety and Health aspects of culture are found in related literature.

INSAG (1991): That assembly of characteristics and attitudes in organizations and individuals which establishes that, as an overriding priority, nuclear plant safety issues receive the attention warranted by their significance.

UK Health & Safety Executive (1993): The product of individual and group values, attitudes, perceptions, competencies, and patterns of behavior that determine the commitment to, and the style and proficiency of, an organization's health and safety management.

Guldenmund (2000): Those aspects of the organizational culture which will impact on attitudes and behavior related to increasing or decreasing risk.

Mearns, et al (2003): Safety culture…forms the environment within which individual safety attitudes develop and persist and safety behaviors are promoted.

Von Thaden and Gibbons (2008): Safety culture is defined as the enduring value and prioritization of worker and public safety by each member of each group and in every level of an organization.

Barnes (2009): The values, attitudes, motivations and knowledge that affect the extent to which safety is emphasized over competing goals in decisions and behavior.

Leadership Actions Drive Organizational Culture

The best safety systems in the world will fail without a supportive culture.

This phenomenon is highlighted in the official investigations into major incidents that have gained worldwide attention in the last few decades.

- A rail disaster outside Paddington Station in London, UK, in 1999 resulted in a newspaper headline that claimed that the organization was "riddled with complacency."
- The Challenger and Columbia space shuttle disasters were described as being due, at least in part, to deficient culture in NASA.
- On completing an investigation of a refinery explosion in the US in 2005, investigators identified deficient organizational culture as a contributing factor.

In other words, an organization might have developed a very robust H & S management system, consisting of best practices and state-of-the-art tools; however, if the culture is deficient, then that system cannot work as it should.

For example, the organization might have a well-designed and adequately resourced lock-out, tag-out, try-out program. All appropriate persons have been trained, adequate locks are conveniently provided, lock-out points clearly identified, procedures annotated where necessary, etc.; however, the culture is such that not everyone is convinced of the need to lock out every time and the habit of ignoring LO/TO/TO in certain situations is condoned. Leadership actions drive a deficient culture.

It is not possible to graft a specific culture onto an organization, as each organization is unique.

Attitudes, both personal and organizational, affect the development of culture in the workplace. The environment in which people work in and the systems and processes of an organization also influence culture. Therefore, each organization needs to consider all of these aspects while developing and nurturing an organizational culture that suits the organization and the individuals within it.

The management system employed by an organization and its culture are the primary drivers of behaviors in the workplace.

The available literature indicates that a number of factors are in place in organizations that have a culture that supports H & S performance.

1. Commitment to H & S improvement exists at all levels of the organization

Positive culture, as well as effective safety and health performance, begins with senior leadership. It is fairly easy for leaders to say or write encouraging words about safety and health, but it is quite another for leadership to exhibit behaviors that demonstrate they actually believe and practice those words.

In an effective organizational culture, the organization adopts safety and health as a core value and actively cares for the workforce. The vision for the organization is that the workplace will be free of incidents/injuries and health and safety are integrated into every aspect of the work process. This attitude is evident throughout the organization from senior leadership through to the newest and most inexperienced member of the workforce.

Safety is not seen as a priority, but as a value. Priorities change constantly depending on various factors. Values, although they do change, do not change as readily as priorities.

Safety is not promoted first, but is seen as an integral part of the way we work. It isn't something separate or different. Safety is simply who we are. In order to do things correctly, they must also be done safely.

2. Health and safety are treated as an investment or even a potential savings opportunity, not a cost

Risk management of safety and health issues must not be treated as a cost, but as a way to improve the performance of the organization. Safety and health should be reported as part of the budget development process and funded accordingly.

There is a cost to health and safety. In some organizations, budget decisions are taken based on initial cost estimates for implementation or improvement without a real consideration of the associated risks. The costs of incidents that may result are much greater than the cost of implementation or improvement.

In the chapter on Basic Concepts of Safety and Health Management Systems, you will find information on the cost of loss and the negative impact that those costs have on an organization's bottom line performance. Actions taken to minimize such losses can have a positive effect on that performance.

It has been said that there are two ways to improve an organization's profit. First, gain more market share and sell more product or service. Second, control loss. In a very competitive marketplace where it can be very difficult to accomplish the first objective, the second objective becomes much more attractive.

3. Safety and health are part of continual improvement

If safety and health are integrated into every part of the organization, then they become part of the continual improvement process. This means that resources are set aside to ensure that the organization can identify weaknesses and develop strategy to resolve and strengthen safety performance.

Safety and health performance is a matter of continual improvement. No organization ever achieves a level of performance at which they can rest assured that all risks are adequately controlled. In fact, if and when an organization becomes so assured, it will most likely receive a rude wake-up call.

Change is inevitable. Changes in technology, work methods, chemical composition, climate, economy, stakeholder demands, medical technology, employee population, regulations, etc., will require continual improvement in an organization's health and safety management system.

4. Training and health and safety information are provided for everyone

People who are provided with regular information about safety and health at work are more likely to be mindful of safety and health issues and the ways in which their actions can affect themselves and others.

Posters, warning signs, and policies are not enough. Safety and health discussions and information distribution should be built into all aspects of the work process, from board meetings to individual interactions.

People who are properly trained in their jobs and are aware of the hazards associated with the role they (or those they supervise) perform are less likely to suffer or cause injury. Training can take a variety of forms and should be ongoing throughout an individual's time with the organization.

5. A system for workplace analysis and hazard prevention and control is in place

Management systems, safety systems and individual attitudes and perceptions can be researched, measured and analyzed to gain a picture of the current state of the organization and reveal barriers that prevent people from performing at their best.

This is often referred to as a climate survey and assists in establishing a base line for the organization to start from. Climate, perception or culture surveys are conducted at regular intervals in organizations that strive for a good organizational culture to measure successes.

Reporting systems should be easy to use (i.e. compact, open-ended, impersonal, and in practice) for leaders who want to know and learn from hazard identification and near misses before they become losses. Attention should be paid to the details and small events.

The way reports are analyzed must be agreed to ensure that individual and system issues are revealed and appropriate control measures taken.

The organization should employ robust methods of risk assessment. See the chapter on Risk Management for more details. This means that there should also be a commonly used set of risk criteria and a risk matrix. Furthermore, there needs to be an understanding and appropriate application of the hierarchy of controls to identified risks. A systematic and comprehensive process for continuous monitoring of the effectiveness of controls and changing exposures should also be installed.

The organization should also use methods such as critical task analysis, behavior observations, regular inspections, employee engagement, and surveys to identify exposures.

6. The environment in which people work is blame free

Trust is an essential part of a proper organizational culture and often the most difficult hurdle to overcome. Everyone in the organization should be encouraged to realize that incidents are worth reporting and should feel comfortable in correcting at-risk behaviors across, down, and up the hierarchy. If this is the case, then management actually knows what is going on and the workforce feels safe to tell the truth, even if it is not what management may want to hear. Holding people at all levels accountable for safety performance sometimes means embracing bad news.

There is a need for disciplinary policies in every organization and individuals must be held accountable for substandard performance.

However, there is a big difference between applying discipline in a consistent and fair way and fostering a blame culture.

Individuals should not be disciplined for having incidents, but for violating rules and procedures.

When latent organizational weaknesses exist, the burden of conformance to rules and procedures lies with the organization itself. Once the organization has satisfactorily addressed these weaknesses, the burden of conformance is transferred to the individual.

7. The organization celebrates successes

Recognition, rewards, incentives, reinforcement and feedback are important. A proper culture makes it worthwhile for everyone to maintain a state of mindfulness by celebrating success, whether big or small.

This concept is not meant to endorse all health and safety incentive programs. Such programs, when based on lagging indicators as the primary criteria for achievement, can have undesired, negative consequences for the organization. Incentive programs that are based on leading indicators, such as achievement of activity-based goals, are more beneficial. Incentives that require individuals or groups to know, learn, or do something for Safety and Health are more effective. For example, awards can be given to groups based on improvement in housekeeping, completion of risk assessments, attendance at group meetings, participation on Safety and Health promotion teams, or improvement in culture survey results.

The safety and health aspects of organizational culture are about improving safety and health management with a holistic, whole of organization, and whole of life approaches.

8. Safety and health activities are a line management function.

Safety and Health professionals are a vital resource for any organization; however, their function is to serve as internal consultants to line management, not to assume responsibility for the implementation of safety. In a proper culture, all leaders, from senior to front-line, have defined performance standards that require their participation in Safety and Health activities.

Typically, senior leaders would be expected to take health and safety tours, participate in audits, issue Safety and Health related communications on a regular basis, and review Safety and Health performance data to identify strengths and opportunities within the system.
Persons with titles such as superintendent or department manager (middle management) would be expected to participate in activities such as incident investigations in their areas of responsibility, evaluation of the Safety and Health performance of their direct reports, and conduct of reviews of behavior-based safety data for their area.

Front-line supervisors would be expected to serve as primary or initial investigators, conduct regular workplace inspections, conduct safety meetings, etc.

9. All employees can define, at least in general terms, the Safety and Health Management System.

All activities or elements in a safety and health management system must appear to be connected in a mutually supportive way. No single activity or element stands alone, but each has the potential to contribute either positively or negatively to the success of the whole.

In a proper culture, employees at every level know the general content and organization of the Safety and Health management system.

10. Compliance is seen as the minimum

Compliance with safety and health regulations should be the minimum the organization must do just to stay in business. Compliance in no way assures the organization it is providing a safe and healthy work environment or that it is protected from catastrophic incidents.

11. Risk competence is a continual improvement goal

The more risk competent the organization becomes—that is, the more effectively it systematically identifies, assess, controls, and monitors risk—the better its safety and health performance. Improving health and safety performance is largely a matter of making better risk decisions. The chapter on Risk Management in this book can provide some valuable insight into what risk competence means and how to pursue it.

12. Health and safety become a way of life

Safety and Health are not something about which employees become aware when they enter the facility or from which they disengage on leaving. Safety and Health permeates their lives such that their risk competence become apparent at home. They become more aware of Safety and Health exposures and make better risk decisions for themselves and their families. Health and safety become part of who they are.

Determining the Organizational Culture With Culture Surveys

This is one of the more difficult challenges for a site manager or Safety and Health Manager.

One common approach is to assess the culture using the Bradley curve (see Figure 4.1 below). Hudson Leader can also be used for this kind of assessment.

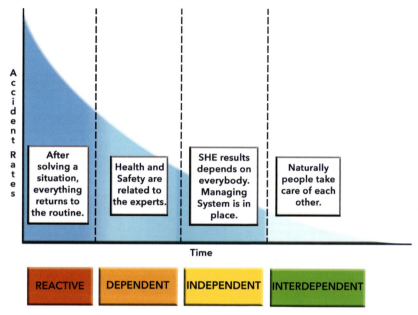

Figure 4.1: Bradley Curve

Safety Engagement Process explores the attitudes, values and behavior of employees regarding safety and their safety management system. This process raises awareness for important safety behavior issues. The process is designed to foster dialogue to help engender common attitudes, values, and behaviors towards safety as well as interdependences within the unit.

Figure 4.2: Safety Engagement Process

The process requires employees to take an anonymous survey. The results are then compiled in a graphical format. Employees can then discuss the survey results with their line manager in a workshop environment and identify improvement actions.

The survey content can be modified if necessary to suit different requirements.

To be exploitable, results can be presented in different ways, as shown in Figure 4.3 below.

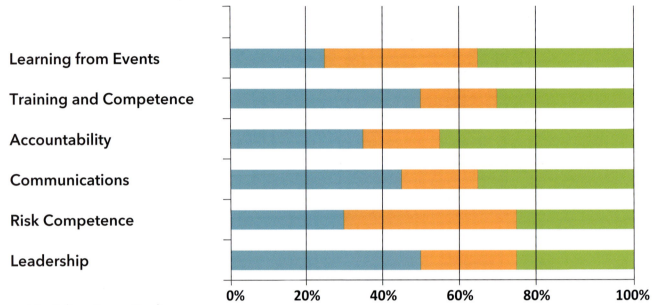

Figure 4.3: Culture Survey Results

At a glance, one can see that Training and Competence and Leadership are perceived as the strongest aspects of the organization's culture while Learning from Events and Risk Competence appear to be the best opportunities for improvement.

Other tools, such as the ISRS Alpha Assessment, can be valuable for this application.

Roadmap to a Positive Organizational Culture

To develop a positive culture, change needs to be driven from the highest levels. The extent to which you can influence the organization largely depends on your place within the hierarchy.

Senior leadership needs to understand the criticality of their role in shaping organizational culture. They need to understand that their words, written or verbal, are strong drivers of organizational culture and they must be careful to send the right messages. This starts with the Safety and Health policy statement that they sign and goes as far as the language they use every day when they interact with others in the organization. Just as a positive message delivered during a plant tour can contribute to a positive culture, a message that is perceived as negative can destroy a lot of good efforts.

In order to shape the culture positively, senior leaders need to have a basic understanding of Safety and Health management systems concepts and the role that the management system plays in loss causation and control. Persons at this level of an organization did not get their position because of their knowledge of health and safety. If they are expected to support Safety and Health efforts, they must be provided with that knowledge.

People are both products and producers of their environment. Any attempts to change attitudes without observing the environment they work in and the systems they work with is doomed to fail. Any change initiatives need to take account of the interrelationship between people, environment, and systems.

The Hudson Scale in Figure 4.4 below may explain the different steps to improve the culture

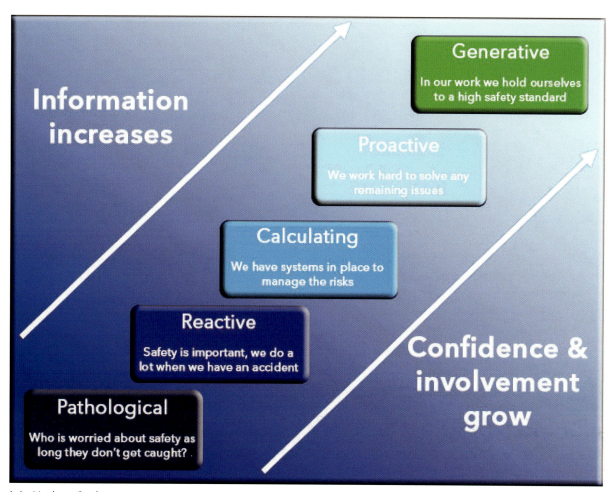

Figure 4.4: Hudson Scale

Culture Determines Characteristics of Management Systems

In the chapter Basic Concepts of Safety and Health Management Systems, the following Loss Causation Model is described. It is a simple way to understand the sequence of latent and active factors that lead to loss and the critical role the management system plays in loss causation and control.

Figure 4.5: Loss Causation Model

One could argue that there should be another block in the model preceding the Lack of Control block. Such a model would look like Figure 4.6.

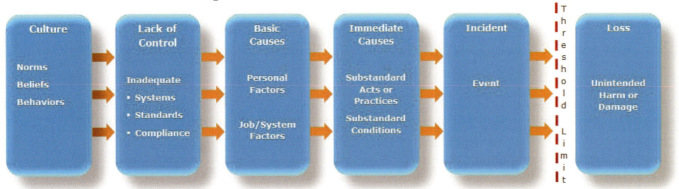

Figure 4.6: Modified Loss Causation Model

The modified model demonstrates that the organizational culture largely defines the kind of Safety and Health management system the organization employs. For example:

- If organizational leadership believes that the basic causes of incidents are substandard behaviors, they are going to focus their improvement efforts on correcting those behaviors in isolation from the management system. They will miss the fact that most substandard or at-risk behaviors are not intentional, but are largely due to deficiencies in the organization and inadequate training, out-of-date or inadequate procedures, poor communication, confusing or conflicting demands, poor design of the work environment, etc. If, on the other hand, leadership understands the role the Safety and Health management system plays in loss causation and control, they will focus on efforts to improve the system.
- If the norm in the organization is that Safety and Health staff appears to have the responsibility to keep employees safe, then Safety and Health activities will not be integrated into line management and the Safety and Health staff largely becomes safety officers. Leadership has no ownership of the process and little to no role to play in continual improvement.
- If leadership at any level fails to comply with Safety and Health requirements, the resulting message to employees is that leadership is somehow above the rules. This will destroy efforts at establishing a positive organizational culture.

Organizational Culture and Sustainability

"Sustainable development is meeting the needs of the present generation without compromising the ability of future generations to meet their own needs."

Bruntland Commission 1987

Organizations that are perceived as good corporate citizens operate on the above premise. It is a critical part of their belief system and decisions are always taken with this objective in mind. Health and safety objectives are established based on future needs and demands, not past records. The moral imperative to protect life is unquestionable and non-negotiable, not only for employees today, but also for succeeding generations.

Some have said that the ability of the individual and the system to change defines, at least in part, the difference management and leadership. Management is about making sure the system works today, that all the standards are met, all the forms are filled out, all the reports made, etc. Leadership is about challenging the system; that is, asking the question, "What about tomorrow?" That's sustainability. A proper organizational culture always asks the question, "What about tomorrow?"

Tool Box: Culture Survey Checklist

The following is a short, simple tool that an organization can use to get a sample of the perceptions and attitudes of employees at all levels. This should not be considered a complete culture survey. In order to have a high degree of confidence in the results, the organization must apply a more robust process.

Please rank each of the following statements on a scale of 1 to 5 according to the value definitions in the legend. When finished, please average your scores for each group of questions as directed in the second chart.

- 1 = **Disagree**
- 2 = **Somewhat disagree**
- 3 = **Neutral**
- 4 = **Somewhat agree**
- 5 = **Agree**

Statement	Ranking
1. Employees are actively engaged in the safety process and are consulted on safety issues.	
2. We receive an appropriate supply of safety-related information.	
3. Incident investigations are focused on solving the problem, not on finding fault.	
4. Safety is perceived as good business.	
5. Safety meetings are positive and beneficial.	
6. There is a clear training plan for each employee or position.	
7. Structured risk assessments are routinely used to determine appropriate safety controls.	
8. Contractor employees are held to the same safety performance standards as our employees.	

Tool Box: Culture Survey Checklist

Statement	Ranking
9. Safety concerns are never compromised in favor of production goals.	
10. Formal workplace inspections are carried out on a regular basis.	
11. Senior managers in my facility are visible and actively involved in safety.	
12. Emergency plans are comprehensive, clear, and well communicated.	
13. Employees can challenge management decisions on safety without fear of negative consequences.	
14. There is a strategic plan (3-5 years) for continual improvement of safety in my facility/unit.	
15. Personal protective equipment is appropriate and conveniently provided for all jobs/areas.	
16. I receive effective training and refresher training appropriate to my job responsibilities.	
17. We hold job-planning meetings that include safety considerations before all major projects (shut-downs, turn-arounds, installation of new equipment, etc.).	
18. A risk matrix, with specific definitions of high, moderate, and low risk is routinely used to facilitate risk assessment.	
19. We hold appropriate emergency drills.	
20. Formal pre-use inspections are conducted by operators of appropriate mobile and materials-handling equipment.	
21. Safety performance and capability are key components of the contractor selection process.	

Tool Box: Culture Survey Checklist

Statement	Banking
22. Safety meetings are interactive and employees actively participate.	
23. The disciplinary process for safety rules violations is applied fairly and consistently.	
24. The findings and recommendations resulting from investigations are followed up on in a timely and effective way.	
25. We have a strong orientation process that includes all appropriate safety information for new employees.	
26. Leadership at all levels of my unit effectively demonstrates their personal commitment to safety.	
27. We hold pre-start up safety reviews before activating any new, modified, or seasonally used equipment or processes.	
28. Annual safety objectives, including both statistical goals and plans, are communicated to all employees.	
29. My facility/unit is sufficiently staffed to enable safe operations.	
30. Employees participate as team members in workplace inspections.	
31. There is an active and beneficial program of behavior observations and coaching in my facility/unit.	
32. Reported near-misses are taken seriously and followed-up appropriately.	
33. The safety aspects of contractor's work are monitored routinely.	
34. Leaders provide positive feedback on performance.	
35. Leadership in my facility/unit effectively demonstrates its commitment to training.	

Question	Group Total	Group Average
Group 1: Questions 1,3,4,9,11,13,23,26,34 All questions in this group assess perceptions around leadership.		
Group 2: Questions 6,12,14,17,27,28 All questions in this group assess perceptions around planning		
Group 3: Questions 7,10,17,18,20,21,27,31 All questions in this group assess perceptions around risk evaluation.		
Group 4: Questions 6,16,19,25,35 All questions in this group assess perceptions around training.		
Group 5: Questions 2,5,11,12,22,25,26,28,31,34 All questions in this group assess perceptions around communication.		
Group 6: Questions 1,2,6,8,15,16,21,23,29,31,33 All questions in this group assess perceptions around risk controls.		
Group 7: Questions 10,20,30,33 All questions in this group assess perceptions around workplace inspections.		
Group 8: Questions 8,21,33 All questions in this group assess perceptions around contractor management.		
Group 9: Questions 12,19 All questions in this group assess perceptions around emergency preparedness		
Group 10: Questions 3,24,32 All questions in this group assess perceptions around incident investigations.		

Please total and average your scores for each of the following groups of questions.

Average scores of 4 or higher might indicate a strong culture. Average scores of 3 or less might indicate an opportunity for improvement.

Key Point Summary

1. It is more appropriate to speak of the organizational culture rather than the health and safety culture. To separate the two reinforces the improper perception that health and safety are somehow something different and that they are not an integral part of the business.
2. The simplest definition of organizational culture is the way the organization's members think and act.
3. Organizational culture deficiencies have been routinely identified as contributing factors in incident causation and the role of culture in causation is much better understood and appreciated than in the past.
4. There are several critical characteristics of a positive organizational culture, especially as it relates to health and safety:
    a. Commitment to Health & Safety improvement exists at all levels of the organization.
    b. Health and safety are treated as an investment or even a potential savings opportunity, not a cost.
    c. Health and safety are part of continual improvement.
    d. Adequate training and information is provided for everyone.
    e. A system for workplace analysis and hazard prevention and control is in place.
    f. The environment in which people work is blame-free.
    g. The organization celebrates successes.
    h. Health and safety activities are a line management function.
    i. Health and safety become a way of life.
5. Individuals at all levels of the organization can make a difference.

Personal Planning

1. What specific aspects of our organizational culture support positive health and safety efforts?
2. Are there any aspects of our culture that appear to be a deterrent to health and safety success?
3. What should I do to help improve the way we think and act about health and safety?
4. Based on the culture survey at the end of the chapter, what actions should our organization take to improve perceptions and drive a more positive culture?

Y – Model for Action Planning

Present Situation

Desired Situation

Need for Change

Present Situation

Stop Responsibility Target Date

RISK MANAGEMENT

Chapter 5

RISK MANAGEMENT

Chapter Objectives

1. The primary organizational competence that distinguishes the proactive safety and health management system from the reactive is the organization's ability to identify, assess, control, and monitor risk. The objectives of this chapter are:
2. To promote the idea that risk management concepts and technology represent the most effective means of achieving sustainable performance in safety and health.
3. To help the reader understand how risk management technology can be effectively applied in his/her area of responsibility.
4. To provide insight to practical tools that can be used on a routine basis to identify, assess, control, and monitor safety and health risks.
5. To help the organization become risk competent; that is, to become practiced and adept at using risk technology to achieve continual improvement.

Joe Looks Ahead

As a manager, Joe has always understood the need to get ahead of the curve. He has seen situations in which leaders primarily reacted to events in their organizations and continuously fought fires. He has watched them became very frustrated because they could not anticipate and plan to prevent those fires. He has even found himself in that position from time-to-time, but has worked hard at learning how to manage from a proactive position. He especially recognizes the need to be proactive in the safety and health aspects of his operation.

Lisa has been very instrumental in helping Joe put some structure to his objectives. She has provided him information on the value of risk management technology. She has implemented some basic risk identification and risk assessment activities in the plant and the positive results are self-evident. Lisa also asked Joe to accompany her to a lunch meeting of her safety and health professionals' organization, at which a speaker presented concepts and best practices for implementing systematic and comprehensive risk management processes. Joe came away with some good ideas for how this could be done in his plant. He also understands how this activity fits with the organization's sustainability initiative.

Joe is a very creative person and has been able to take that information and, with Lisa's help, develop a practical approach to making his organization risk competent. Joe understands that improvement in safety and health performance is largely dependent on how well the organization identifies, assesses, controls, and monitors risk. He understands that safety is about making better risk decisions.

Joe held a meeting with his plant leadership team and presented his plan. He gave each participant written material on the best practices for risk management programs. He then challenged his team to move quickly and methodically to implement the activities outlined in his plan. An implementation strategy was developed and, over a period of months, there was noticeable movement toward becoming a risk competent organization.

Joe and Lisa would like to share with you what they learned about risk management and its vital role in improving safety and health performance and sustainable business development.

CARLOS, THE RISK MANAGER

Carlos has only been a supervisor for a short while, but he has demonstrated both the required people skills and technical knowledge and ability to be a very important asset to the company. He has a strong desire to learn and understands the need for change if the organization is to continually improve.

Both Lisa and Joe recognize Carlos' abilities and energy and consider it vital to the success of their risk management initiatives at the working face. They ask him to sit down to discuss how he can be instrumental in making this effort a success.

After explaining the purpose of the meeting and outlining the plan, Joe asks, "Carlos, what do you think about what you have heard?"

"Well, it certainly makes sense to me. I mean, if we can identify where things could go wrong and put barriers in place to prevent them, it can only be a good thing. What I don't understand is what you want me to do."

Lisa explains, "Right now, we would like you to be a bit of a guinea pig. We would love you to work with us to develop details like risk identification checklists, risk criteria, structured risk assessments, and so on. When we have some basic materials ready, pioneer them in your area. Explain the activities to your people and engage them in the implementation process as much as possible."

Joe adds, "Carlos, you are a very influential and respected leader. I am sure you can develop very quickly. And that includes the associated benefits!"

Carlos soon found himself so interested and excited about the risk management activities that he was actually spending some of his own time planning for the project. Joe's prediction about Carlos' career also came true when Carlos' name headed the list for promotion to Department Superintendent.

Carlos would like to share with you some of the concepts, tools, and techniques he found helpful to his success. support for these new initiatives. You should be involved in training the appropriate people in the new knowledge and skills required to make this work. Of course, we are prepared to offer you the necessary training to get this off the ground."

"Okay, I'm convinced. Just tell me what you want. Oh, by the way," Carlos joked, "how much of a raise am I getting?"

Joe understands that this was said in jest, but responds in all seriousness, "If you make this work, I'm willing to bet you will move up the leadership ladder

What is Risk?

The ISO31000 Risk Management standard is a valuable resource for understanding how risk management works. At one time, the standard defined risk as "chance or probability of loss." ISO31000:2009, ISO Guide 73, defines risk as "the effect of uncertainty on objectives," which means that risk can apply to potential positive outcomes as well as negative ones.

Organizations have long understood the potential benefits of speculative risk; that is, risk intentionally undertaken when there is a possibility of gain. However, for our purposes, risk will be defined in terms of potential negative incidents, such as injuries, illnesses, property damage, and associated financial losses. These types of negative risk involve factors such as the probability an exposure will result in a loss, the potential severity of such a loss, and the frequency with which such a loss may occur.

What is Risk Management?

Risk Management is the process by which risks or exposures are identified and analyzed, followed by a determination of how best to handle each risk or exposure. The overall mandate of risk management is to comprehensively, consistently, and effectively manage all types of risks, including safety and health risks.

An effective risk management program describes the way in which the organization intends to carry out risk assessments and related processes. It can fulfill the following objectives:

1. Help an organization identify, understand, and manage specific risks;
2. Support risk-informed decision making by compiling risk information when making decisions affecting safety and health;
3. Maintain acceptable risk exposure for the organization;
4. Support compliance with external risk requirements and standards such as OHSAS18001 and Process Safety Management (PSM);
5. Apply risk management systematically, consistently, and efficiently across the organization.

There are additional benefits to such an approach since the same tools and techniques that enable identification, assessment, and control of safety and health risks can be used to help develop aspects and impacts information for the environmental factors.

A risk management program allows an organization to identify and control significant risk in a manner that provides useful information to management, optimizes controls to reduce risk, and reduces overall risk exposure.

An effective risk management process must address four steps or phases as illustrated in Figure 5.1. As represented by the cycle, risk management is a continuous process.

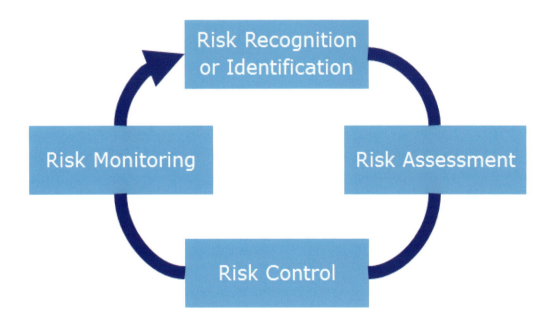

Figure 5.1 Risk Management Process

Although risk management, in the broadest sense, deals with all types of risks an organization might face, the focus of this book is on specific safety and health risks, sometimes called exposures or hazards.

Risk management technology (i.e., the tools and techniques available for implementing a robust risk management process) is quite varied. The technology used can range from simple techniques that can be used routinely at the working face by all employees to more comprehensive techniques that require special expertise and significant investment to apply. This chapter explores the full range of techniques, with an emphasis on those that are more operational and practical.

Risk Recognition or Identification

Effective risk management begins with the recognition or identification of threats. Once a threat is identified, the potential consequences that could result from that threat manifesting and the expected frequency of that consequence occurring are analyzed.

Threats and hazards are forces or events that may result in loss or have the potential to negatively impact an organization's ability to meet its objectives. Since the threats and hazards identified in this part of the process feed into the entire risk management process, accurate identification using effective, consistent methodologies is essential.

A systematic practice of threat identification must be comprehensively applied across all of an organization's functional areas and involve all levels of the organization. A consistent and uniform basis for threat identification is considered a prerequisite for correct and prudent prioritization and management of risk. The organization should define the preferred tools and techniques to be applied consistently across all operations.

As mentioned in the paragraph above, effective risk recognition or identification must involve persons at all levels of the organization. In practical terms, the people closest to the work are the most likely to be able to identify safety and health risks, exposures, or hazards.

The prudent organization will develop requirements for systematic, comprehensive risk recognition activities on a repeatable and routine basis for all operations. However, there are a number of events that should trigger such activities, including:

- Audits and assessment findings
- Incident investigations
- The management of change process
- Lessons learned events
- Employee concerns

Any of these triggers may present the possibility that a hazard or threat exists and precipitate the need for further analysis, in which case a hazard identification study can be conducted to gain a basic understanding of the hazard or threat. This section describes these methodologies and provides high-level guidance for their use.

The following section provides a brief overview of the more comprehensive techniques that are available for high-level threat assessments.

Organizational Risk (Threat) Identification Techniques

The methodologies described in Figure 5.2 below are appropriate for very high-level risk identification. They are more suitable for major projects, such as building of new plants, significant expansion of production processes, or other major changes. They are not practical for routine application and require special expertise and significant investment to apply. This chapter does not offer detailed explanation

Methodology	Purpose	Rating	Strengths	Weaknesses
HAZID	Identify and qualify threats, hazards, and risks	Skill – Medium Complexity – Low Cost – Low Value – High	Flexible tool for determining where quantified risk assessment is warranted. Useful when data is limited.	Does not produce detailed recommendations. Dependent on experienced team.
HAZOP	Identify operational / process risks	Skill – Medium Complexity – Medium Cost – High Value – High	Forces thorough evaluation of hazard and operability issues in the design of or changes to a process.	Requires detailed information. Dependent on experienced team.
FMECA	Any activities involving key equipment / machinery should go through RCM / FMECA	Skill – Medium Complexity – Medium Cost – Medium Value – High	Systematic evaluation of individual components to assess the effects of failures on systems or subsystems.	Not appropriate for analysis of multiple failures or highly complex systems.

Figure 5.2: Advanced Methods for Risk Identification

Operational Risk (Threat) Identification Techniques

The risk identification methodologies described in Figure 3 below are more practical for use on a routine, ongoing basis. All employees engaged in or responsible for operating and maintenance work should be well versed in their proper application. Each of these methods will be described in more detail.

Method	Description
Job Safety Analysis (JSA) or Critical Task Analysis (CTA)	Most all organizations employ some type of JSA/CTA. A JSA focuses on the safety and health risks of work while a CTA seeks to identify all risks of work, including safety and health.
Checklist	Simple set of prompts or checklist questions to assist in hazard identification. Used for OH&S type activities (e.g. permit to work, job safety analysis) where the type of hazards that may be present are fairly well understood. Tends to stifle creative thinking.
Pre-Start Up Safety Review	Performed as a means of identifying uncontrolled hazards prior to the operation of equipment or processes. Required by PSM standards in the United States.
Planned Inspections	Perhaps the oldest tool used for identification of hazards, especially physical conditions that could lead to loss. Best practices for a planned inspection process are the subject of a separate chapter in this book.
Simple Risk Assessment	The simplest and easiest tool for risk identification. It pushes risk identification competence right down to the workforce.

Figure 5.3: Operational Methods for Risk Identification

Job Safety Analysis/Critical Task Analysis

This tool is described in some detail in the chapter Task Competencies, Analysis and Training. Job Safety Analysis (JSA) is used by many organizations to focus on the identification and control of safety and health risks. Critical Task Analysis (CTA) employs a similar approach as JSA, but looks beyond safety and health to include environmental, quality, production, and business risks. We will focus on the JSA approach.

JSA is applied in two distinctly different ways:

1. Some organizations use JSA as a means to develop safe job procedures for use in training, development of Standard Operating Practices (SOP'S), or as a basis for task observation. In this application, the organization may determine to conduct JSA only on those tasks that have been identified as critical from a safety and health perspective. The JSA is a rather robust process involving supervisors and operators and a series of task observations and discussions in order to arrive at the finished product. This activity may be done periodically (or annually) and reviewed when changes occur. A document is then generated and filed for further use and future reference.

2. Other organizations choose to use JSA on a more routine basis. Prior to conducting a task, especially non-routine tasks, the supervisor and work crew will conduct an assessment of the safety and health risks and determine how they will proceed with the work to control those risks. This is a much less robust process than the option discussed above and usually requires only a few minutes. A document is generated for that specific task in that specific situation.

A team approach is always a good practice to use while implementing the JSA. As mentioned before, the persons who do and/or supervise the work are the most likely to know the hazards or exposures involved. In either case, the process is essentially the same and consists of three steps as in Figure 5.4.

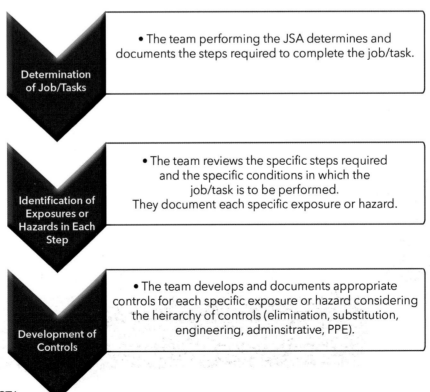

Figure 5.4: Steps in JSA/CTA

The result of the JSA/CTA process, when used properly, is improved control over the exposures inherent in the work being performed. It is helping the organization become competent in dealing with its safety and health risks.

Checklists

Checklists have long been used to help the organization be more thorough in identification of exposures or hazards. Types of checklists include:

1. General inspections checklists
2. Pre-use equipment inspections checklists
3. Health hazard (chemical, physical, biological, and ergonomic) checklists
4. Pre-start up safety review checklists
5. Change management reviews checklists
6. Engineering review checklists
7. Equipment specification checklists
8. Contractor review checklists

Organizations should develop and use checklists for all activities requiring minimum performance standards.

Pre-Start Up Safety Review

Although required by regulatory standards in some jurisdictions, a pre-start up safety review is a best practice for all organizations. In general, a pre-start up safety review focuses on equipment or processes that are new or modified, and/or have been inactive for a period of time such as those that are used on an infrequent or seasonal basis.

Figure 5.5 outlines the essential steps in the process.

Tool Box: pre-start up safety review

Assemble a Team

- The pre-start up review team should consist of persons with vested interest in or knowledge of the equipment or process being evaluated (operators, maintenance personnel, engineers, purchasers, area supervisors, etc.).

Apply a Pre-Start Up Checklist

- The team should ensure a systematic approach to consideration of all safety and health related issues such as design specifications, guarding, emergency alarms and shut off gauges, proper installation, etc.

Develop Remedial Actions for Identified Deficiencies

- The team should develop corrective and preventive actions to address any identified deficiencies prior to start-up.

Completion of Remedial Actions

- All corrective and preventive actions should be completed prior to initiating start-up.

Apply a Pre-Start Up Checklist

- Documentation should be completed for all identified deficiencies and actions taken to control risk prior to start up.

Figure 5.5: The Pre-Start Up Safety Review Process

Start-up of any new equipment or process has been show by experience to be a very critical time and often the time when major incidents occur. Proper use of the review process helps minimize the potential for these undesired events.

Simple Risk Assessment

Simple risk assessment is an effective means of pushing risk identification and, therefore, risk competence right down to the workforce. It requires very little time and almost no structure.

There are several commercially available programs that are used to implement this approach. They are based on the philosophy that the persons who actually do the work and are the most directly involved with the exposures or hazards are also the most likely to identify them. Because they are the most likely to be affected by these exposures, they also have a vested interest in identifying and controlling them.

As the name implies, the process is simple. All persons in the workforce are trained, encouraged, and empowered to take a bit of time prior to performing any task to ask themselves a few very important questions as in Figure 5.6 below.

Tool Box: Simple Risk Assessment

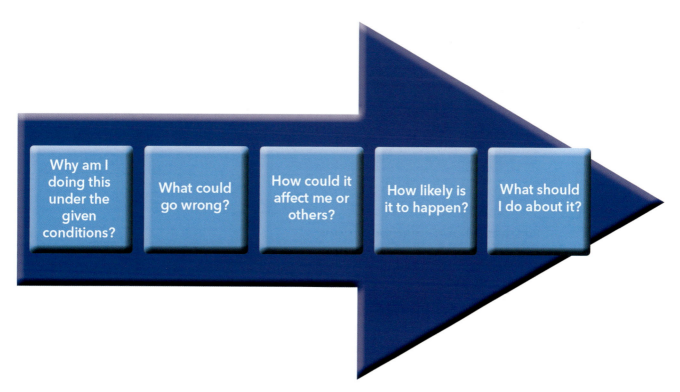

Figure 5.6: Simple Risk Assessment Questions

Should the individual find any problems with the work, they are directed to consult their supervisor before proceeding to ensure that all exposures are adequately controlled.

Risk Assessment

Once a risk is recognized and suitably identified, risk assessment is the process by which the potential consequence(s) that could result from that threat manifesting and the probability of that consequence occurring are estimated. Many of the risk identification techniques earlier in this chapter deliver a qualitative risk assessment of both the consequences and the probability associated with a specific risk.

Risk assessment is comprised of two distinct activities: risk analysis and risk assessment. The tools and techniques presented in this chapter combine these activities.

Detailed risk analysis

The development of a quantitative estimate of risk based on engineering evaluation and mathematical techniques for combining estimates of incident consequences and frequencies.

Detailed risk assessment

The process by which the results of a detailed risk analysis are used to make decisions, either through a relative ranking of risk reduction strategies or through comparison with risk acceptability targets.

Non-Quantified Risk Assessment Techniques

Using the risk information gathered during the recognition process, the risk (probability and consequence) can be plotted on a risk matrix. Criteria that support a proper matrix will define risk acceptability (or tolerance) enabling consistent decision making regarding the need for interim risk reduction measures, detailed assessment of the risk and its controls, and permanent risk reduction measures.

The organization should develop its own risk matrix, supported by specific definitions or risk criteria, for measuring the severity of the consequences and the probability of risk resulting in losses. The supporting criteria should also define a level of risk acceptability or tolerance. This provides guidance for decision-makers to determine if existing controls are adequate and what additional controls may be appropriate. Some matrices will be simple, non-quantified tools, usually in a 3x3 or 5x5 arrangement with two axes, probability and severity. Figures 5.7 and 5.8 illustrate a simple 3x3 matrix.

Tool Box: Risk Matrix Examples

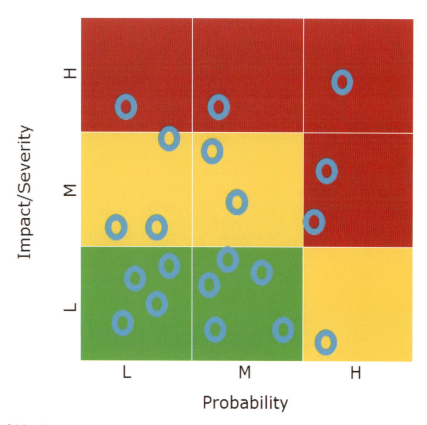

Figure 5.7: Example of 3x3 Matrix

In this example, the organization has determined that any threat that ends up in the red blocks is unacceptable and must be addressed immediately. Any threat that ends up in the yellow blocks must have a control plan developed with defined time frames for completion. Any threat that is judged in the green blocks may be acceptable as it is, but should be monitored to ensure that the risk doesn't increase as the organization changes.

The 3x3 matrix allows a fairly quick assessment of the relative risk in any given threat or exposure. Each identified threat can be plotted on the matrix to provide a visual depiction of its risk level. This enables more effective decisions to be taken in proper response to that threat.

This type of matrix, including the 5x5 that follows, is usually applied in two stages. First, the assessment is conducted and the specific exposure is plotted assuming no controls are in place. No assumptions are made regarding the effectiveness of existing controls. Following the development and implementation of controls and based on the evaluation of pre-existing controls, a second assessment is performed. The second assessment is for the purpose of determining the remaining level of risk and whether that level of risk is acceptable.

This type of matrix could be used routinely in situations such as pre-start up safety reviews, minor changes in plant or equipment, or in job safety analysis.

It is critical that specific definitions be written for what constitutes low, medium, and high probability and low, medium, and high severity.

The following is an example of such definitions. These definitions are not recommended as appropriate for any organization. The organization should write its own criteria.

Ranking	Severity Definition	Probability Definition
Low	Any threat that could result in a minor (first-aid) injury or illness, or property damage less than $1000USD.	Unlikely to occur. Has happened less than every five years in the company. Rare in the industry.
Medium	Any threat that could result in a recordable/reportable injury or illness, or property damage of $1000-$10,000USD.	Possible. Has happened at least annually in the company. Happens frequently in the industry.
High	Any threat that could result in a serious injury, illness, or fatality or property damage that exceeds $10,000USD.	Likely. Has happened more than once annually in the company. Happens frequently in industry.

Figure 5.8: Criteria to Support a 3x3 Matrix

The 5x5 risk matrix in Figure 5.9 below is used much the same as the 3x3. It simply enables a broader range of possibilities and rankings and provides the practitioner with a more precise assessment.

This type of matrix is often combined with the semi-quantified method described later.

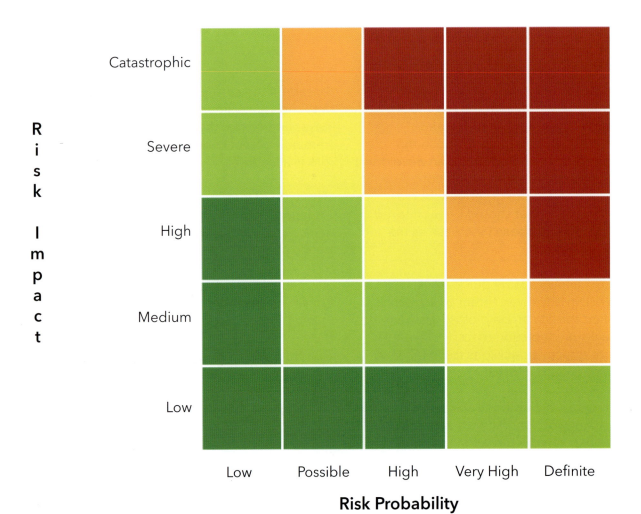

Figure 5.9: Criteria to Support a 5x5 Matrix

Once again, it is critical that specific definitions be written for the various criteria or categories in the matrix. In other words, the criteria by which the practitioner decides how to rank the threat should be defined.

Semi-Quantified Risk Assessment Techniques

Some organizations prefer a semi-quantified method of risk assessment. Such methods can be very simple and do not employ the same rigorous engineering and mathematical-based approaches that more comprehensive methods do.

Tool Box: Semi-Quantified Risk Assessment Example

Figure 5.10 and the descriptive information below is an example of how a semi-quantified risk ranking approach can be used.

The assessors using this technique assign an identified exposure or hazard a value from each of the three categories in the table. Multiplying these three values yields a risk score for each hazard on a scale from zero (0) to ten thousand (10,000). This enables an even more specific assessment of the relative risk in each exposure or hazard.

The organization should support the process by developing standards for defining levels of risk based on the risk scores. For example:

0 – 50   Very low risk. Controls not required.

50 - 100   Considered acceptable risk. Should be monitored routinely to assess effect of change.

100 – 500   Additional controls should be considered in a short-term strategic plan.

500 – 3,000 Additional controls required. Must be addressed in a short-term strategic plan.

3,000 – 5,000   Additional controls required immediately. Consider suspending operations until adequately controlled.

5,000 – 10,000 Unacceptable risk. Operations must be suspended immediately until effective controls are in place.

This is only an example and does not constitute advice for any specific organization. Again, each individual organization must develop risk criteria and definitions appropriate for their situation.

Frequency		Probability		Severity	
1	Very Rare. Never faced in history of the company. Documented only twice in history of the industry.	0	Considered almost impossible. Has never happened anywhere on record. Less than one in a million chance of happening.	1	Negligible impact on employee safety and health, little to no property damage, process, or environmental loss.
3	Very Infrequent. Faced or performed only once in every three years.	2	Conceivable, but very unlikely. Has been documented a few times in recorded history.	10	Potential for first aid treatment injury or illness, property damage below $100, self-contained environmental release, downtime of less than $100 impact.
5	Infrequent. Faced or performed three to four times per year.	4	Unusual, but possible. Has been documented several times in recorded history. Wouldn't be considered surprising.	20	Potential for medical aid (recordable) injury or illness, property damage, process downtime of $100 - $5000, or environmental release resulting in less than $500 cost.
7	Frequent. Faced or performed weekly.	6	Possible. Has been documented many times in recorded history. Should be seriously considered.	30	Potential for lost-time injury or illness, property damage or process downtime of $5000 - $50,000, environmental release resulting in less than $50,000 cost. Potential for environmental citation.
10	Routine. Faced or performed continually throughout the workday.	8	Quite possible. Very likely to occur. An occurrence at least once per year has been documented. Must be considered.	50	Potential for permanently disabling injury or illness, property damage or process loss of $50,000 - $500,000, or environmental loss of less than $500,000 excluding citations.
		10	Almost certain. Has been documented many times in recent history. Demands immediate attention.	70	Potential for fatality, extensive property damage or process loss (>$500,000), or environmental loss of greater than $500,000 excluding citations.
				80	Potential for multiple fatalities, loss of entire facility, permanent loss of resource. Potential for public injury/illness, loss of property.
				100	Potential for catastrophic loss. Numerous fatalities, loss of entire facility, permanent loss of resource. Potential for public fatalities and extensive loss of personal property.

Figure 5.10: Semi-Quantified Risk Assessment Scales and Definitions

This type of matrix is often used with simple risk registers. Figure 5.11 is an example of a risk register that could be practically applied by any organization.

Tool Box: A Simple Risk Register

Changing a Tire on Roadside

Concern	Risk	F	L	S	R	New Control/ Procedure	Risk	F	L	S	R
Traffic	Being struck by vehicles	2	6	15	180	• Pull off roadway at least 20 feet. • Set Flares. • Wear reflective vest.	Risk still exists but much less likely to occur.	2	2	15	60 / 67%
Uneven Surface	Jack could fall, serious injury potential	2	6	9	108	• Where possible, park on even, paved surface. • Carry shovel to create a level spot if necessary.	Risk still exists but much less likely to occur.	2	1	9	18 / 83%
		Total Initial Risk Score					Total Residual Risk Score				

Figure 5.11: Simple Risk Register

The risk register pictured above allows the organization to record all identified exposures or hazards, the specific level of risk each exposure or hazard presents (frequency, probability, severity, and risk scores), the appropriate controls to be developed and applied, an assessment of the residual risk following application of the controls, and the percentage of risk reduction. There are many regulatory requirements and voluntary performance standards, such as OHSAS18001, that require proof of systematic, comprehensive efforts to identify, assess, control, and monitor risk. A document such as a risk register helps prove due diligence in the proper management of safety and health risks.

Risk Assessment: Science and Art

Risk assessment is a not completely objective process that enables the practitioner to always arrive at the answer. In fact, all of the risk assessment techniques discussed above only provide tools to consider more pertinent information and a structured means by which to make a better decision.

The science of risk assessment is in the applied methodologies. These methodologies must be practiced routinely in order for the art of risk assessment to become a skill. The more experience the practitioner has with the tools and techniques, the more comfortable and confident they become with their resulting decisions. The more experience the organization has with the methodologies, the more risk competent it becomes.

Risk Assessment Methods

The available risk assessment methods and models have different strengths and limitations; therefore, an iterative process of more focused quantification is appropriate until the risk is understood well enough to confidently identify effective and efficient mitigations.

In all types of risk assessments, the information, data, and assumptions that are collected can affect the outcome and validity of the assessment. The following list provides a brief description of common mistakes made when performing these assessments:

- Inadequate information
- Incorrect logic
- Failure to recognize common-mode effects
- Failure to use realistic data
- The wrong combination of data
- Using inconsistent or incorrect units
- Overestimating the reliability of existing protection
- Overconfidence in numerical values
- Failure to check the credibility of the result
- Failure to verify the validity of assumptions
- Failure to check that subsequent modifications or changes do not invalidate the analysis
- Failure to recognize one's limitations and seek more qualified advice or guidance

Risk Control

The third phase of the risk management process is risk control. In some cases, pre-existing risk controls may be deemed adequate if proper assessment of their effectiveness can be demonstrated. In other cases, effective controls must be developed and implemented if the level of risk presented by specific exposures or hazards is to be deemed acceptable. There are a number of tools and techniques that can be helpful to the organization in making these decisions.

A Bow-tie diagram is a useful tool that can provide the organization with a simple visual representation of a fairly complex process. It is intended for use at a fairly high level in the organization, by a team of trained personnel, and for dealing with the most serious exposures or hazards. Figure 5.12 illustrates a Bow-tie diagram.

Tool Box: The Bow-tie Diagram

Figure 5.12: Bow-tie Diagram

The team must be trained in the proper use of the Bow-tie. The following steps describe the process in its simplest terms and an understanding of them does not constitute proper training.

1. Beginning in the upper middle of the diagram, the practitioner identifies a specific exposure or hazard as the basis for the Bow tie.
2. In the very center of the diagram, the potential top event that could occur from the exposure or hazard is identified and described.
3. Working from left to right in the diagram, each threat that could cause or result in the top event is identified, along with any potential escalation factors.
4. The team then carefully considers and designs threat barriers to be installed between each threat and the top event. The purpose of these barriers is to reduce the potential of the threat. Some organizations require a minimum of three threat barriers between each threat or escalation factor and the top event. Some threat barriers may be effective against more than one threat.
5. The opposite side or right side of the Bow-tie is for the purpose of designing controls to minimize the effect of a top event should it occur.
6. Beginning at the extreme right side of the diagram, the team identifies all potential consequences and escalation factors of the top event.
7. The team then carefully considers and develops recovery measures to be installed between the top event and the potential consequences.

Figure 5.13 below is an example of a completed Bow-tie. It is included as an example only and does not constitute advice for any given situation.

"There is no 'perfect' decision. One always has to pay a price ... one always has to balance conflicting objectives, conflicting opinions, conflicting priorities. The best decision is only an approximation - and a risk."

Peter Drucker

Completed Bow-tie Diagram

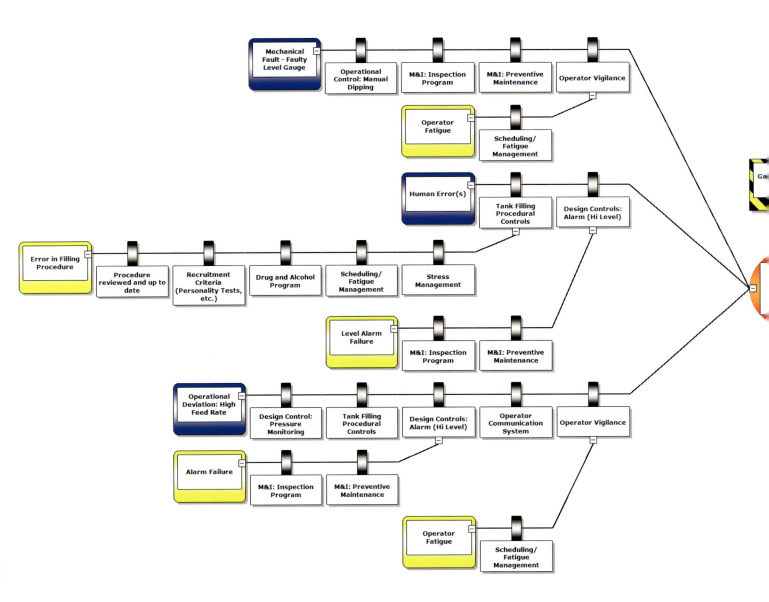

Figure 5.12: Bow-tie Diagram

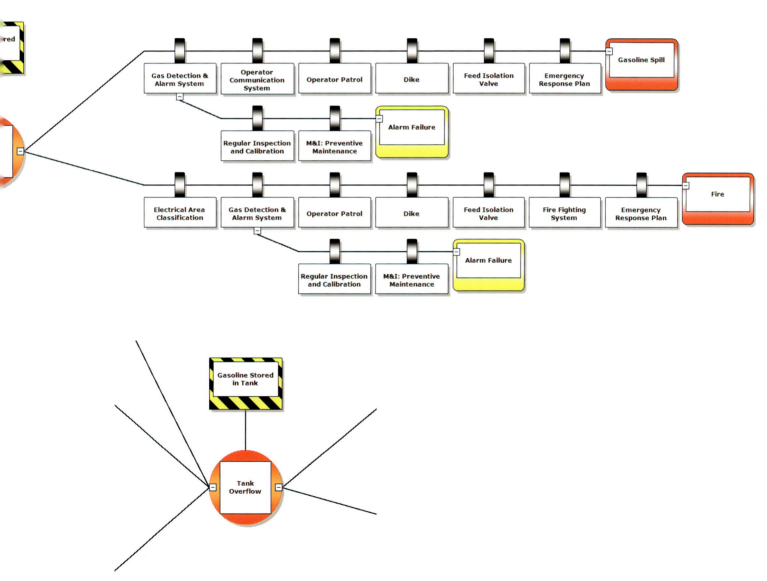

Center of the Bow-tie

The Hierarchy of Controls

Figure 5.14 illustrates a widely accepted order in which barriers or controls should be considered due to their level of effectiveness.

Elimination	Elimination should always be the first consideration in dealing with exposures or hazards, especially those assessed as having high or extreme risk. It is the most effective control because the exposure is completely terminated or removed from the operation. Elimination is also the most unlikely possibility. Each industry has risks that cannot be completely eliminated due to the nature of the business. For example, underground mining cannot completely eliminate the exposure of roof collapse nor can a steel mill completely eliminate heat exposure. Most often, barriers or controls will consist of a combination of the remaining options.
Substitution	In some cases, less hazardous processes or substances can be substituted for existing high-hazard situations. This optional control allows for lower levels of energy or toxicity to be introduced to the workplace. For example, it may be possible to substitute a less toxic cleaning solvent in a maintenance operation to replace an unacceptable chemical exposure.
Engineering Controls	Engineering controls include such things as the installation of physical barriers to separate people from exposures in time and space. Sound baffling, guarding, improved lighting, air quality controls, etc. are examples of engineering controls.
Administrative Controls	Administrative controls include such things as training, development of proper SOP'S and task procedures, behavior observation programs, job rotation, fatigue prevention programs, etc.
Personal Protective Equipment (PPE)	PPE should be the last line of defense considered. It is the least effective because it does nothing to reduce the exposure itself. It only puts a barrier between the person and the exposure. Furthermore, it only serves to reduce the amount of energy or substance with which the individual comes in contact, thereby, hopefully, keeping the contact below the threshold level of the individual.

Figure 5.14 Hierarchy of Controls

The following paragraphs provide more examples of prevention controls, mitigation controls, and consequence reduction controls.

Tool Box: Examples of Risk controls or Barriers

Prevention Controls

Examples of Prevention Controls include:

- engineering or designing with inherently safer options, which eliminate or control hazards;
- controls that avoid the identified hazard;
- appropriate qualifications, training, knowledge, and skills required for the job;
- warning signs, markers, or placards;
- training for emergencies and abnormal situations, including rehearsals, simulations, and drills;
- preventative hardware controls, such as pressure relief, shutdown devices, and interlocks;
- adequate communications;
- and authority requirements for purchases/contracts.

Mitigation Controls

Mitigation controls include:

- Automatic Controls – controls that act automatically and do not require human intervention, such as fire and gas suppression and detection, automatic isolation and blowdown.
- Design Controls – controls that are part of the system design, such as siting, equipment placement/layout, and area classification.
- Administrative Controls – controls that depend on the competence or ability of a person to intervene or respond, such as controlled access, operator initiated fire and gas suppression, spill and emergency response teams, and manually initiated isolation and blowdown.
- Passive Controls – once passive controls are in place, they only require regular maintenance to remain effective. These controls require no response from a person or a control system, such as dikes, bunds, flame arrestors, fireproofing, and blast walls.

Consequence Reduction Controls

Consequence reduction controls include:

- controls that limit the number of people and the amount of time they are exposed to hazards;
- personal protective equipment, such as clothing, eye protection, ear protection, hard hats, gas monitors;
- warning signs, markers, or placards;
- fire and gas detection and suppression systems;
- containment booms, dikes, and other secondary containment;
- adequate communications;
- emergency response plans;
- control of information procedures;
- and standard contractual terms.

Risk Monitoring

Risk monitoring consists of risk tracking and assurance activities.

Risk Tracking

Risk tracking is typically achieved via maintenance of a register of risks. A simple risk register was described and illustrated earlier in this chapter. For organizations engaged in higher risk activities, a more robust risk register is recommended. Management should also practice active monitoring of the organization's risks and the health of important risk controls, achieved through assurance activities.

Maintaining a register of hazards and risks is the best way to ensure risks are identified, action plans are developed and tracked, and risks are communicated to appropriate levels within the organization. The risk register also provides the information used to generate an organization's risk profile and sub-profiles for various segments of the organization.

A risk register helps achieve the following:

- An organization-wide perspective of all types of hazards, risks, and critical controls;
- A compilation of data used to create an organization-wide risk profile and the ability to sort for projects or specific facilities;
- A data source for valuable risk management performance analysis and reporting;
- The ability to identify, assess, and prioritize risks, and utilize the information during the annual business planning process;
- Communication of appropriate risk information to employees at all affected levels of the organization;
- The ability to ensure line management is engaged in the risk management process, aware of risks that affect their employees, and can communicate risk information to employees;
- Clear responsibilities and accountabilities of key risk management roles and risk owners;
- Communication of risks to the appropriate levels of accountable management for the purpose of risk-based decision making;
- And proof of due-diligence and compliance with regulatory and voluntary standards.

Use of the risk register encourages a common risk language applied to all types of risks at all levels of an organization. Risk management decisions are made at all levels of the organization and are aggregated from the asset level to the corporate level. This allows for a consistent evaluation of risk at various levels within the organization.

The following information should be included in a more robust risk register:

Tool Box: Content of Robust Risk Registers

Risk Information:
- Chronological identification number and date of initial entry
- Type of risk
- Asset Name
- Cause(s) associated with the risk
- Consequence severity information for each type of consequence
- Controls currently in place
- Frequency information, including frequency modifiers
- Risk ranking information

Tracking Information:
- Risk owner
- Responsible parties
- Interim mitigations
- Summary of planned mitigation actions
- Work order number or other authorization to perform work
- Mitigation status updates
- Date of next required update

Risk Assurance

In addition to risk tracking, assurance is another practice monitoring activity. Assurance includes:

1. Audits and assessments
2. Performance measurement (KPIs)
3. Management reviews

These three methods provide different types of performance information that, when combined, provide a sound understanding the status and effectiveness of the program, as well as insights for continuous improvement. The resulting information can be used to determine areas for improvement or enhancements and provide management with assurance of performance. Audits and assessments are valuable means to evaluate the performance of the risk management program and answer the following questions:

- Is the program meeting performance objectives?
- What are the best opportunities for continuous improvement of the program?
- Is the program comprehensive or are there gaps?
- Are the practices described in the program adequate?
- Is conformance to the program adequate?

Audits, assessments, and performance measurement are addressed in detail in the chapter, Reviewing Performance.

Achieving Maturity and Risk Competence

A risk management program is mature when the following conditions have been met:

1. All personnel with risk management responsibilities have documented risk competence.
2. An ongoing process of systematic risk or threat identification is in place and working with adequate resolution, recorded, described, and with direct causes sufficiently expanded on identified risks or threats.
3. The risk associated with all identified threats has been evaluated, assessed, and ranked/prioritized in accordance with an organization's policy. Furthermore, necessary mitigation actions have been identified, approved, and implemented.

4. Suitably effective, efficient, and robust controls are in place for all identified relevant threats with appropriate metrics and standards to demonstrate that the ongoing required performance of these controls is being maintained.
5. Organizational risk competence is a critical ingredient in the recipe for sustainable business development.

Key Point Summary

1. Risk management is the process by which threats, exposures, or hazards are systematically and comprehensively identified, assessed, controlled, and monitored.
2. Risk competency must be the goal of the organization; that is, to become mature in the proper use of risk management concepts, tools, and technology.
3. All persons in the organization, from the CEO's office to operating and maintenance personnel, should be involved in the process with the goal of becoming personally risk competent. All persons are risk takers and all employees should become risk managers.
4. Risk competence defines the difference between a proactive safety and health process and a reactive one.
5. There are tools and techniques that can be used to more adequately identify, assess, control, and monitor exposures and hazards. Some of these tools and techniques are designed for use at a higher level in the organization by trained personnel. Others are more suited for routine, day-to-day use by all employees. The organization should choose which tools and techniques that are most appropriate for their business and risk profile.
6. The organization should develop its own tools such as risk matrices, supported by specific criteria by which risk is to be assessed and determinations of acceptability made.
7. The hierarchy of controls should guide decisions about the most effective controls or barriers to be used for each identified exposure or hazard.
8. A robust risk monitoring process must be used to ensure sustainability of the risk management system.

Figure 5.15 is a simple flow chart that summarizes the risk management process we have presented in this chapter.

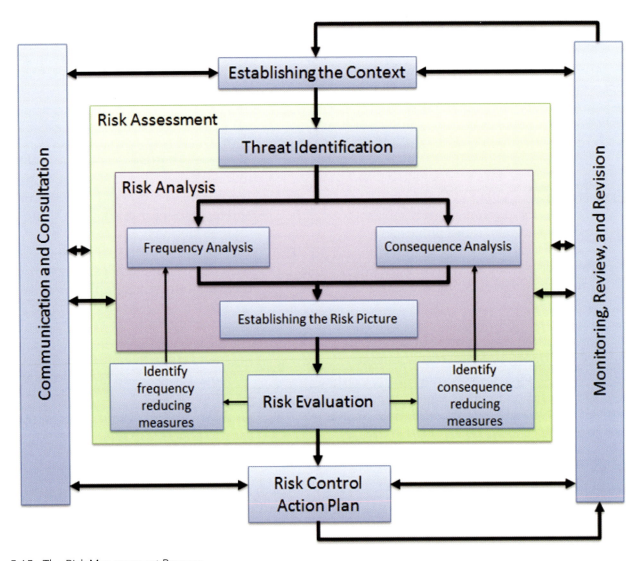

Figure 5.15: The Risk Management Process

Personal Planning

1. Does my organization have a comprehensive risk management plan applied to safety and health?
2. Can I describe that plan?
3. What methods do we use to identify safety and health exposures?
4. What method do we use to assess the risk in our exposures and prioritize them?
5. How have we effectively used the hierarchy of risk controls?
6. How do we monitor the effectiveness of risk controls?
7. What are my responsibilities for identification, assessment, control, and monitoring of safety and health exposures?
8. What can I do to improve my personal risk competence?

Y – Model for Action Planning

Present Situation

Desired Situation

Need for Change

Present Situation

Stop   Responsibility   Target Date

STAKEHOLDER ENGAGEMENT

Chapter 6

STAKEHOLDER ENGAGEMENT

> **CHAPTER OBJECTIVES**
> 1. To emphasize the critical role of stakeholder engagement in the organization's safety and health process.
> 2. To offer practical knowledge on effective management of the stakeholder engagement process.
> 3. To encourage the reader to explore creative means of engaging stakeholders while protecting the right and responsibility of the organization to manage its affairs.

Joe Seeks to Manage Engagement

Joe decides to meet with Lisa over coffee. While sipping coffee, they reflect on the feedback from the previous week's management review meetings.

"Lisa, a couple of things have been playing on my mind," Joe starts. "Do you mind if I run a few ideas by you?"

"Sure, go ahead, Joe. I know there are lots of new ideas coming out of the recent management meeting and we need to understand how we can best implement those changes. I am particularly concerned about their impact on our safety and health system."

"Well, that's one of the key challenges we are facing," Joe adds. "Many of the new expectations require us to work with others a lot more to deliver those expectations. We can't do it on our own. I wanted to talk to you specifically because we want to initially focus our efforts on safety and health."

"I appreciate that. You know, many of the risks and opportunities they talked about in the meeting are out of our direct control," replies Lisa. "Sure, we can influence them, but I'm not sure if influence will be enough."

"From what I can tell, we need to collaborate with our business partners more. For example, we are being judged by the safety and health performance of our suppliers and our customers expect us to reduce risks in our supply chain."

Joe's cellphone rings, interrupting him. He apologizes, takes the call, and then turns back to Lisa. "That was the local residents association. They got wind of our plans to expand our operations on this site and are worried that the noise from the works might impact their home values. More issues just keep coming up."

"Joe, I can tell you that I've heard similar concerns from our employees. They've already started asking questions about construction-related exposures like noise and dust."

"They are certainly major stakeholders and their concerns have to be addressed. However, when it comes to safety and health, there are several other stakeholders we must work with. We have our regulators, investors, suppliers, and pressure groups. Even our customers have a vested interest in our safety and health performance. I understand that we should engage them in the process, but we need to come up with some creative ideas that will allow us to maximize the potential of their input while protecting the organization's right to manage its affairs."

"Well, maybe I can help there," Lisa offers. "I have a friend in the safety and health network who had to attend a training course on sustainability and stakeholder engagement. She loved it and said it gave her a whole new perspective on her work. Apparently, there are some great materials on stakeholder engagement based on standards that are freely available and probably worth looking at. They're all about working more effectively with partners and others along your value chain. I'll ask her to share some information with you."

"Great," says Joe, "Maybe this will offer us some tools and techniques and help us manage some of these new issues."

Introduction to Stakeholder Engagement

The practice of stakeholder engagement (SE) has been around for a while, although lately it has matured immensely. It used to focus on alleviating pain locally while managing risks and understanding strategic directions. It has since been used by private and public sector organizations in order to understand and agree upon solutions for complex issues. Vital to such engagement is that stakeholders have a chance to influence a decision, whereas mere communication seeks to issue a message on a decision that has already been made. The purpose of shareholder engagement is to share risks and benefits.

Leading organizations are realizing that they are not only judged on quarterly financial returns to shareholders, but they are also judged on how the extent that they can deliver a return to society. This "stakeholder model" of business is gaining a lot of traction and is central to concepts of the sustainable business, shared value, and corporate responsibility. Leading stakeholder engagement looks beyond the company and towards systems based sustainability challenges, such as poverty and accelerated climate change. For the purpose of this book, the focus will remain on stakeholder engagement and its potential contribution to continual improvement of safety and health performance.

THE TOP TEN KEY POINTS FOR EFFECTIVE STAKEHOLDER ENGAGEMENT

1. **Have a strategy.** Engagement helps to further align business practice with societal expectations and to generate long-term commercial value.
2. **Make it operational.** With benefits such as improved employee satisfaction, safer workplace, greater community cohesion, and improved license to operate, stakeholder engagements can be beneficial to everyone involved.
3. **The devil is in the detail.** Representatives of the organization should make sure they plan ahead and come well prepared. They need the right skills and resources to be effective.
4. **Agree the rules of engagement.** . Everyone must understand each party's role and how the engagement processes will run.
5. **"Buy-in" is essential for success.** Every party must have a stake in the process; participants must have a chance to affect decision-making.
6. **Decisions should not be made prior to the engagement.** The dialogue must be legitimate and fair, with each party provided an equal opportunity.
7. **The organization probably already does it.** Learn from existing channels of communication and dialogue.
8. **Senior commitment is vital.** Demonstrating this through leadership actions is critical.
9. **Be practical.** Start early and be realistic in making goals. Set clear objectives for each engagement.
10. **Always take time to review.** This will give all parties an opportunity to share the outcomes, report on them and consider how best to use assurance

---

"[We engage] to find solutions to shared challenges, everything from creating awareness about a topic to improving company performance on the environment and human rights, to finding solutions to societal challenges."

Bo Wesley, Manager, Trendspotting and Dialogue, Novo Nordisk

Benefits of Mutual Sharing and Learning Through Stakeholder Engagement

Engaging with the outside world enables companies to improve decision-making and performance using external perspectives. When considering how a company is governed and managed, it becomes evident that engagement and consultation present tangible benefits:

- **Good neighbor** - Engagement helps the organization to be a "good neighbor" (during the good times and the tough times) and to understand impacts on their community and employees. This will allow them to decide if the organization has to undergo structural change.
- **Performance –** Stakeholders help develop performance indicators that help assess organizational performance. Stakeholders share resources such as best practice, skills, money, and technology.
- **Managed Risks and Reputation** – Through the process of systematic, transparent engagement, the organization can gain a real understanding of issues in a timely manner. They can also detect emerging issues immediately. This builds trustworthiness—or "dollars in the reputation bank." When an organization manages its safety and health risks in a proper way, employee morale improves and they represent the organization in a positive way to the community. The organization is perceived as a good place to work and confidence of the marketplace is improved. The community is more receptive to the organization's initiatives. Relationships with regulatory authorities are enhanced.
- **Strategy –** Demonstrate strategic thinking on big issues, such as climate change, technology, and human rights. By explaining their needs and expectations, stakeholders help organizations identify which issues are most important or material to them and potential challenges and opportunities. For example, HSBC bank learned much from its partnership with WWF, an environmental NGO, and improved risk management activities in its lending practices as a result.
- **Innovation –** Stakeholders can help in navigating through strategic challenges and opportunities, which might result in new products, services, or even new markets. For example, IBM worked with non-profit SeniorNet to produce disability-friendly services such as web page accessibility for easier reading and understanding and gained access to quickly growing market segment.

Companies are already expected to engage with their community; for example, local consultation is often a requirement of planning permission for site expansion. Figuring out how to capture and exploit the potential value of engagement is emerging as a key business focus area.

"We strongly believe that the only way to guarantee long-term prosperity is to grow businesses in line with the needs and aspirations of the communities they serve. Although there is considerable progress, we also face challenges that we cannot solve alone. To achieve large-scale change, Unilever believes more collaboration is needed between companies, governments, NGOs and consumers."

Gail Klintworth, Senior Vice President of Sustainability, Unilever

Core concepts

What is a stakeholder?

Stakeholders are individuals, groups, or organizations who affect, or who are affected by, an organization's performance or products and services now or in the future. Also included are those who can legitimately claim to represent the interests of "voiceless" stakeholders, such as future generations and the environment.

There are a number of ways to identify stakeholders, which will be covered later. They might include, but are not limited to, investors, customers, suppliers, employees, regulators, the media, NGOs, and unions.

Who Owns The Engagement?

Prior to the engagement, all parties should define the single force that will lead the engagement. It could be one company, a partnership, or collaboration. They are the ones who will commit their authority and resources to the engagement task ahead. They should make the objective of the engagement clear from the outset. There will be a related group of people or organizations that participate in the decisions associated with the planning, preparation, implementation, review, and communication of the engagement. Therefore, for a single issue or problem related engagement, the organization will likely "own" the engagement. For a wider issue engagement, there will often be a more complex form of "ownership." Wider issue engagements might involve safety and health concerns that extend outside the physical plant and into the surrounding community and employees' families.

Do We Already Engage?

All organizations are already executing stakeholder engagement in one form or another, e.g. customer service, employee opinion surveys, news releases, etc. However, very not every organization performs stakeholder engagements in a systematic and strategic way that contributes towards improved sustainability. It is worth tapping into existing channels, such as procurement, HR, customer relations and external affairs. Representatives of the organization might work through these existing mechanisms to engage with specific stakeholders on issues.

Most organizations already engage employees on safety and health issues to some extent. They usually employ activities such as joint safety and health committees, group or team meetings with a safety focus, perception surveys, contests and promotions, etc., as means of engagement. These can be very positive efforts if managed effectively.

However, these efforts have are sometimes implemented as stand-alone, ad hoc activities with little or no strategic planning or organization. In this case, the results can be very negative. Joint safety and health committee meetings become the place where employee complaints are dumped rather than analyzed. Safety or team meetings become repetitive, boring, and have no obvious relationship to the overall safety and health initiative. Perception surveys become appeasement exercises. Contests conducted with no strategic purpose become laborious and ineffective.

An organized approach to engagement around safety and health will drive improved performance.

A Commitment to Engagement

Before undertaking any individual engagement, representatives should commit to an inclusive approach to better inform decision-making, systematically applied across the organization. This has implications on governance arrangements, strategy development, and operations management processes. By being proactive, stakeholder engagement can help identify ways for top-line revenue growth, risk mitigation (including safety and health risks), and cost reduction. Trends are moving away from engagement as a reactive, bolt-on public relations mechanism.

Senior executive commitment is key. It helps to change the ethos and mindset of the entire company towards one promoting engagement. If the board considers engagement a "tick-box exercise," then everyone else in the organization will treat it the same way rather than using it to improve performance.

Accountability at executive level for SE activities and outcomes can be supported by a set of principles that commit the organization to:

- Openly involving all stakeholders **(inclusivity)**, focusing on the most relevant and significant issues **(materiality),** and responding adequately **(responsiveness)**. These help ensure full and fair involvement and improved decision making.
- Systematically integrate into business process and communicate internally and externally.
- Respect others' cultures and values and enable appropriate participation.
- Connect the engagement with governing methods to ensure accountability.
- Integrate policies and practices into the operations management.

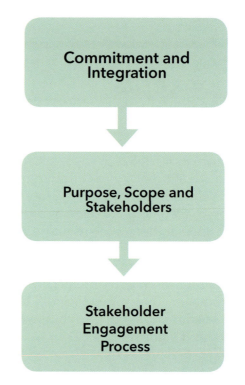

SECRETS OF THEIR SUCCESS.
In 2013, Deutsche Telekom presented the results of its sustainability management efforts over the last five years, which can be attributed to:

- Aligning its business to sustainability principles towards a "climate friendly" information society.
- Deeper collaboration and engagement. They now involve stakeholders in core decision-making, innovations, and other common challenges, for example, carbon-foot-printing products and services.
- More meaningful, long-term targets that challenge the business.

Below is a review of the key parts of the process of engagement. Once the organization has committed and integrated engagement as part of general practices, how can it be applied? There must be clear planning, preparation, implementation, and review tasks. The organization should be clear as to why it wants to engage on the issue at stake. The organization should understand what it wants to learn from the engagement. Lastly, the organization should assess whom they need to involve for this particular engagement.

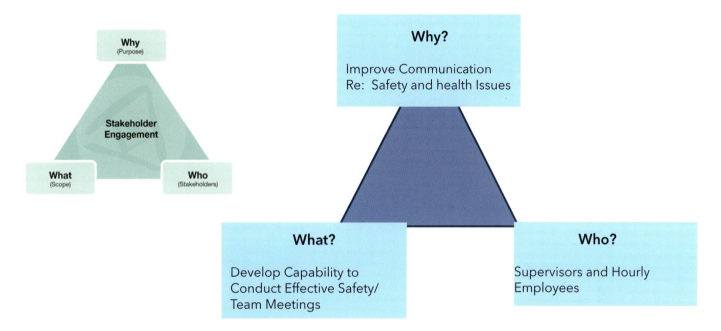

Purpose, Scope, and Target Stakeholders

Purpose: Why Engage?

Setting a purpose will govern the process and determine not only how representatives of the organization review it, but also any changes they make along the way.

Representatives should consider strategic business objectives and how they relate to stakeholders and specific issues, and then decide whom their primary stakeholders are and which issues are most important for them.

Businesses most often engage to:
- Improve strategic decision-making, or
- Better understand operational issues.

If the purpose is **strategic,** try analyzing the big issue in smaller chunks. If the purpose is operational, such as driving efficiency improvements, resolving an issue, product innovation, or fostering better relationships due to site developments or business change, further steps must be taken.

Knauf Insulation in Czech Republic worked hard to foster excellent relations and strong involvement within their community because their plant was close to residential areas. Since their employees worked in a hazardous environment, safe operations were critical.

Chapter 6   123

A clear objective for each engagement is paramount and defines the whole process. Examples could include informing the community about a change in shift patterns or process that may impact on them, generating and prioritizing ideas for the next generation product, or informing a corporate investment decision. Any of these issues could potentially affect safety and health exposures for both employees and the community.

Learning from the engagements may mean that a course correction is required or that plans are adapted and changed. As the process is iterative, the organization may undertake certain steps to refine later plans.

> **WHY MIGHT WE ENGAGE?**
>
> - **Strategy.** To inform strategic business decisions.
> - **Operational management.** To deal with a specific issue or change an event and to understand improvement options.
> - **Obligation.** To comply with legal and voluntary obligations to disclose information and engage with stakeholders, such as the US Sarbanes Oxley Act or the UK Companies Act.
> - **Market opportunities.** Companies need to understand their consumers, workers, and related communities to properly target new potential in emerging markets.
> - **Scrutiny.** More people have become interested in the conduct of business, fueled by the Internet and social media.
> - **Expectation**. Private sector involvement in delivery of essential services has grown, such as with healthcare and security.
> - **Technology advance.** New technology, such as nano-technology or genetically modified organisms, raises new questions about risks and tolerance.
> - **Catastrophic events.** From Bhopal to Deep Water Horizon, better systems of governance and engagement are required to manage risks revealed by such events.

Examples of purpose will vary depending on the activity. For example, a cement manufacturer proposing to build a new factory site would need to engage with local community groups and individuals, regulators, and others on issues such as noise, traffic disruption, employment opportunities, etc. Creating goodwill and successfully obtaining planning permits are examples of specific engagement objectives. Another example is an apparel manufacturer that realizes that its reputation is at stake due to high human rights risks up its supply chain. It would be prudent for this manufacturer to engage and even partner with labor rights NGOs to development more systematic responses to the issues.

> STAYING ON COURSE.
> Be aware that getting involved in the wrong engagements can lead to a misuse of resources and can distract you from more pressing priorities. When considering an engagement, think about the following:
>
> - Be clear on your strategic objectives for the business or project in question, e.g. "secure our long-term license to operate in countries that host our sites."
> - Talk with colleagues about the objectives and risks of engaging.
> - Be clear about whom the stakeholders are and the key issues at stake.
> - Articulate engagement objectives with the stakeholders.
> - Supply the engagement sufficiently with resources and ensure appropriate deadlines to complete agreed upon tasks.

> Take a plasterboard manufacturer in Europe, for example. As it grows and expands its premises and processes, it will likely need to engage to ensure it achieves the goodwill of the community, the continued loyalty of employees, and credibility with the planning regulators.

The Scope of the Engagement

What are the boundaries should be discussed when engaging with stakeholders? What is the "scope" of the task?

CHECK BOX — Coping with scoping
Are we clear on the scope? We can't cover everything.
Our engagement covers all issues and parts of the business that are relevant to our defined objective.
We are clear on the scale the engagement relates to. For example, selected global, regional, or local parts of our business, specific or all business activities.
We involve colleagues who look after specific product or service areas or have responsibility for a business function relevant to the issues at stake.
We clarify the proposed time frame; know what will happen when, and when to close the task.
We involve our stakeholders to confirm the scoping and that the appropriate people are involved.
We know how to identify the relevant issues at stake.

Thinking ahead about the scope makes for a more efficient approach. Specificity about the subject matter, scale, extent, and geography of the task, will guide the level of detail necessary when developing the questions or discussions of the engagement task and who should be involved.

The discussion agenda must cover all material issues. For example, if the purpose is to improve management of staff, the organization's material issues could involve line management quality, staff feedback options, staff safety and health, benefit/care packages, perks and bonuses, and so on. Perception is as important as reality; therefore, engagements must be open to covering all issues deemed important by stakeholders. If an issue raised falls outside of the scope being considered, then this should be politely communicated to the stakeholder.

The time frame chosen will determine the degree of detail that the organization requests from stakeholders internally and externally. It will be good to know how long all parties plan to engage for and what parties need to be consulted. All parties should be aware of specific deadline they need to meet, such as planning application date.

Example subject matter, or "material issues," is demonstrated in this graphic:

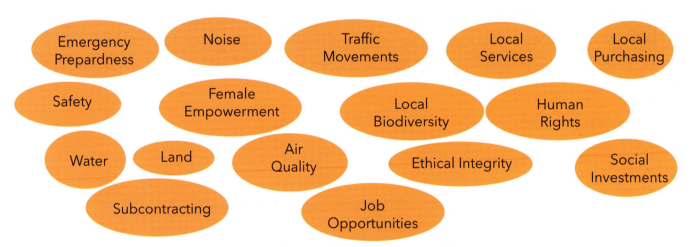

For example, if you want to engage with suppliers, your procurement team might reach them using site visits and physical meetings with tier one suppliers and a survey for other suppliers. This will help establish what suppliers need to do to comply with your supplier code of conduct. The length of the engagement might take two months. This scope clarifies the purpose, identifies who from your business will get involved, the activities anticipated, and the time frame.

> For the plasterboard manufacturer, the key issues may relate to dust, traffic noise as the business grows, emergency preparedness, local water abstraction, jobs, construction contracts, or local supplier recruitment.

Who Are My Stakeholders?

An easy place to start is by mapping out the current organizational relationships, the existing channels available to use to communicate and engage with the stakeholders, and the issues they are raising with the organization. Consider getting input from colleagues in external affairs/communications, procurement, EHS, HR, legal, risk and investor relation's roles. External consultants may be able to add value in mapping, facilitation, and other aspects of engagement.

The organization may want to propose a list that could be ratified by the internal working group they convene – doing so saves their time and enhances their cooperation. Use the following priority groupings for example:

People to whom you have legal, financial or other operational responsibilities.

Some examples include:
- Employers
- Investors
- Customers

People who are likely to influence your organization's performance or who can influence decision makers.

Some examples include:
- Suppliers
- Business Partners
- Host Communities
- Competition & Peers

Stakeholders who are affected by your organization's operations.

Some examples include:
- Government
- Regulators
- Trade Unions
- NGOs
- The Media
- Opinion Leaders
- Scientific Community
- Supranational Institutions
- Remote Communities

The intent is not a scientifically accurate outcome; there may, for example, be overlap in the tiers of stakeholders. For example, the Employee group might include the board and executive team, management, staff, trade unions, new recruits, potential recruits, and employees who have left the company.

Organizations will typically have many stakeholders, each with different interests. The organization should chose theirs depending on the purpose and scope, in order to limit conflict or inefficiency. A systematic method of stakeholder identification helps to enhance accountability and overall performance.

Look at the following attributes of stakeholders to help the process of systematically selecting them. Understand who they are, their importance, and how they are being engaged.

Dependency
- Stakeholder is dependent on organization's activities, products and associated performance

Responsibility
- Stakeholders organization has, or in future may have, legal, commercial, operational or ethical/moral responsibilities

Tension
- Stakeholders who need immediate attention from the organization with regard to financial, wider economic, social or environnmental issues

Influence
- Stakeholders who can impact the organization's strategic or operational decision-making

Diverse Perspectives
- Stakeholders whose different views can give new understanding of a situation, and identify opportunities for action that may not otherwise occur

Chapter 6   127

For example, the plasterboard manufacturer, if engaging about emergency preparedness, might consider the local fire department, health/welfare/hospital, schools and facilities, forest management, suppliers, accident prevention agencies, citizen groups, water authority, and community housing groups.

The diagram below illustrates one way an organization can prioritize what matters to stakeholders.

This offers a quick means to identify which stakeholders are important due to their interest in particular issues as well as stakeholder concerns. Note that stakeholders and issues may emerge at any time, so the matrix and prioritization should be reviewed periodically.

What Are Their Concerns?

Which issues are most important to delivering business strategy and ensuring long-term success? How do your priorities the issues that focus on the things that matter most to your business? How do you understand where your priorities and stakeholders' priorities are not aligned?

An allied effort to engagement is the process to understand relevant and significant issues called *materiality assessment*. Materiality assessment considers, from an internal and external perspective, which issues are most important. The outputs of engagement feeds into the pool of issues considered and prioritized by the materiality process.

This is an example of an issues prioritization process (known as materiality) in action. Issues plotted in the top left part of the grid indicate stakeholders' hot topics. They show more concern on these than the company does. Similarly, those plotted bottom right indicate the topics of most relevance to the company. There are of course specific potential risks for each issue.

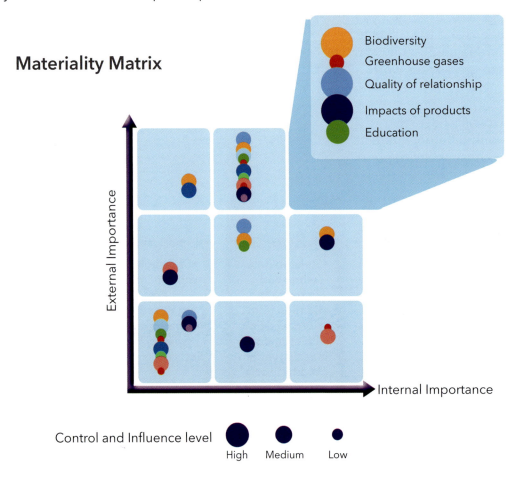

128 SAFER, SMARTER, GREENER

Materiality Matrix Example

Concern to Stakeholders →

Increasing or Current Impact →

Top row (high concern):
- Public Policy, Climate Change, Business Integrity, Responsible Marketing
- Product Safety, Packaging, Responsible Sourcing

Middle row:
- Locations, Executive Compensation
- Mfg waste, Life cycle impacts, Sustainability, Waste, Pollution, Taxes
- Energy Consumption, Community Engagement

Bottom row:
- Nano-Technology, Bio-Technology
- Transport & Distribution, Diversity
- Health and Safety, Security, Employee Benefits, Workplace Wellness

Chapter 6   129

WHEEL OF RELATIONSHIPS

This is an example of how a major automobile manufacturer could map its stakeholders on a circular matrix that identifies their relative importance by type of relationship to the business. This makes it possible for the company to prioritize and structure its engagements. For each stakeholder, the company has a separate engagement strategy.

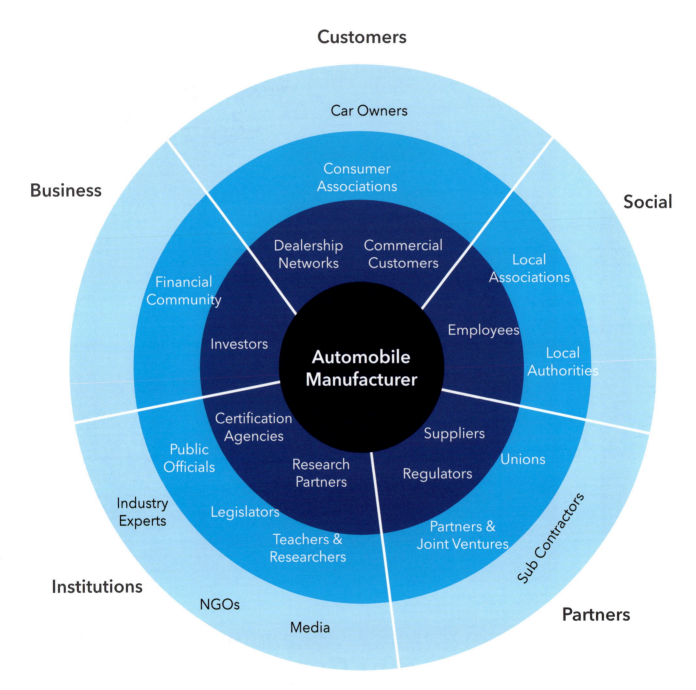

Is Our Current Engagement Adequate?

Armed with an improved understanding of the range of stakeholders, current channels of engagement, and the issues they consider important, areas within the business that may need more or less attention can be analyzed systematically. Is the current approach right for the issues? Are competencies and capacities correct for those involved? Do we have clear, stakeholder-specific objectives? For instance, one stakeholder may only require that they are kept informed, while another may require that a policy be amended to meet their expectations.

Preparing for an Engagement, Delivery, and Review

Considerable effort, time, and resources should go into planning and preparation. Proper preparation will help ensure that the business gets the most value from its relationships. There is also considerable skill involved in running engagements effectively. By now, the organization should be aware of:

- How the issue is currently managed within the organization,
- What policies and systems are already in place,
- Existing channels of engagement,
- And options the organization has and steps it need to take for the issues.

Stakeholder engagement, in common with safety and health and other management systems, follows the Plan, Do, Check, and Act cycle:

Planning an Engagement

Based on the intended response, representatives of the organization will need to plan their approach. They will most likely use a variety of methods of engagement at different levels to meet the various needs of different stakeholder groups. These methods may also change as engagements develop. For example, they might want to start by providing information and plans and then invite feedback on it. This may be followed by a structured consultation or negotiation. The more fundamental the transformation is, the more important it is that the organization and their stakeholders work together closely.

CHECK BOX: Check your levels	
Achieve this level of engagement…	**By doing this …**
COMMUNICATION: "We want to provide you with information to keep you informed." One-way information flowing out from the organization.	Publishing narrative and data based reports, issuing press releases, putting notices up, sending letters and mail outs, publishing research findings, issuing statements
CONSULTATION: "We want to keep you updated, listen to your concerns, consider your insights, and provide feedback on our decision." Limited two-way engagement: organization asks questions, stakeholders answer. Surveys, focus groups, meetings with	selected stakeholder(s), public meetings, workshops, online feedback mechanisms, advisory committees

NEGOTIATE: "We want to work with you directly or through representatives in order to come to a mutually agreeable outcome." This can be simple contract negotiations to complex negotiations that impact on	large parts of your workface. Collective bargaining with workers through their trade unions, product and service procurement from suppliers
INVOLVE: *"We will work with you to ensure that your concerns are understood, develop alternative proposals, and provide feedback about how stakeholders' views influenced the decision making process."* Two-way or multi-way engagement: learning on all sides	but stakeholders and organization act independently. Multi-stakeholder forums, advisory panels, consensus building processes, participatory decision making processes, focus groups, online feedback methods
PARTNERSHIPS: *"We will look to you for direct advice and participation in finding and implementing solutions to shared challenges."* Two-way or multi-way engagement: joint learning, decision making and actions	Joint projects, joint ventures, partnerships, multi-stakeholder initiatives
EMPOWER: New forms of accountability; decisions delegated to stakeholders; stakeholders play a role in governance.	Integration of stakeholders into governance, strategy and operations management

Don't forget the level of engagement that the organization and its stakeholders choose depends on the strategic engagement objectives. Is the aim for *incremental* changes or *systemic* changes? What is the *social maturity* of the issue at stake?

PROGRESS THROUGH PARTNERSHIP #1.
Cross-sector collaboration helps tackle the most pressing issues and such collaborations are gradually spreading. For example, The Coca-Cola Company has a cross-sector initiative with Heinz, Ford, Nike and Procter & Gamble to drive forward sustainable packaging through the development of a commercially scalable, 100% sustainable, plant-based plastic used in its PlantBottle™ which comprises 25% of the new plastic.

Preparing for an Engagement and Challenges

Here are few practical considerations to keep in mind:

Challenge 1 – It takes time. Don't fail to prepare.

It takes time to develop the "common ground" necessary to create relationships. Relationships with stakeholders will generally always grow, rather than fade, and others will want to join in. However, be aware that the organization will not have an unlimited amount of resources and do not underestimate the high expectations that some groups may have of the organization. In developing countries, for example, companies instead of governments often provide infrastructure such as roads and healthcare. Last but not least, it is important to ensure that the engagement results in the agreed outcomes. If the consultation yields nothing, stakeholders will leave tired and frustrated. It is essential that expectations are managed; an organization should not make promises that they cannot deliver on. Poorly managed engagements are worse than none at all.

Challenge 2 – The right stakeholders.

It can be hard for companies to identify stakeholders who represent common interests. Sometimes, individuals report to represent stakeholder interests but lack legitimacy. The most vocal, articulate, and resourceful stakeholders are not always the most legitimate. Representatives of an organization should be aware of conflicting interests so they don't become involved in local tensions. Effective stakeholder engagements often demand certain capabilities, culture, and mindsets. This requires successful facilitation and cultural awareness. Mature relationships will present benefits; for example, after two decades in Angola, Ode Brecht, an engineering company, has developed a strong understanding of shared needs, goals, and rules of engagement with stakeholders. They claim to be "like a local company." Once there is an understanding of local culture and history, there can be an understanding of the context of stakeholder issues and demands.

> Jason Scherr of Natural Resources Defense Council (NRDC) cautions that the person who is at the table is often as important as what is being said: "Organizations like ours have to be careful getting involved with dialogue where there is no end – where you're talking with people who don't have power." The key is to manage the tension in order to reach practical common ground and tangible outcomes.

Challenge 3 – Regional differences.

There tend to be varying levels of concern over similar issues in different regions of the world. Environmental concerns tend to dominate in the US and the UK, while in Africa, economic development, AIDS, healthcare and social justice may be more dominant issues. Partnerships will also vary in their intensity. Well-organized church NGOs and development institutions may prevail in Africa, while US stakeholders may prefer advisory panels. Crucially, where people may have poor literacy skills or restricted freedom to engage, companies may need to develop different methods of communication and work to enable an open engagement.

"Stakeholder engagement doesn't always have to result in actions and deliverables. Sometimes talking can be very important. Many NGOs still amaze me by not recognizing that participation in stakeholder engagement is a powerful way of doing what their mandate requires – engaging businesses and promoting a sustainable development agenda."

Susan Côté-Freeman, Transparency International

> *"Companies seem unable to maintain a meaningful conversation with different stakeholders over time. If an interaction is not project- based, that's where the wheels fall off the bus."*
>
> Paul Kapelus, African Institute of Corporate Citizenship (AICC)

Challenge 4 - Make sure you have the internal skills/resources.

Representatives from the organization should ask themselves, "Do we have the systems, people, and budget necessary to put insights and possible commitments into practice?" They may need people who push the boundaries of what can be achieved. The varied skills required will be in the fields of project management, analysis, personal behavior, technical knowledge, and engagement approaches. They should list their intended outcomes, assess gaps in skills, and propose learning resources to close those gaps. Credibility will help the engagement.

Challenge 5 – Know your stakeholders.

It is vital to understand their expectations, their levels of knowledge, their legitimacy, their willingness to engage, their impact on your business, their cultural context, their capacity to engage, and how familiar they are with each other. It is important to research stakeholders to unearth these details about them and inform the approach.

Although safety and health should be a win-win proposition for all stakeholders, close cooperation on these issues is not always the case. Every stakeholder at the table has an agenda, which may be directly opposed to the agenda's of others. For example, regulators are mainly concerned about compliance with the letter of the law, not the success of one's business. There have been situations where labor-management relations are so historically poor that safety and health has become a hammer for each side of the table to use against the other. Knowing the stakeholders and their agendas is a real challenge.

The following is a profiling tool, complete with a safety and health-related example:

CHECK BOX Simple Profiling tool	_____ Date:
Stakeholder group:	*Employees*
Primary issue for this group:	*S & H exposures created by construction project*
Stakeholders objective:	*To ensure exposures are effectively controlled*
Preferred level of engagement with Group:	*Involvement – we must actively listen and respond*
Representative's name:	*J. Bloggs*
Their expectations of our business:	*A risk management plan to address their concerns*
Engagement history with them:	*Good – recent successes on other S & H issues*

Their preferred engagement approaches:	*A joint team approach*
How are they funded:	*Internally*
Their relationship with other stakeholders:	*Rely on regulatory support and enforcement*
Their knowledge level of issue (High/Medium/Low):	*Medium - no S & H professionals in the group*
Their legitimacy (High/Limited/Low/None):	*High - our employees are our greatest resource*
Willingness to engage (Willing/Moderate interest/Hostile):	*Very willing. We have a good relationship.*
Other practical issues/comments:	

Preparation for an engagement requires setting clear objectives, knowing stakeholders, issue prioritization and practicalities. It is essential to understand that the representatives of the organization do not have to agree with everything presented by your stakeholders. An engagement is about being better informed for making decisions.

1. **Resources.** Time and funding are necessary for the engagement itself and for any agreed changes in response to the engagement. The organization will need to be clear in the process about its limitations. Focus on the scope of the engagement to avoid the discussion spiraling out of control.

> **HOW FAR CAN WE GO?**
> Make sure your organization has the ability and willingness to respond adequately to the outcomes of stakeholder engagement. Talk with your budget holders: are costs clear and approved? Consider the best and worst case scenarios of engaging (or not engaging). Consider the business plans relating to the issues that you are engaging on. What margin of movement can you tolerate in any change you make? What is and what is not up for discussion with stakeholders? List what actions and resources are required in response to the outcome. Where are the resource gaps?

2. **Capacity building.** Does the organization have the systems and skills to engage successfully? Identify the resource limitations of the team and of stakeholders and work to build their capacities. As outlined above, for each key issue you engage on, the organization will need appropriate arrangements relating to governance and management commitment, policy, performance indicators, clear internal responsibility, review and learning processes to allow responsiveness. It may take time to enable the organization to contribute a successful response, but there will be quick wins, such as educating senior budget-holders on the issues at stake or developing a policy draft based on industry and peer norms. The engagement itself will help strengthen the organization, so it pays to get started in a structured and measured way.

BUILDING STAKEHOLDERS' ENGAGEMENT.
Some individuals and groups may find it difficult to take up your invitation to engage. Circumstances may hinder them in contributing, for example, due to language, literacy or cultural barriers, distance, lack of time, Internet access, or knowledge gaps. To help overcome these barriers, consider providing the following:

- Timely information
- Training
- Translations
- Sensible and culturally sensitive locations for engagement
- Appropriate time slots
- Ensure anonymity
- Compensate for lost working time or travel.
- Round tables and providing a meal often help

Delivering an Engagement

As described above, the method used will depend on the level of engagement sought, resources, likely information needed, stakeholders' mobility and resources, familiarity with the stakeholders, as well as the sensitivity and maturity of the issue(s) at stake.

APPROACHES CAN INCLUDE:

- Inviting written responses from stakeholders, e.g. via reply slips in reports
- Telephone hotlines
- One-to-one meetings
- Online engagement mechanisms
- Involvement of stakeholders in issue research, reporting, and policy development
- Focus groups and public-meetings
- Surveys
- Stakeholder advisory or assurance panels
- Multi-stakeholder forums and alliances, partnerships, voluntary initiatives and joint-projects

For example, an organization could use web based feedback or discussions. In this case, the stakeholders must be able to access the technology required for this form of consultation. Note that web based discussions are useful up to a point and can be improved with a more quantitative survey, for instance. There is a wide array of online options, such as time-limited bulletin boards, wikis, social media chat rooms, blogs, Q&A sessions, or polls.

BREAKFAST BRIEFINGS IN THE FIELD.
In Peru, Rio Tinto meets with a reference group of NGOs every month over breakfast to share updates on the company's activities. Members include a major international NGO, a local think tank, the head of a dialogue group, NGOs critical of mining and an NGO active specifically in the region where Rio Tinto operates.

For each of these options, there are pros and cons. In the end, representatives have to come up with a formula that works uniquely their own organization.

> **Progress through partnership #2.** As part of the response to the Deepwater Horizon disaster, Repsol S.A. collaborated with peers, IPIECA and the Ministry of Agriculture of Spain to draft industry guidelines on marine spills. While incidents like Deepwater Horizon require fundamental reviews of the way oil and gas companies approach operating in challenging environments, collaboration to create best practice can help the entire sector to prepare better for the risks and opportunities of the future.

Working "Face-to-face"

Be clear what issues are up for discussion and which are not (margins of movement). Be clear in communications with stakeholders, such as invitations concerning the aims of the engagement. Make sure that external facilitators, internal staff, and workshop leaders are clear about the objectives.

- Recap prior discussions with stakeholders.
- Make plans in case things go wrong (key people not speaking, combative positions, etc.).
- Make sure the stakeholders with authority and influencing ability are there.
- State a clear objective and have an agenda that is shared beforehand.
- Be flexible if out-of-scope issues arise; agree to refer to topics later or for others to consider if out of scope.
- Work towards a definitive outcome for the engagement.
- Allow time for questions and discussion.
- Keep presentations short and to the point.
- Be alert to local customs and cultural sensitivities regarding public meetings.
- Be effective but avoid making it all too "slick" – this helps avoid accusations of "PR spin."
- Use a good facilitator.
- Lay out the ground rules: confidentiality, commitments, honor freedom of speech, equal opportunity for contributions, think towards solutions, focus on the matters at hand.
- Use a planner to check off each aspect of the event, see below an example.

CHECK BOX STAKEHOLDER ENGAGEMENT PLAN
Preparation

Invitation/publicity	Agenda/plan for the event
Pre-information	Ground rules and terms of reference
Logistics	On the day roles and facilitation
Venue, timing	Record Keeping
Transport, food, lodging, etc.	Assurance procedure
Equipment, etc.	Feedback to participant
Participants reimbursement	Wider communication of results
Process to meet desired outcomes	Participation satisfaction feedback method

If the plasterboard manufacturer is to expand, they will want to discuss how to expand while maximizing benefits to the community and minimizing the negative impacts. While preparing the face-to-face work, they will be clear on what other issues should be saved for future discussions, should they arise. For example, whilst increasing energy efficiency may well be relevant to the new plant, the company's overall impact on climate change may be out of scope of this specific engagement and may need to refer to the corporate level.

Defining Success

How will you know if the engagement has been successful? You could consider setting targets for inputs, outputs and outcomes, such as engagement plan, number of participants, extent of feedback, media coverage achieved, or consensus reached. Ask the stakeholders how they felt the engagement went and incorporate ways to track feedback about participants' satisfaction with the process.

Wrapping Up

Core to any engagement is to put learning, insights and agreements into action and to ensure that the stakeholders understand the methods to achieve success. At the end of the engagement, representatives should not forget to secure the relationships they make, enhance the contact and trust, and keep in touch as new material issues arise. They may want to share details with others who couldn't attend the engagement.

The next task is to review and improve the engagement process itself. A detailed record of the engagement may be used in an annual sustainability report. Evidence of the process may also need to be collated for an assurance check (if desired).

Delivering on any agreed action plan will be a key task moving forward. Focus on the strategic questions: what are the operational and strategic implications of the engagement? Confirm the agreed actions or commitments: who is responsible for taking this forward? Do we set targets relating to the engagement response? Who, internally, needs to know what happened? Do we need a team meeting or workshop to keep things moving and manage associated risks?

REBOOTING RELATIONSHIPS. One of South America's most publicized gold mines, Minera Yanacocha, has experienced a mix of conflict and peace with its neighboring communities. In 2012, it was found that the local Cajamarca community held the company responsible for environmental damage and community discord. In an effort to build closer relationships with host communities, the company (dramatically) shifted its headquarters from Lima to Cajamarca, sponsored a radio station providing information on relevant topics, encouraged staff involvement in local organizations, and ran an external advisory panel to act as a "barometer" of how stakeholder interests were being addressed. If the measures put forward by Yanacocha are successful, then trust and license to operate will be regained from regional government and local stakeholders.

Be aware of the range of possible responses across the organization and how they may be perceived. For example:

Function	Levels of action likely
Governance arrangements	**Strong:** Formal commitment at board level, with systematic engagement with relevant stakeholders. **Weak:** a senior individual may have awareness of the issue, but no formal responsibility for it, no engagement.
Policy	**Strong:** A formal policy may exist with objectives connected to the business. **Weak:** Discussions on policy but nothing developed.
Management	**Strong:** Formalized into management system with smart indicators, reporting, and assurance. **Weak:** Some discussion, perhaps partial indicators, no targets.
Responsibility & Competency	**Strong:** Continuous learning on the issue, which connects to performance related senior pay. **Weak:** No responsibility, limited or no learning related to the issue, limited discussion.

Key to any engagement is the subsequent implementation of a response that has been agreed upon. As the engagement unfolds, make to inform the stakeholders involved, keep track of potentially building relationships, monitor any changes, report progress, and learn from issues that arise.

Joe and Lisa Apply Stakeholder Engagement

A week after their meeting over coffee, Joe makes the effort to speak with Lisa again.

"Hey, Lisa," he says, pulling her aside. "That information you shared on stakeholder engagement helped pull together much of what I realized I knew but didn't really act on in a structured way. While a lot of it was common sense, it was great to understand that this can be systematically applied."

"Great, I'm glad it was helpful," replies Lisa. "How are we going to apply it?"

"To start with, I think we need to be more open and inclusive in the way we roll out our plant expansion plans. I have already revised our approach and am sharing more information and inviting feedback on it. I've followed up with the local residents association and am keen to hear what they have to say. I know we may not be able to do exactly what they want, but I can help them understand the benefits of expanding the plant. I'll point out our ability to make jobs for the area and hopefully they can help me devise ways to reduce any negative impacts on the community. I might need some support, though, and I know you grew up in the area and know the people. Can you help me prepare?"

"Sure, Joe, I'll share what I know and help ensure you speak to the right groups and people."

"I feel much better bringing people in on the plans and learning from them rather than trying to impose change on them. Thank you."

Key Point Summary

1. Stakeholder engagement should be an intentional and strategic activity to drive safety and health performance.
2. There are fundamental human relations concepts that support effective stakeholder engagement and logical steps to carrying out any engagement activity.
3. The first challenge is to identify and locate all stakeholders for any and all organizational issues.
4. Adequate resources must be dedicated to the stakeholder engagement activity.
5. In planning to engage on any issue, it is helpful for the organization to develop a profile of each stakeholder and use the information to develop an engagement strategy.
6. Clear objectives for each engagement activity must be agreed upon.
7. Properly managed engagement activities can serve to deepen relationships and improve future cooperation.

Personal Planning

1. Has my organization identified all the stakeholders in its safety and health management systems?
2. How well do we understand our stakeholders and their perceptions of our safety and health performance?
3. Is there adequate strategic planning and organization around our safety and health engagement activities?
4. What should we do to improve stakeholder engagement around safety and health?

Y – Model for Action Planning

Present Situation

Desired Situation

Need for Change

Present Situation

Stop | Responsibility | Target Date

BEHAVIOR-BASED SAFETY

Chapter 7

BEHAVIOR-BASED SAFETY

> **CHAPTER OBJECTIVES**
>
> 1. To propose a different way of looking at behavior-based safety.
> 2. To focus attention on deficiencies in the management system that prompt substandard or at-risk behaviors rather than on individual behaviors themselves.
> 3. To illustrate how behavior-based safety approaches can either positively or negatively impact organizational culture and vice versa.
> 4. To outline the critical factors for organizing and implementing a behavior-based safety process.

Henry Learns From Lisa

Henry has heard through the grapevine that behavior-based safety (BBS) is a great tool for improving safety performance. Professional contacts in other organizations have told him of significant reduction in incident rates following implementation of BBS. They mentioned that, because the vast majority of incidents are due to human error, BBS allows them to identify unsafe acts that could lead to incidents and coach the people so that they avoid such acts. He wants to explore implementing BBS in all the organization's plants.

Henry communicates his interest to all his plant managers, including Joe. Joe discusses the matter with Lisa and asks for her input.

"Joe, while I agree with Henry that BBS could be a good tool for us, I think the premise for implementing it is a false one," begins Lisa. "The primary purpose of a BBS program is not to fix the people. It is to identify barriers to safe performance and remove them. You see, while it may be true that the vast majority of incidents involve unsafe acts of people, it is also true that the vast majority of those unsafe acts are not intentional on their part, but are due to what some people call latent organizational weaknesses. In other words, more often than not, it is weaknesses in the management system that produce those unsafe acts, such as inadequate training, unclear or out of date procedures, improper design, and inadequate communication. Any BBS program that focuses solely on the people and their behavior is missing the point and I think going into it with that mindset is dangerous. It might look like the organization is blaming people for all the incidents."

"Okay, Lisa. I think I understand. It sounds like you have a good handle on BBS. Would you go with me to discuss this with Henry before we go too far with the initiative? I wouldn't want us to get off on the wrong foot."

A couple weeks later, Henry, Joe, and Lisa have their meeting. Lisa gives a well-prepared presentation on the basics of effective BBS implementation. Following a few questions, Henry is convinced they need to modify their approach. He asks Lisa to serve on a team to evaluate BBS for the organization and develop an implementation strategy. She agrees and a team is formed consisting of a couple other safety and health professionals, Joe, and one other plant manager.

Three weeks later, the team makes its recommendations to Henry and a strategy is adopted. Within eight months of roll-out, BBS is perceived by all stakeholders to be a positive process that contributes to continual improvement.

Henry, Joe, and Lisa would like to share with you their experience and the critical factors they believe contributed to success.

Introduction

Earlier in this book, there is information about building an improvement culture. There is a symbiotic relationship in which such a culture and Behavior-Based Safety (BBS) are mutually influential.

The culture of an organization largely determines how Behavior-Based Safety programs are conceived and implemented. At the same time, the way in which BBS is conceived and implemented has a potentially significant effect on organizational culture. Ideally, this relationship is a mutually supportive one in which a positive culture drives effective BBS, while effective BBS helps shape a positive culture.

What is Behavior-Based Safety (BBS)

Behavior-Based Safety is a generic term used to describe any number of approaches to behavior observation and coaching programs. There are many different vendors of such approaches and each vendor has a specific brand name for their product. Although each of these products/approaches has its own distinct set of characteristics, they all involve essentially the same following activities:

1. Identifying the critical behaviors that cause or could potentially cause harm;
2. Developing an observation program including report forms, standards for managing the program, and means of collecting and properly interpreting data;
3. Training observers;
4. Performing observations and providing immediate feedback (positive reinforcement and/or correction);
5. Collecting report forms and interpreting data;
6. Developing and implementing methods to remove barriers to safe behavior;
7. And monitoring implementation and effectiveness of actions.

There is, however, enough variance between the many BBS approaches promoted by vendors that it is actually inaccurate to refer to "Behavior-Based Safety" as though it were a singular, specific program that is implemented exactly the same way in all circumstances. There is no template for BBS that fits all organizations and there is no handbook that prescribes exactly how any one organization should implement BBS. In order to be effective, the implementation of a behavior-based safety program in any organization should be a consultative exercise to customize the program to fit the organization's S & H management system and culture. The implementation of BBS is a process, not simply a training class.

Principles and Characteristics Supporting BBS Implementation

There are some basic concepts that shape positive organizational culture and drive effective BBS implementation. In no specific order, they are:

1. Avoid Using the Term Unsafe

Using the term unsafe to describe behaviors that lead or can lead to incidents is undesirable. Unsafe can be interpreted as finger pointing, blame fixing, accusatory and personal (for instance, inferring that someone is an unsafe person). Unsafe is also an unclear word and open to interpretation. No situation is entirely safe or unsafe. There are *degrees of safety*; therefore, a behavior one person interprets as acceptable or safe might not necessarily be perceived in the same way by another.

The preferred terms are substandard or at-risk behaviors. Substandard refers to the fact that there is an agreed standard of performance or expectation. An organization can also define critical at-risk behaviors. These critical behaviors become the basis for the observation process.

2. Avoid Using the Term Carelessness

The term carelessness has no place in a BBS program. The vast majority of people do not engage in substandard or at-risk behaviors because they do not care. People want to avoid incidents. Even the terms mind not on task or eyes not on task are not necessarily sufficient to describe why someone might engage in substandard behaviors. Most often, substandard behaviors are due to latent organizational weaknesses or culture deficiencies that shape an individual's behavior.

3. At-Risk Behaviors Are Symptoms

Substandard or at-risk behaviors are important to identify and correct, but they are just symptoms of deeper problems. There are basic or root causes of these behaviors that must be identified and corrected if the full value of a BBS program is to be realized. In fact, the use of basic/root cause analysis to identify and effectively remove barriers to safe behaviors should be the ultimate goal.

4. Apply Positive Behavior Reinforcement Routinely

A BBS process must include the opportunity to identify and recognize safe or proper behaviors if the program is to be deemed acceptable to the work force. More people are doing it right than wrong and they need to be recognized accordingly. If positive behavior reinforcement is not a major ingredient of the observation and coaching process, the entire BBS program will quickly become one in which employees perceive they are being blamed for problems. This negative atmosphere surrounding BBS will doom it to failure.

Figure 7.1: Modified Ratio Pyramid

5. At-Risk Behaviors Precede Incidents

All organizations experience many more near-misses than actual losses (injuries, illnesses, property damage incidents, etc.). However, even before near-misses occur, there are significantly more substandard behaviors occurring. If the organization can identify these at the behavior stage and take the necessary steps to correcting them (removing the barriers to safe behaviors), a more proactive safety culture will be developed. In the chapter on Basic Concepts of Safety and Health Management Systems, an accident ratio study was introduced using a pyramid. Figure 7.1 uses that pyramid to illustrate a critical concept.

6. Include Leadership Behaviors

It is important to recognize that substandard behaviors are not reserved exclusively for operators at the working face. Leadership behaviors are also critical and should be included in any BBS process. If leadership behaviors are not included, this reinforces the perception that management is trying to blame individual workers for problems.

7. Establish Unquestioned Leadership Commitment

Absolute, visible commitment and involvement from all levels of leadership is important to the implementation, their words and actions may not support the effort, which may, in turn, damage it. The leader who continually asks the question, "Who did it?" is unconsciously placing blame without knowing facts. On the other hand, the leader who contributes to an effective BBS process is one who supports robust efforts to identify basic causes of substandard behaviors and accepts bad news when it is deserved.

8. Establish Requirements for Managing BBS

Management performance requirements must be developed for any BBS program. The term requirements as used here and elsewhere in this book refers to very simple statements of performance expectation that include at least three vital things: what work is to be done, who is to do that work (by title), and when or how often the work is to be completed. BBS requirements should define things such as:

- How many observations will be required from an observer in a given time frame?
  - It is best to start slowly and give observers time to adjust to the process. A good suggestion could be limiting it to initially one or two observations per week per observer. As the process matures and observers become more comfortable with the process, the frequency can be increased. One or two observations per week may seem too few, but if we recognize that we may have many observers, the amount of data will be multiplied. For example, if the organization has 20 trained observers conducting two observations per week, then that results in 40 observation reports that must be analyzed and followed up. This number can quickly overload the system and cause frustration with the process.
- How will the information gathered in the observation process be analyzed?
  - The organization should determine the means by which BBS data will be analyzed and how reports will be generated.
- Who will conduct the analyses? How often?
  - Someone should be assigned the responsibility for analyzing the observation reports, determining basic causes, and preparing reports for leadership. Such analysis should probably be conducted at least quarterly, if not monthly.
- How will the analysis and remedial action information be shared with employees?
  - There must be an organized feedback system so that all stakeholders are kept informed of results. If employees do not see tangible results from the BBS process, they can quickly become disinterested or even non-compliant. If leaders do not see such results, they may decide the investment in BBS isn't worth it. Successes must be celebrated.
- Who will be responsible for communicating results? How often?
  - Someone should be assigned responsibility for the feedback process.
- Who will manage the process?
  - Someone should be assigned the responsibility for managing the BBS process. This person should ensure that the process works as designed and is kept up-to-date.

9. BBS is Not a Management System

It must be recognized by the organization that BBS is not a replacement for a safety management system. In fact, if the organization does not have a fairly mature safety management system and culture, it is probably not ready for BBS. BBS is simply another tool in the tool kit for maturing the safety process. Also, it is not the "silver bullet" that will solve all an organization's safety problems. Among elements of a safety management system that must be mature in order to support BBS are:

- Leadership – Leaders must be visible in S & H work and perceived to be committed to continual improvement. Otherwise, their commitment to BBS will be questioned; the BBS process will become just the latest safety program to be tried and will probably go away fairly quickly.
- Risk Management – The organization must have a robust process for identification, evaluation, control, and monitoring of exposures. BBS is another tool for identification of exposures and must fit comfortably within the system.
- Incident Investigation – Investigations must be carried out in a systematic way and must result in the identification and correction of basic causes and management system deficiencies. If investigations tend to stop

with immediate causes (substandard acts and substandard conditions), employees will rightly perceive that leadership is not really interested in dealing with organizational weaknesses and will resist any attempt to focus even more attention on individual behaviors.
- Corrective and Preventive Action Systems – The organization must have a robust process for developing and completing meaningful actions to correct basic causes and prevent future incidents. BBS will be introducing a large amount of additional data to the system that must be handled properly if the program is to have credibility.
- Communications – There must be effective communication systems in place and working. It is vital that information on the results of BBS observations and the corrective or preventive actions that follow be communicated promptly to all stakeholders.

10. The Purpose of BBS

BBS is not about fixing people. BBS is about identifying barriers to safe performance and fixing the system.

BBS does not necessarily reveal how a person normally performs. It will reveal if they know how and can perform properly. While being observed, most workers will perform the best they know how. Any mistakes they might make can usually be attributed to lack of knowledge or skill, bad habits that have been condoned, conflicting demands or directions, or other issues typically beyond their control.

Although an observation process focuses on substandard or at-risk behaviors, it also provides the opportunity to identify and correct substandard conditions. The activity can be a very good means of supplementing the workplace inspection program.

11. Openness

BBS is not a spying program. All observations are done openly with all persons aware that they are being observed. Some organizations have made the BBS observation a voluntary activity. In other words, the observer must first ask the person if they can observe him/her. The person being observed has the option of declining. Other organizations have made the process mandatory. If this is the approach, it must be made abundantly clear that all persons are subject to observation, that all will be observed over a period of time, and that no one is being singled out because they have perceived problems. Also, the consistent application of positive behavior reinforcement and regular communication of BBS results (successes) will help to encourage receptivity.

12. Engage People

In order to be effective, the implementation of a BBS program must involve employees at all levels. Their buy-in and support are gained by engaging them in the design of the process. They should have input into the identification of critical behaviors to be observed, the design of observation forms, the approach to be taken (voluntary or non-voluntary), the analysis of data, and the design and implementation of corrective and/or preventive actions.

13. BBS for Quality and Production

Proper application of a BBS process has spillover effect for quality and production improvements as well. Often, the same behaviors that have safety implications have implications in these other disciplines. Also, improvements in the system brought about by effective behavior analyses will most often result in quality and production improvements. For example, if analysis of observation data reveals deficiencies in the organization's training process, then fixing those deficiencies so that proper training is provided will naturally result in improved production and quality performance as well. If that same analysis identifies problems with the corrective and preventive action system, fixing those problems may resolve some production and quality issues as well.

14. Not a Quick Fix

Although the coaching provided at the time of an observation can have rather immediate, positive results, the real value of a BBS, and the long-term improvements desired, will not have significant impact on the organization's loss indexes immediately. Organizations that wish to implement BBS should understand that improvement in the safety bottom line requires a long-term investment. BBS is not a quick fix.

15. Need for Focus

An observation process that simply instructs observers to "watch and make sure they are doing their work safely" will not work. Without some guidance as to what specific behaviors to observe, the observer will have no frame of reference for what is acceptable or substandard behavior. It is critical that the organization develop a short list (10 to 15) of specific, critical behaviors against which observations are to be conducted. As improvements are made, the list can be modified to focus on different behaviors.

Sometimes called a Behavior Identification Study or Critical Behaviors Inventory, this activity consists of an analysis of substandard or at-risk behaviors that have been identified as repetitive contributors to incidents and analysis of risk identification and assessment data from such tools as Job Safety Analyses (JSA's), pre-start up safety reviews, management of change initiatives, etc. These analyses are for the purpose of identifying the critical behaviors that will be the focus of the BBS observation cards.

General Guidelines for Effective Implementation of BBS

There is no single implementation strategy that works for all organizations. The way in which BBS is designed and applied must fit within the S & H management system and the culture of the specific organization. The following are general guidelines.

Education of Leadership

A significant first step must be the education of senior leadership to develop their subsequent ownership of BBS. The very top management in the organization must understand what BBS is, the basic concepts behind it, and the requirements for successful implementation and operation. This is to ensure that they are committed to a BBS program and the resources necessary to make it successful.

Assessment of Readiness

As mentioned previously, a BBS program must be based on a mature S & H management system and culture. An assessment of the maturity of these elements would be important to ensure the organization is ready for BBS. This enables the implementation team to design the process to take advantage of the strengths and to be aware of the opportunities to improve so that there are no false expectations. A brief assessment questionnaire is included at the end of this chapter under the toolbox subtitle. It is only an example and should not be viewed as a comprehensive or complete checklist.

Behavior Identification Study/Critical Behaviors Inventory

A Behavior Identification Study/Critical Behaviors Inventory must be the basis for the observation checklist. See the Tool Box at the end of this chapter for critical factors to consider when conducting such a study. Behaviors to be considered for the observation list include behaviors that have led to a large number of incidents in the past, behaviors that have contributed to serious or major incidents, and behaviors that have the potential to cause incidents.

A generic critical behaviors list might look like Figure 7.2 below.

- Proper Use of PPE
- Proper Position for Task
- Using Proper Lock Out Procedures
- Properly Securing Equipment
- Proper Use of Safety Devices
- Proper Placement of Hands, Feet, Etc.
- Using Proper Lifting Techniques
- Attention to Mobile Equipment Travelways
- Proper Chemical Handling

Figure 7.2: Generic Critical Behaviors List

Education of the Workforce

The workforce must be educated on the basic concepts and practical aspects of BBS. It is important that all employees, even if they are not going to be observers, be aware of the basics of BBS so that they can see the program as a positive improvement effort and not an effort to place blame on the worker or spy on them.

Education of the Implementation Team

There should be a team of organization personnel involving workers on the floor, HSE professionals, and line managers, to design and guide implementation of the BBS program. These persons need detailed training that includes their roles in managing the program.

Responsibilities of the Implementation Team

The implementation team should design its own BBS program. The team should develop requirements for managing the program, identify the critical behaviors list, design the observation checklist, design the process for analysis of data, determine how the results of observations and analysis will be incorporated into the corrective and preventive action system, and design a means of regular communication of results to all employees.

Training of Observers

It is recommended that a limited number of observers be trained initially and that they be allowed to pilot the program for a time. It may be wise to choose these initial observer candidates based on their interest and interpersonal skills. This helps ensure success and demonstrates the positive nature of BBS. This approach provides experience within the program and allows for adjustments to be made before a large-scale roll out is attempted. Eventually, and ideally, all employees should be trained and participate in BBS.

Auditing BBS

An audit of the BBS should be performed at least bi-annually with results communicated to the implementation team and senior leadership.

Observation and Coaching

Performance observation focuses on acts and practices in an organized and systematic way. It enables the organization to know, with a fairly high level of confidence, how well people are performing and adhering to established expectations of conduct. While safety and health are the primary focus of such observations, they can also identify behaviors that could lead to inefficiencies, waste, and other problems.

Behavioral observations enable a tight focus on a selected few behaviors that have been identified as critical for safety and health performance.

Observers must understand the difference between seeing and observing. Seeing is a physiological process that involves the sense of sight. Observing is more of a psychological process that involves understanding the significance of what one sees. Observing involves the mind.

Observation skills usually require development. They are not intuitive in most people. Training and practice, therefore, become extremely important. The more one practices, the more adept one becomes at being able to separate the significant from the insignificant.

Observation involves:

- Intention – observing on purpose with specific goals in mind. The BBS observation checklist references specific behaviors to focus the mind of the observer.
- Attention – concentrating the powers of observation on the task at hand. BBS observations are not casual; they are not performed for the purpose of watching people work. They are performed to focus on critical behaviors that could contribute to incidents.
- Detection – noticing and recording details.

Observers must be detail-oriented.
- Comprehension – the observer must be able to mentally figure out the significance of observed behaviors.
- Retention – written notes. Some types of BBS observations preserve information critical to analysis and proper corrective and preventive actions.

Guidelines for the Observer

1. Stay out of the way. Observers can become obstacles and distractions if they are not careful. It is important that the observer does not enter the work area and put themselves or the workers at risk.
2. Talking to the worker being observed can be a distraction and should be avoided unless they are doing something that is putting themselves or others at immediate risk. The observer should not interrupt except in case of imminent danger. The observer should stay out of the worker's line of vision.
3. Focus your attention. Clear your mind of other problems or issues. Keep your mind, eyes, and ears open. Be alert to any indication of developing problems.
4. Take notes. Brief notes using key words are preferable; the observer should stop taking notes if he or she finds it distracts from their ability to focus. Extensive notes should be written after the observation.
5. Avoid satisfaction of the search syndrome. This refers to the tendency of people to see only that for which they are looking and not look any further. The observer should not approach any observation with preconceived idea of what they will find. If the observer believes the worker to be observed is an inherently unsafe worker, the observer will look only for substandard behaviors and fail to see the complete picture. By the same token, if the observer believes the worker to be safe, the observer will be tempted to overlook any performance issues.
6. Know how to give feedback and coaching. Performance discussions can be challenging and observers must be given training, support, and coaching to develop and maintain their coaching skills.

Guidelines for effective feedback and coaching include:

a. Feedback needs to be specific and deal with specific behaviors. General statements such as "you did just fine," or "you need to improve," should be avoided unless supported with specific corrections or commendations.
b. Whether supportive or corrective, feedback should be given as quickly as possible. The worker will be curious about their performance and about the notes you were taking. Feedback given hours or days later lose their impact because the worker might have trouble connecting the feedback with their specific behaviors.
c. Give feedback one-on-one and in private. Even positive feedback can be embarrassing for some people.
d. Begin with acknowledgment of positive behaviors.
e. When identifying the specific substandard or at-risk behavior, be prepared to state why the behavior is unacceptable and explain the expected alternative.
f. Explain that the purpose of any corrective coaching is out of concern for the individual's safety and health and well as that of co-workers.
g. Request the person's commitment to avoid the substandard behavior in the future.
h. Thank the person for their commitment to continual improvement of safety and health performance.
i. Where appropriate, feedback and coaching on specific at-risk behaviors can be provided to work groups. This should always be done without names or inferences as to who engaged in the behaviors and always with concern for the safety and health of all employees.

Making Behavior Based Safety Work

The first step in the implementation strategy is to pilot BBS in Joe's plant before extending it to the entire organization. Joe decided to take the leadership role. One week after Henry approved the organization's BBS implementation strategy, Joe and Lisa arrange to meet to determine exactly how they will go about their pilot project within the guidelines of the adopted strategy.

"Lisa, I think we should expand our local implementation team to include at least one other department manager, a supervisor, and an employee representative."

Lisa responds, "That fits with our strategy to engage the entire workforce from the beginning and, if you don't mind, I have some recommendations."

"Okay, who?" asks Joe.

"I am sure Carlos would agree to be our supervisory representative. Don Jones from our maintenance crew has always been a positive supporter of safety and health initiatives. We should ask him."

"Sounds good. I was going to suggest someone from HR, but I think it would be more powerful to have an operating department manager on the team. What do you think about Marcia McGill over in Packaging and Shipping?" asked Joe.

"Great! Should I invite Don and Carlos?"

"Go ahead. I will talk to Marcia."

Fortunately, all their original recommendations agreed to participate on the implementation team. Their first meeting was three days later.

During the meeting, Joe reviews the overall implementation strategy and the group agrees that, with a few modifications, they can make the strategy work in their plant.

Lisa set about securing BBS training for the team and, two weeks later, they met with a consultant to learn the basics of BBS and begin designing the initiative. One week following, the entire management team, including all supervisors, engages in an intensive BBS training class. Although there are understandable questions and concerns, they seem to have been resolved and the group signs on to the initiative.

The second major step was to conduct a Critical Behaviors Inventory. Lisa and Don are assigned the task and work with the BBS consultant to analyze data from their investigation reports and their risk assessments. They identify over twenty behaviors that had or could contribute to incidents. Lisa and Don make their report to the team at large and the team decides that twenty behaviors are too many to include in the observations, at least for the initial effort. After conducting a group risk assessment, the team agrees to focus on twelve behaviors they deemed most critical. An observation report card is developed to include only those twelve behaviors.

The implementation team then works to design the management structure of the initiative. They determine that two observations a week will be required initially from each observer, that the reports will be turned in to the administrative assistant in human resources, that Lisa will collect the reports on Friday of each week, that she will present the results to the team on the following Monday, and that the team will analyze the data to identify basic causes and develop corrective and preventive actions. The organization's Remedial Action Tracking System (RATS) will be used for follow-up. It is also determined that the status and results of BBS will be reported once a month to all employees through e-mails, postings, and safety meeting announcements.

The team meets again to design the training portion of the initiative. During the meeting, it is decided that the entire team will participate in two-hour sessions with all employees. Over the next week, these two-hour sessions introduce BBS as "one more step in the continual improvement of our safety and health program." The team is careful to follow the guidelines provided by the BBS consultant so that BBS will be perceived as a positive initiative. Although there are the usual skeptics and a few challenging questions from some employees, the overall response is very good. They decide it is time to select and train the initial group of observers.

There was some discussion within the team of who should be in the initial group. The BBS consultant advises that they select persons with demonstrated interest in the initiative as well as persons with interpersonal skills that will support effective coaching and feedback. A list of twenty-six persons is developed. When contacted, all but three on the list agree to participate.

A workshop is organized to prepare observers to begin the process. The workshop consists of some class time devoted to observation, coaching, and feedback skills, as well as the proper use of the observation card. The majority of the workshop involves participants actually conducting practice observations under the watchful eye of implementation team members. Participants then discuss their experience and pass on helpful suggestions to their colleagues. A schedule of observations is developed and begins the following day.

Over the next three months, the initiative goes through some growing pains. A couple of the initial observer group decides they won't continue. There are some problems with getting adequate and accurate information on the observation cards. The implementation team misses a couple meetings to review data. There is even some sparse negative feedback that observers are "too picky" or "too negative." Despite these setbacks, the initiative is largely perceived as a success. Adjustments are made and the next three months see marked improvement.

Don, the maintenance man, is particularly helpful in making mid-course corrections. As a representative of the workers, he is adept at interpreting and communicating the specific concerns workers have with BBS. Also, because his co-workers hold him in high regard, he is able to explain BBS and correct any misunderstandings they have.

Eight months after BBS is initiated, an audit of function and results is conducted. Again, there are some relatively minor problems identified, but overall the initiative appears to be functioning effectively. A perception survey is also conducted that shows widespread acceptance of BBS and common belief that it is helping to identify problems and solve them.

Henry participated in the audit and perception survey. Seeing the positive results, he decides it is time to expand the initiative to all plants. He recruits Joe, Lisa, Carlos, Don, and Marcia to help communicate the BBS message to the rest of the organization.

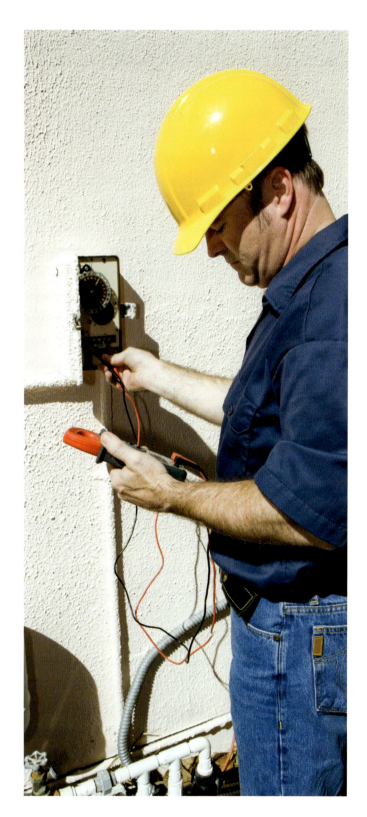

Tool Box: Readiness Assessment Checklist

The following brief checklist is an example of an assessment protocol to determine whether or not an organization is ready to implement BBS. It is not considered complete or appropriate for a full assessment.

Question	Y/N

1. Does senior leadership participate in the following S & H activities?
    a. Workplace inspections or tours?
    b. Safety or group meetings with all employees?
    c. Risk assessments?
    d. Incident investigations?
    e. S & H training?
    f. Audits of the S & H management system?	

2. Do department heads, superintendents, etc., participate in the following S & H activities?
    a. Workplace inspections or tours?
    b. Safety or group meetings with all employees?
    c. Risk assessments?
    d. Incident investigations?
    e. S & H training?
    f. Audits of the S & H management system?	

3. Do front-line supervisors assume primary responsibility for the following S & H activities?
    a. Workplace inspections?
    b. Safety or group meetings with their teams?
    c. Incident investigations?
    d. Enforcement of rules, procedures, work permits, etc.?	

4. Are S & H staff used as consultants or primary advisors to leadership on the development, implementation, and continual improvement of the S & H management system?	
5. Do leaders at all levels accept that S & H performance is their responsibility?	
6. Have all leaders been trained in basic S & H concepts and how to carry out their specific roles and responsibilities?	

Question	Y/N

7. Are the following forms of risk assessment carried out in the organization?
    a. Formal, structured risk assessments on capital projects?
    b. Risk assessments as part of a management of change process?
    c. Critical Task Analysis or Job Safety Analysis (JSA)?
    d. Health hazard surveys?	

8. Does the organization use a predetermined set of risk criteria and/or risk matrix to evaluate the relative level of risk identified exposures?	
9. Is there a robust, functioning corrective and preventive action system being applied consistently in the organization?	
10. Are workplace inspections carried out on a consistent basis?	

11. Are employees engaged in S & H activities such as:
    a. Risk assessment teams?
    b. Workplace inspection teams?
    c. Leadership of safety meetings?
    d. Joint S & H committees?
    e. Development of procedures?
    f. Promotional campaigns?	

12. Do incident investigations routinely identify basic or root causes and system deficiencies?	
13. Is there a training needs analysis that identifies all training, including S & H, that should be provided to specific employees based on their roles and positions in the organization?	
14. Is training routinely provided as prescribed by the needs analysis?	
15. Is the effectiveness of training evaluated on a periodic basis?	
16. Is there a robust communication process in place such that all employees are provided timely information to support proper performance?	
17. Do employees perceive that investigations really get to basic causes and solve problems?	
18. Is there a disciplinary policy, understood by all leaders and employees, and consistently applied to deal with non-conformance issues where appropriate?	
19. Is there a positive culture around reporting of incidents, including near-misses?	
20. Is there commitment to continual improvement of the S & H process?	

Tool Box: Behavior Identification Study/Critical Behaviors Inventory

The following is a checklist of critical questions the organization can use to conduct a Behavior Identification Study/Critical Behaviors Inventory.

Incident Investigation Analysis

What substandard acts/practices are shown to be repetitive contributing factors to incident causation? Examples:

- Improper Lifting
- Failure to Follow Procedures
- Speeding
- Removing/Disabling Safety Devices
- Failure to Wear Proper Personal Protective Equipment
- Distracted Working (Improper Use of Mobile Phones, Radios, Computers, etc.)
- Horseplay
- Operating Equipment without Authority
- Using Equipment or Tools Improperly
- Improper Demeanor or Appearance
- Improper Loading
- Servicing Equipment in Operation
- Failure to Identify Hazards

Analysis of Risk Assessment Data (JSA's, Management of Change Data, Pre-Start Up Safety Review Data, Structured Risk Assessments, etc.)

What specific at-risk behaviors have been identified as having potential to occur? Examples:

- Mis-operation of equipment.
- Misunderstanding of data displays or operator feedback.
- Line-of-Fire placement
- Removal or disabling of safety devices
- Improper use of PPE
- Potential for inattention to task and hazards
- Distracted working due to sensory overload

Employee Surveys

What behaviors do you believe to be most threatening to the safety and health of yourself and your co-workers?

Key Point Summary

1. Behavior-based safety is not a one size fits all program. A BBS process must be designed specifically for the organization's safety and health management system and culture.

2. An organization may not be ready for BBS if there are serious weaknesses in management system elements such as communications, investigations, remedial action tracking, data analysis, etc. Another sign the organization may not be ready for BBS is the existence of a blame culture.

3. BBS is not a magic bullet that will solve all safety and health problems.

4. Leadership from top to bottom must understand and demonstrate support if BBS is to work.

5. Employees must perceive BBS as a positive process, not an attempt to focus only on fixing their behavior.

6. Data collected from BBS observations must be used to address weaknesses in the management system.

7. Successes that result from BBS must be routinely and frequently communicated to stakeholders.

Personal Planning

1. Is my organization ready for behavior-based safety? Why or why not?

2. If we currently have a BBS process, how is it perceived by employees? By leadership?

3. What can the organization do to improve the BBS process?

4. What can I personally do to contribute to BBS success?

Y – Model for Action Planning

Present Situation

Desired Situation

Need for Change

Present Situation

Stop   Responsibility   Target Date

SUSTAINABLE SUPPLY CHAIN

Chapter 8

SUSTAINABLE SUPPLY CHAIN

CHAPTER OBJECTIVES

1. To discuss how organizations can respond to increasing expectations from customers or consumers regarding various areas of concern, including safety and health.
2. To discuss how organizations can structure their own expectations of their suppliers to improve performance in various areas of concern, including safety and health.
3. To demonstrate how best practices in supply chain management can have a positive effect on safety and health performance.

Henry Feels the Pressure

Henry is returning home one evening from an internal meeting at headquarters when he happens to meet Joe, the site manager for one of the largest facilities, waiting to be seated at the airport restaurant.

"Joe, what time's your flight? Mine is delayed for a couple of hours because of the storm, so how about joining me for some dinner here? Plus, we haven't spoken for months, so we should catch-up."

"Sure, Henry, that would be great. How are things going for you? Did you have a good meeting? I heard there were some good external speakers."

Henry had just spent three days at the biannual meetings with top management. Beyond the usual performance reviews, external speakers had been invited during open sessions. One was the Chief Sustainability Officer at the company's second largest customer. The other was a supply chain risk management consultant.

The customer's CSO had presented his company's new five-year plan and strategy. Following some NGO investigations two years ago, the customer had spent considerable effort behind the scenes to understand how to recover the image, market share, loss of talent and disruptions that resulted.

This strategic shift had left the customer with the clear vision that it had to change its way of looking at corporate sustainability. It would incorporate sustainability into its decision-making process and handle it just as it would handle any other risk or any other opportunity. That was why the customer had been presenting in front of Henry for the last couple of days.

This CSO had been appointed to ensure that sustainability criteria were effectively applied and grounded in existing governance models. As a result of a risk assessment under these new criteria, the supply chain was identified as being the biggest source of risk to the customer's brand. As one of its biggest suppliers, Henry's company was the biggest hotspot in that supply chain.

"It was certainly an eye-opener," says Henry. "I had no idea how important this was to our customer. We are used to hearing about quality, product safety, and increasingly about safety and health and environmental issues. But now they're talking about labor rights as well. It's all about corporate sustainability, apparently."

Joe winces. He knows what it means when customers as critical as this one demand something. He even knows what it means when other important customers start demanding that new issues are managed. Sometimes the demands were even conflicting. A site manager has to respond to all these demands, while running an efficient and profitable facility as well. He knows where this is going. This would need to involve others as well.

Joe understood that, with customer expectations like these, a checklist approach was no longer enough. A supplier had to demonstrate a systematic approach and report accurate and reliable performance metrics. Soon suppliers would be using evidence of proactive sustainability risk management as a selling point to gain new customers and retain existing ones. This is how the market works.

Joe is concerned enough about how his site would stand up to the new expectations. However, he wonders also how his own suppliers would measure up if he had to look at his own risks.

"Henry, I think I have some experience from my former work that can help us be more proactive with these customer requests and make sure we get more market share as a result. Can we discuss this in our scheduled meeting next week?"

"That would be appreciated, Joe. I'll find out more about what principles or standards we're expected to apply. I think understanding that from this customer will best help our people manage this issue."

Introduction

Sustainable Supply Chain Management is an integration of many disciplines and can therefore be embedded in different company functions depending on the level of risk, how it is managed and how it evolved in an organization.

For some companies, it can be the result of the risks and opportunities of managing a branded product. Brand product owners frequently outsource production and source materials to countries with reduced labor costs and those less able to enforce compliance with even minimal safety and health and environmental laws. For global brand product owners that are listed on the stock market, valuation is so dependent on intangibles that any misconduct by suppliers can have a measurable impact on shareholders.

These companies are expected to have some degree of integration of environmental, health, safety, and human and worker rights issues into existing procurement practices. From the risk assessment process, through the stages of supplier evaluation, qualification, compliance and performance review, the buyer shares the management of these risks with its supply base through contractual relationships, monitoring, proactive engagement or shared value models as the situation befits.

Other companies are at the receiving end of these customer specifications and the degree to which these demands are met can cover every maturity model in between. Brands can be both customer and end-consumer facing at the same time, which itself can drive a different model of management response. Even commodities at the source of many supply chains are seen to proactively define and address their sustainability risks. Thereafter, any degree of response could be dependent on a variety of factors such as the supplier's exposure to the brand, society's level of concern for the issue at hand, or increased regulatory scrutiny.

The objective of this chapter is to discuss how organizations can respond to increasing expectations from customers or consumers, citing best-practice examples that can help the reader to understand internal gains and how to effectively communicate this to key stakeholders.

Principles of Sustainable Supply Chain Management

For the purposes of this chapter we consider Sustainable Supply Chain Management (SSCM) to be an extension of core procurement practices and supplier risk management, including but not limited to some of the items below:

1. Supplier Selection and Qualification
2. Supplier Quality/Safety Management (ISO9001, TS/AS, Food Safety)
3. Business Continuity/Crisis Management
4. Environmental, Health and Safety MSC Requirements (ISO14001, OHSAS18001)
5. Human Rights and Working Conditions (SA8000, Industry or Corporate Code of Conduct (CoC)
6. Environmental Product Compliance (WEEE, EPD)
7. Product Content Compliance (RoHS, REACH)
8. Commodity Chain-of-Custody and Certification (FSC, MSC, Bonsucro, Fairtrade, Conflict Minerals, etc.)

For many, familiarity with the above is not likely to extend much beyond number 4. But for some, depending on the nature of the product and its content, raw ingredients or manufacturing process, some of items number 5 through 8 may be relevant.

Whether you work for an organization that drives these and other requirements up the supply chain, or whether you work for a supplier facing those requirements, the selection of agreed principles should be informed by stakeholder relevance and your company's commitment and ability to uphold the principles in question.

Why It Can Be Important to Your Organization

Whether for defining policy or understanding customer requests, it's essential to understand the background and scope of the standards that may apply and how they may be important to your company or your customer:

For legal compliance:

- Many applicable standards and principles (such as EHS and those covering minimum human rights and working conditions) incorporate minimum legal requirements and should therefore be considered under any organization's responsibility to manage.
- Product compliance requirements for environmental performance and content are increasing
- Product and supply chain requirements are increasingly regulated (e.g. Dodd-Frank conflict minerals provision, California Supply Chain Transparency Act).

For more efficient operations:

- Not many organizations can or know how to accurately measure the internal improvements and efficiencies delivered by effective SSCM, including how it contributes to and defines business continuity, enterprise risk management and continuous improvement.
- For a select few brands, effective SSCM is a "license to operate" requirement, but for many companies the valuation of any additional efforts or investments may require better articulation.

For market share:

- An appropriate response to SSCM is considered essential to some brands and a minimum requirement for its suppliers. Similarly, consumers even if not always willing to pay a premium for SSCM are likely to show little tolerance for basic violations
- A full application of SSCM principles and practices can build trust in your product or show a customer that you are considering the sustainability risks and opportunities that your own organization, as part of their supply chain, contributes to their success.

Why It Can be Important to Your Stakeholders

We can consider the customer or the consumer as the ultimate stakeholder, the one that provides the most measurable of performance indicators (sales). The buyer can be seen as the ultimate arbiter of effective SSCM and the first to respond when compared to other stakeholders. Understanding and meeting current expectations, and anticipating future ones, should be the primary focus, insofar as much as they can apply to customers and consumers, when determining the extent of SSCM required. However, other stakeholders are capable of influencing your customers or consumers and may change those spending habits and your ability to maintain market share. It is therefore important to understand the stakeholder landscape beyond contractual or transactional relationships.

Be proactive in understanding issues that may be important to wider stakeholder groups:

- Think about your client's client. What's on the horizon?
- What can be important to your employees?
- What are your competitors doing?
- Are shareholders concerned? How important is this to owners?
- What can be expected to be regulated?
- Who needs to know about your performance? How often and in what format?

For reputation and brand:

- For consumer-facing brands, SSCM can seem like an undisputed cost of doing business and should be managed as systematically as any corporate risk should. But the social boundaries of responsibility for even these companies are being extended. Today's emerging issue may soon be on tomorrow's dashboard.
- For B2B companies, demonstrating proactive management of the customer's extended risks, will generate trust in direct negotiations and to the wider market

The main takeaway about analyzing your stakeholders' opinions is: ask early; ask often.

For some guidance on how to conduct effective stakeholder engagement and integrate this into the decision-making process, refer to the chapter, Stakeholder Engagement.

Setting Priorities

Henry is sitting at his desk, thumbing a worn copy of his customer's sustainability report with fluorescent sticky notes sticking out among its pages. Joe knocks at the glass door and is quickly waved in.

"Hey Joe, welcome back from your trip. How's it going with those internal audits at your site? Anything new showing up, or is everything as you expected?"

Henry was referring to some internal EHS audits that Joe had been preparing for during the last month. He knows that there are problems with recent near-misses and lost time incidents having spiked for reasons that are not yet quite clear.

"Thanks, Henry. Nothing to report yet. The auditors have just finished the opening meeting, so we'll get the full picture then. Speaking of which, did you manage to find out more about what our customer's CSO is expecting us to manage in the supply chain?"

Henry had managed to talk with the CSO that morning: "Yes, their CEO signed an agreement with an activist NGO to monitor the supply chain for human rights and working conditions. But they haven't yet decided exactly which approach to take. We should use this as an opportunity to engage with them on issues beyond price."

Henry and Joe both know that this customer is extremely brand-sensitive and a market leader in a mass volume low-margin product segment. Before long, all existing and most aspiring suppliers would be expected to demonstrate compliance to the NGO-defined principles and, in turn, extend that responsibility up their own supply chains.

"This is what I was talking about last week at the airport. We had a similar thing happen at the last place I worked. A European company had just acquired us. Their due diligence process included some corporate sustainability risk assessment, and as soon as they bought us, the internal audit and security team and their external auditors were flying in to investigate some compliance concerns."

"Turns out we were in violation of their code of conduct. And our own code, as it turned out," explains Joe as he settles into his chair. This meeting could get long. Henry is not the type to enter into operational matters without being well informed, so that's what he knows he can rely on Joe for.

"So what did you do?" asks Henry, crossing his arms and leaning back. Joe reaches for his laptop bag and powers up.

"I hired the same people the new owners came with, their external management system auditors. I figured that if we could pass a pre-assessment with them, we'd be pretty ready for internal audit to revisit us the second time."

"How did that turn out for you?" asks Henry. He leans forward as Joe turns his laptop 90 degrees to share the screen.

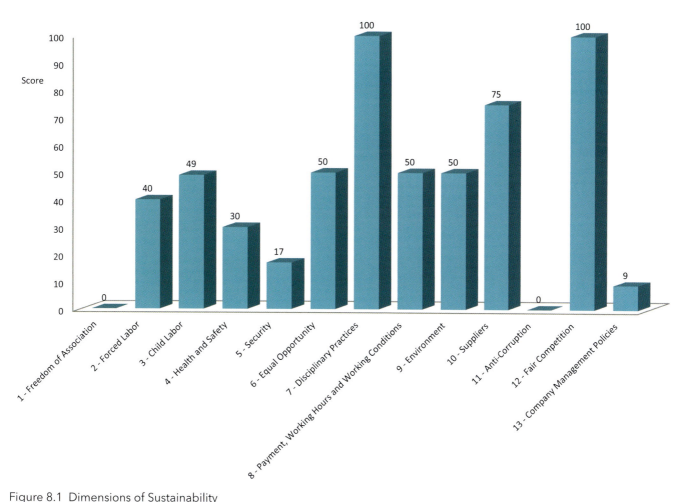

Figure 8.1 Dimensions of Sustainability

"This was the result of our first audit just after the acquisition. We were only in full compliance in two of the code requirements. The second time, when we brought in the external auditors a month later, we were in compliance with 8 of the 13 requirements."

Joe explains how the pre-assessment went and how the external auditors reviewed systems and processes that were new to the acquired company, yet familiar to them.

Following the management of the issue through the experienced eyes of the auditor, many of those interviewed during the exercise were questioned on their responsibilities and contribution to the management of these recent requirements. After the management system was understood, the auditor requested representative samples that were analyzed and crosschecked with workers and other management representatives who were interviewed.
Joe concludes the story. "By the time we had our third and last audit, this time with our new owners' internal audit team, we felt prepared. And even if we received three major non-conformities after that final audit, we still felt that it was an unqualified success."

"How so?" asks Henry. As a perfectionist, Henry believes the phrase "continuous improvement" only applies once.

Joe goes on. "Those three non-conformities were on issues that we would require long-term solutions for, but more importantly, they were on issues that reduced our liability to lawsuits, that addressed key safety and production concerns, and that even were appreciated by employees."

"The external auditors helped us to prioritize those areas where we could see the clear associated correlations with our business targets. They conducted the audit as rigorously as ever but were able to apply a justified focus on those areas where we all knew we were struggling." Joe opens his files and drops his eyes down the cascaded menus. He knows he has a file containing the external auditor's name somewhere.

"While you're looking for those files, Joe, tell me how you think we ought to approach getting our suppliers aligned on this matter? This corporate sustainability thing is going to be a hard sell. Furthermore, it's going to be even harder to prove that we can really make that change with them," says Henry.

Joe pauses his search. He had come to the realization that this was where he had been before with Henry. This was how Henry built his career in the company, by finding the right people for the right solution and right position. Often these people were unaware of being candidates for positions that did not exist yet; Joe is not one these people.

"Henry, can you give me two days to get back to you? My feeling is that we need to take control of the agenda by being seen as proactive by our customer," Joe says, buying some time. He knows that Henry will end up asking for a budget estimate and that his time now was not best spent on a helicopter view with Henry. "Can I assume you'll need a financial justification for this as well?"

Henry smiles. "If you think it will help, Joe."

Risk Assessment and Identifying Key Suppliers

Understand Material Issues in Direct Operations and the Supply Chain

Many of the management approaches in SSCM can be applied and replicated in order to prioritize actions, whether code of conduct compliance is requested by your company's customer or expected of your suppliers.

Some inputs into a risk assessment can include, but are not limited to:

1. Legal compliance: As a minimum, benchmark the countries where you and your suppliers operate for
    a. regulatory framework (alignment with requirements)
    b. enforcement (willingness and capability to control and prosecute)
2. Nature of operations: Whether looking at your own operations or those of suppliers, legal compliance should also include:
    a. Working conditions
        i. White-collar or blue-collar?
        ii. Adequacy of facilities
        iii. Shifts? Homeworkers?
        iv. Workplace hazards? Occupational risks?
    b. Controlled substances
        i. Chemicals used in product or process
        ii. Fertilizers/pesticides/dyes/ bleaches
        iii. Silica/paint/lubricants
3. Historical performance: Historical performance can cover direct operations as well as suppliers. Even if they are not always easily quantifiable, consider the following:
    a. Past and current fines, penalties and prosecutions of specific site and/or supplier
    b. Level of perceived corruption in country/industry
    c. Anticipated increase in regulatory scrutiny
4. Environmental performance: If you are part of the manufacturing supply chain of a major brand you may soon be required to provide them with product-related environmental data. Consider:
    a. A lifecycle assessment or other analysis per unit of production
    b. Impact of raw material sourcing
    c. Organizational or product carbon footprint
    d. Organizational or product water footprint
    e. Use of pollutants, controlled substances in production or product
5. Stakeholder Engagement: Effective stakeholder engagement is a valuable tool and a fundamental principle of sustainability management. Use it effectively to understand:
    a. the relative level of concern over sustainability issues
    b. accepted and expected management approach
    c. measures of success, performance

A self-assessment can be carried out by any company, using some of the above as inputs, and against any agreed customer code or industry standard as applicable.

In order to extend the assessment to the supply chain, further inputs may be required to fully understand its impacts and the company's ability and capability to manage these risks:

1. Criticality: Where are the most critical suppliers? Are any of these considered a sustainability risk?
2. Volume: Where is the spending concentrated?
3. Mapping: Is there visibility over the supply chain? Where may there be hidden subcontractors?
4. Supplier Communication: Outreach and contracting
5. Supplier Engagement: Understanding expectations and addressing responsibilities and resources
6. Supplier selection: Considering of high risk, critical suppliers, sampling and scaling over time
7. Monitoring Options:
    a. Supplier self-assessments
    b. Using second-party auditors versus in-house auditing
    c. Certification/audit to a standard industry code or scheme (e.g. SA8000, EICC, WRAP)

Developing an Effective Supply Chain Management Process

Fundamental Concepts

- Do not work in isolation: Working in silos does not serve any corporation's interests. Understand and be prepared to articulate how sustainability fits in with HR, EHS, R&D, RM and CI.
    - What corporate functions are/need to be consulted?
    - What functions impact the risk?
    - How is risk defined and communicated in the organization?
    - How is ROI currently defined?
- Integrate into existing procurement practices: Ownership of sustainability should reside within procurement (or supply chain) if that department has the capability of otherwise managing the supply chain.
    - Get on the risk radar
    - Define a policy and set targets
    - Set a benchmark and measure performance
    - Align supplier qualification and monitoring models
    - Train and/or calibrate supplier auditors
- Understand that risks are interrelated and can drive opportunities. See the following examples:
    - Safety and Health working hours
    - Working hours and productivity
    - Business continuity and resilience

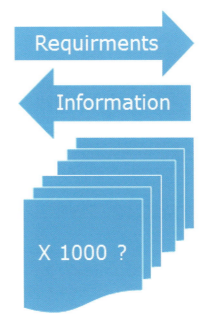

Figure 8.2 Dimensions of Sustainability

Practical Actions

Map your supply chain.

Many organizations, of all sizes, are frequently unaware of the extent and size of their supply chains. This should be seen as an opportunity. A poor understanding of the supply chain can result in much inefficiency, redundancy and even mixed messages to different suppliers.

In terms of worst cases, a case of two different departments auditing the same supplier within the same week has been observed, both departments with external auditors in tow. At least half the time spent by the first auditor was repeated by the second. However, at least that was partially offset by the discovery that the supplier had different contracts for each department with noticeably different prices as well.

As so much of SSCM risk is defined by national jurisdictions (and, even more relevantly, their ability to enforce regulation) and management cultures, a clear vision of the supply chain, how many layers it has, and how far it extends before reaching source will determine later challenges in effecting change and exercising influence.

Be clear about what you need

Communication is even more critical in an effective SSCM, as new requirements are expected to be met that are frequently voluntary in nature. At the same time, buyers themselves are not always clear about their requirements—not so much the standards that they expect to be met, but what burden of proof needs to be provided.

Buyers also need to be clear on what the escalations levels are to be, and in what form this will have consequences to the commercial relationship. There are important principles that need to be followed should critical violations be detected through monitoring. So make sure the suppliers understand that they will bear the burden of any compensation due to workers, indemnification due to use of banned substances, etc.

Make sure you and your suppliers are clear on the expectations and responsibilities for the following:

- Contractual compliance
- Scoring, weighting and supplier qualification
- Audit costs and logistics
- Findings, types and their handling
- Corrective, preventative and remediation actions

Build capacity

Make sure that all of the people involved in the procurement department and associated functions (internal stakeholders, enablers) are adequately prepared to manage the wider scope of their jobs. Each will benefit from understanding how they fit in and how they can contribute. It should be clear that procurement practices may impact on supplier compliance, such as with short lead times, unverified production capacity or sudden changes in specifications that can lead to unintended violations.

Tailored training may be required for internal or supplier auditors, mostly to calibrate on the type of evidence to seek and sample in order to determine labor and human rights compliance if the auditor already possesses EHS skills.

Measure the results

In the last few years, the level of transparency provided by sustainability risks in the supply chain has only increased. So too has the upstream extension of responsibility assigned to some industries where brands and now even expected to respond to the impacts of sourcing at the commodity level, whether it be mineral, vegetable or animal. It can only be expected that this level of scrutiny will require big data.

To the degree possible, invest early on in the ability to measure results. Just as importantly, invest in the analysis of the results. Link associated metrics in different departments to find correlated benefits, particularly those that can quantify a financial return.

Performance should be accurately measured for the purposes of external communication and avoidance of restatements. Add credibility to your claims and performance over time by designing in data audit-ability from the outset.

Supplier Selection and Monitoring

Selection

Some companies (those closer to primary production and extractives) can opt to manage their supply chain through existing and established chain-of-custody certification schemes. Examples include the Forest Stewardship Council for the paper industry, the Kimberly Process certification for diamonds, the Marine Stewardship Council for fisheries and similar schemes for sugar (Bonsucro), cotton (Better Cotton Initiative), and for a host of other commodities.

Other industries can follow schemes tailored to the realities of their operations, such as the EICC code for the electronics industry or those derived from retailers (BSCI, GSCP) and demand corresponding audit reports, certificates or other proof of compliance.

For yet other companies, the selection process is critical to scale capability and resources when these may be constrained.

Categorize suppliers by risk and response:

1. Selection of suppliers/partners: Desk-based risk assessment (see previous section: "Understand material issues in Direct Operations and the Supply Chain").
2. Self-assessment: Ensure all critical and high-risk suppliers submit to a scored self-

assessment that is instructive to the suppliers and can identify focus areas.
3. Inspections/assessments: The results of the selection process, combined with the results of scored self-assessments, results in another subset to be assessed through existing supplier monitoring visits.
4. Close follow-up: The last subset can be those suppliers deemed particularly high risk or as a rolling sample, and that would justify in-depth, even unannounced audits with specialized teams.

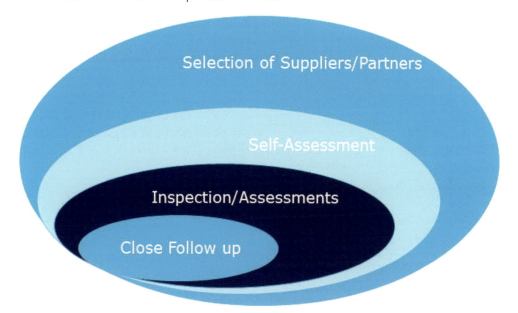

Figure 8.3 Dimensions of Sustainability

Monitoring

Depending on your supply chain model there are many options open to you in how your suppliers can be monitored. If your organization is in the fortunate position of having one of the aforementioned well-established sourcing standards, then your choice is fairly straightforward. But it could be likely that you will have to consider more closely monitoring at least a select number of your suppliers.

The following are some of the options available, and many companies can adopt a combination of these:

In-House Supplier Auditors:
If you already have a complex supply chain and have the internal resources to already be carrying out supplier inspections and assessments, then this is where monitoring should begin. These same resources should be supported, with external support in the beginning if required, to allow them to include sustainability as part of their scope.

External Auditors (Certification Bodies/Registrars):

Experienced auditors with knowledge of local legal requirements can carry out the full supplier monitoring program, from protocol design to performing supplier audits if this is done to a corporate code. Using second- or third-party auditors can enhance the credibility of monitoring.

Shared Audits:

These may be industry-specific (EICC) or industry-agnostic (SEDEX) schemes that allow suppliers to share audit results with buyers. The scheme's portal brings transparency to buyers and reduced audit fatigue to suppliers. Monitoring is conducted by external auditors, typically at supplier's choice and expense.

Two months had passed since their last meeting at the Shanghai Supplier Summit and Henry is eager to catch up on progress with Joe on the Sustainable Supply Chain Management program. After a day of meetings with the regional teams, they somehow manage to meet in the hotel lobby for half an hour.

"Great presentation today, Joe! Good to hear how far you've got on the supplier monitoring part already. That was impressive." Henry seems to mean it. He makes a point of it by quoting from Joe's presentation on several statistics from the risk assessment.
"But I never had the chance to ask you something, Joe," continues Henry. "What's your next move?" It was no secret that Joe was the right person to set up this kind of project, fast yet deliberate. However, Joe never saw himself settling into this stage of the program.

"I've already interviewed the new Sustainable Supply Chain Manager and I'm pretty sure we have the right person already. I want to be operational in six weeks. Then it's a short vacation for me," replies Joe.

"Then what? I can't see you being quite ready to let this go yet."

"Then comes the tough but fun part. I want to see things happen in the field. I want to see the change we leave behind with our suppliers." Joe undoes his tie. He is not going to be quite satisfied reviewing reports at Corporate HQ. He wants to see the change happen for himself.

Creating Shared Value in the Supply Chain

According to Porter and Kramer's Creating Shared Value (CSV) business concept, to create shared value, companies can:

1. Re-imagine products and markets to provide appropriate services and meet unmet needs.
2. Redefine productivity in the value chain to mitigate risks and boost productivity.
3. Enable local cluster development by improving the external framework that supports the company's operations

As none of these are likely to be achieved to any degree of success in isolation of the suppliers themselves (and the last two outcomes are dependent on suppliers entirely), it is often not so much a sustainability innovation model as a supply chain model. Even with GE and Unilever often touted as best-case examples of CSV models that identify emerging markets and unmet needs, those that provide an equally valid value in supply chains, through capacity building that provides measurable social co-benefits.

This chapter concludes with an invitation to read the Responsible Sourcing section of Nestlé's Creating Shared Value Report, which includes examples of how suppliers, once considered barriers to generating value are increasingly considered part of the solution.

http://www.nestle.com

FRAMEWORK

Our commitment: Roll out the Rural Development Framework. Read more...

COCOA PLAN

Our commitment: Roll out the *Nestlé Cocoa Plan*. Read more...

NESCAFÉ PLAN

Our commitment: Roll out the *Nescafé* Plan Read more...

SOURCING

Our commitment: Implement responsible sourcing. Read more...

DID YOU KNOW?

300 000

Farmers trained through capacity-building programmes in 2013

DID YOU KNOW?

47.6 million

Milk farmers benefiting from financial assistance.

Source: http://www.nestle.com

Key Point Summary

1. The principles of supply chain management are applicable to safety and health management.

2. The safety and health concerns of the organization should extend to include both suppliers and customers.

3. One of the most proactive things an organization can do to prevent introduction of safety and health exposures to their operation is to demand a high level of safety and health performance from their suppliers and monitor their performance routinely.

4. Continual improvement in safety and health performance helps protect brand and market share.

5. Risks are interrelated and what an organization does to improve quality, environmental, branding, or other concerns can have a corresponding positive effect on safety and health.

6. Practical actions taken to manage an organization's supply chain include:
    a. Mapping the supply chain
    b. Specifically and clearly defining requirements
    c. Building capacity and utility within the supply chain management group
    d. Measuring results

Personal Planning

1. Do I understand the safety and health implications of our supply chain?

2. What safety and health exposures could potentially be introduced to my organization through the supply chain?

3. What are we doing to manage these exposures?

4. What safety and health exposures could our organization potentially introduce into our customer's organization?

5. What are we doing to manage these exposures?

6. What should we be doing to improve our supply chain management from a safety and health point of view?

Y – Model for Action Planning

Present Situation

Desired Situation

Need for Change

Present Situation

Stop Responsibility Target Date

TASK-COMPETENCIES, ANALYSIS AND TRAINING

Chapter 9

TASK-COMPETENCIES, ANALYSIS AND TRAINING

CHAPTER OBJECTIVES

1. To present best practices for identifying training and competency requirements through systematic analysis of tasks.
2. To illustrate how task analysis can be used as both a risk management and a training process technique.
3. To illustrate how adult learning principles can be used as the basis for a robust training and competency process.

Joe takes pride in the fact that for several years now, the overall score of the employee satisfaction survey for his plant has been improving, to the point that they are now above average compared to other plants and, as he has heard; even above average compared to peers in the industry.

However, the latest scores on questions that address safety and Health seem to be equal to, or in some cases slightly lower than, the scores in previous years, while actually the number of safety and health accidents has not actually increased. As in previous years, Joe has budgeted for all his workers to participate in annual refreshment courses that cover all risks and hazards within the organization. He has also approved of ad hoc training requests when safety or health incidents occurred.

Joe wonders if this stagnating score is merely the result of his decision to stop the, in his eyes, the erratic spending on safety and health trainings. He has made it clear that the organization would maximize the annual increase, which is still quite generous, of the overall training budget.

Well aware of the fact that the employees are one of the major stakeholders, Joe contemplates allowing for an extra increase of the overall training budget, specifically related to safety and health, in order to improve the employee satisfaction survey scores.

"Lisa, you have seen the results of the employee satisfaction survey. We need to further improve the scores on Safety and Health and I assume that an extra increase of our training budget might be what our colleagues are looking for. This would of course impact other investments we had planned."

"Joe, I believe we can utilize the budget a lot better if we would invest in an effective competence management system. I believe that if we take the time to conduct a thorough inventory of the critical tasks, especially related to safety and health and the critical competencies needed to perform those tasks, we would get the most out of our training budget. Who knows, maybe we could still find budget for the other investments."

"Sounds like music to my ears, Lisa. It happens that this week Henry has organized a session with all plant managers with the objective of determining our organization's competencies that are key for achieving our business goals. We should ensure that these key competencies are embedded in the critical competencies of our colleagues."

Introduction

Most organizations rely significantly on the competencies of its employees to achieve its business goals and conduct the work at hand safely. The objective of a competence management system is, in essence, to match in a systematic way the business goals and the competencies needed to achieve them. And while most of today's organizations are also dependent on contractors, the competence management system should also extend to the supply chain.

Employees are among any organization's major stakeholders. The desire to utilize one's talents and competencies, the desire to be able to further develop them, and to be able to work in safe and healthy work conditions are fundamental to employee loyalty, and thus to achieving sustainable business performance. Employee loyalty begins with employer loyalty and the commitment of management to uphold these fundamental values.

Tomorrow's successful companies will create value by meeting the world's economic, social and environmental needs and must be creative and learning organizations. The process of meeting and balancing the needs of the stakeholders exerts tremendous pressures for change on all types of organizations and virtually every person in them. If companies want to achieve excellence in this new environment, they simply need to start training for this.

Executives must learn, for instance, totally new sustainability strategies; how to both compete and collaborate globally; how to develop and implement mission-vision-values-paradigms-social, environmental and ethical principles; how to change and communicate the company culture; how to include employees and the supply chain to drive change.

Front-line leaders must bridge the huge gap from "boss" to team leader–mentor–support provider–facilitator.

Associates (workers/employees) must learn how to function in new organization structures; how to handle team membership and empowerment; ever more rapidly changing technology, statistical techniques, problem-solving systems, and on and on.

Everyone must learn to be more flexible and creative; how to do more with less; how to cope with stress; how to fully satisfy their stakeholders and customers (internal and/or external); how to improve continually.

Yes, there is a vital need for employee engagement and lifelong learning: changing-adapting-improving. Learning and training are proven instruments for excellent sustainable individual and corporate performance. Training fosters knowledge transfer, giving rise to further innovation, efficiency and competitive insight. If companies want to achieve excellence in this new environment, they simply need to start training for it.

In her book "Good Company," Laurie Bassi discusses requirements for companies to be successful in the "worthiness era" of which sustainability and being a good employer are key parts. Interestingly, her research started by studying the correlations between corporate training investments and stock market performance. Bassi found that companies with strong commitments to training attained a positive 47 percent mean change in market value (as compared to book value) whereas companies with comparatively weaker commitments averaged a 4 percent decline in value during the same three-year period.

Developing a Competence Management System

A competence management system is a framework of processes and procedures, accountable and continuously improving, to ensure that the organization has the required competence to achieve its objectives.

The competence of the organization is the aggregated and structured interaction of individual competencies, which results in the ability to apply knowledge and skills to achieve intended results.

In order to have an effective competence management system, the organization should, both on different organizational levels and for individuals:

1. Have a clear understanding of the organization's key competencies.
2. Have a clear overview of the critical tasks and linked competencies.
3. Conduct an individual gap analysis, indicating required as well as desired competencies.
4. Develop a plan to bridge the gaps.
5. Implement the actions of the plan.
6. Evaluate and improve.

The Key Competencies of Your Organization

Key competencies provide your organization (or an individual for that matter) with a competitive advantage. These key competencies are the results of underlying skills, abilities, knowledge and experiences and enable you to provide unique products or services. Based on these key competencies, provided they are hard to imitate, your company can achieve strategic competitive advantage. In order to achieve sustainable business performance, your organizations may need to develop new key competencies to meet future market wants and stakeholder needs.

Determining the key competency(s) of your organization can be done by interviews and may include members of your leadership and sales team, employees, key customers, suppliers and contractors, competitors and general public. Depending on your organization, you typically may find one to three key competencies.

Having determined the key competencies, your organization needs to assure that these competencies are nurtured and strengthened throughout the entire organization through goal setting, task/job descriptions, training, performance assessments and feedback discussions.

Critical Tasks and Competencies Analysis

In order to support achieving the sustainable business goals, critical tasks and the necessary essential competencies need to be determined through a systematic task analysis from the perspective of safety, quality and efficiency all at the same time. Without such an integrated approach, changes might be made for the sake of production or quality that could have a negative impact on the safety and health aspects. Also, because it requires important input from the people who actually do the work, this technique utilizes employee involvement and participative management. This results in work instructions and practices which are among the most valuable tools imaginable for such important activities as job orientation, task instruction, performance observation, team meetings, organizational rules, corrective and developmental coaching, incident investigation and skill training.

There are other techniques to determine critical tasks:

Critical Incident Technique (CIT), which is based on primary interviews focusing on "critical incidents" in the job. A critical incident can be described as one that makes a contribution—either positively or negatively—to an activity or phenomenon. CIT is a flexible method that usually relies on five major areas. The first is determining and reviewing the incident, then fact-finding, which involves collecting the details of the incident from the participants. When all of the facts are collected, the next step is to identify the issues. Afterwards a decision can be made on how to resolve the issues based on various possible solutions. The final and most important aspect is the evaluation, which will determine if the solution that was selected will solve the root cause of the situation and will cause no further problems.

Functional Job Analysis (FJA), which is based on observations, interviews and focus groups used to identify job tasks as they relate to people, data and things. FJA is carried out by a focus group of experienced job performers guided by a facilitator. The focus group collects information on the (1) Outputs of the job performers; (2) knowledge, skills, and abilities required to perform the job; and (3) Tasks performed in getting the work done. This information is then used to document the performance standards applying to individual tasks or the job as a whole resulting in written task statements that collectively comprise a task bank for the job being analyzed.

DACUM Job Analysis, which uses single focus group to identify job tasks and corresponding knowledge, skills and abilities, tools and equipment required to perform the job. The philosophy of DACUM is that expert workers can describe and define their jobs more accurately than anyone else. An effective way to define a job is to precisely describe the tasks that expert workers perform. All tasks, in order to be performed correctly, demand certain knowledge, skills, tools, and worker behaviors. In the DACUM process, a panel of six to eight high-performing workers analyze their own job. These skilled workers identify the duties and tasks that make up their job. Under the direction of a facilitator, the panel analyzes their job-related tasks while using a modified brainstorming process that encompasses a storyboarding technique. The final result is an occupational profile presented in a chart.

As noted in Figure 9.1, this approach involves these eight stages:

1. Inventory occupations/positions
2. Inventory all jobs within each occupation/position
3. Inventory all tasks within each job or occupation
4. Identify the critical tasks
5.1. Analyze the critical tasks
   (a) Break tasks down into steps or activities
   (b) Pinpoint loss exposures
   (c) Make an improvement check
   (d) Develop controls
5.2. Identify critical competencies (knowledge, skills and behavior)
   (a) Define competence standards, performance, test and training requirements
   (b) Write job/task competence profiles
6. Write work instructions or practices
7. Put to work
8. Update and maintain records

Each of these stages will be explored in detail, but a basic understanding of several key terms is first required. These terms include occupation and position, job, task, critical task, competence, work instruction and practice.

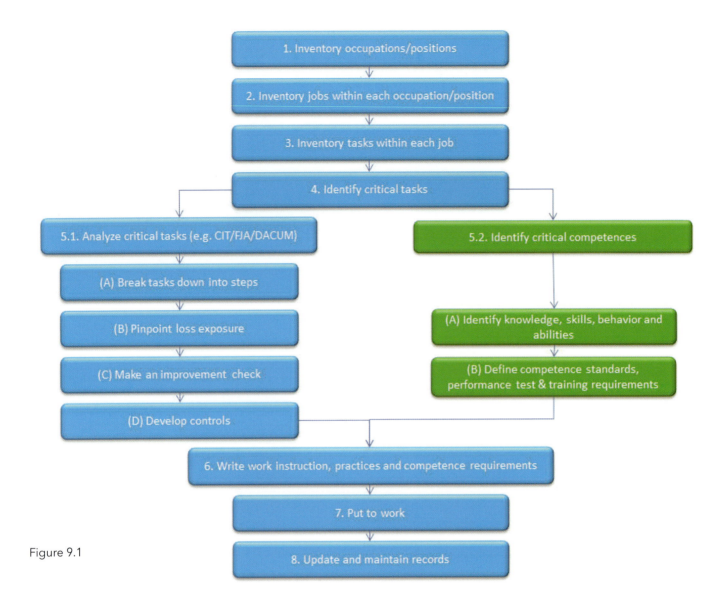

Figure 9.1

OCCUPATION/POSITION:

A person's occupational title or position in the organization, such as maintenance mechanic, trimming machine operator, painter, shipping clerk, data entry operator, freight scheduler, lift truck operator, quality analyst, etc.

JOB:

A work assignment, such as rebuild a packaging machine, or load a flatbed trailer. With today's increased use of teams sometimes a team's "job" is the process for which the team is responsible. One example might be "order procurement" which involves a group of tasks that is more comprehensive than "sales."

TASK:

A segment of work that requires a set of specific and distinct actions for its completion. For example, a task for an electrician might be to "wire a junction box." This task could be done in isolation or could be one of a series of tasks necessary to complete a much larger work assignment, such as wiring a house. Many people use the terms job and task interchangeably. For our purposes, however, while both terms are used in describing this segment of work, we prefer the term task and will use it to avoid confusion, and for the sake of consistency and simplicity. This is an especially important distinction, as enormous confusion is created when the word job sometimes means occupation and sometimes means task. The relationship between occupations/positions, jobs and related tasks is shown in Figure 9.2.

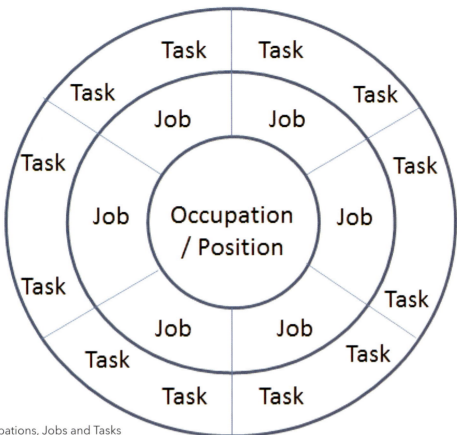

Figure 9.2: Occupations, Jobs and Tasks

CRITICAL TASK:

A task that has the potential to produce major loss to people, property, process and/or environment when not performed properly.

WORK INSTRUCTIONS:

Step-by-step instructions for how to properly perform a specific task from start to finish. The exact sequence of each step is usually a very important consideration when developing work instructions.

PRACTICE:

A set of positive guidelines helpful to the performance of a specific type of work that may not always be done in a set way. The use of practices helps to avoid attempts to develop detailed work instructions for tasks that do not always follow an established sequence and thus have an end product that is not practical. Task practices are especially useful with trades, crafts, and maintenance and materials handling where the same task may be done in a wide variety of settings and circumstances.

It is fitting at this point to stress that the entire process of task analysis is a demanding one and should not be underestimated. Because of the extensive time and energy required to develop good practices or work instructions, and because it requires the cooperation of persons from various areas, a written directive or letter stating management's position on this subject is valuable for establishing the proper climate for maximum cooperation. This communication not only should show that management supports this activity wholeheartedly, but also should re-emphasize the major potential benefits for all areas of the operation.

COMPETENCE:

The ability of a person to apply knowledge, skills, and appropriate behavior in order to achieve intended results. While knowledge (e.g. knowing what traffic rules and signs mean) and skills (knowing how to apply brakes, steer around a corner) are commonly accepted competence elements, the person's behavior is considered an equally essential part of the competence. For example: anticipating, being careful and forgiving would be considered appropriate behavior and therefore an essential element of driver competence. For many jobs and tasks, formal competence standards (diploma's, certificates) exist, defining in detail the minimal required knowledge, skills and behavioral competencies.

QUALIFICATION:

Demonstrated education, training and work experience, where applicable. A qualification may supply the person with formal authorization to enter into a specific occupation, or perform a specific task and is assumed to assure on a somewhat generic level that the person is competent. Competence relates to competencies acquired within the specific workplace and tasks performed. A person may have a driver's license and ten years of driving experience, but may not have the competence to drive a small van with a heavy load on icy roads.

1. **Inventory occupations/positions**

    The first step in developing a comprehensive task inventory is to produce a complete list of all occupations/positions.

2. **Inventory all jobs within each occupation/position**

    The primary purpose of this stage is to avoid confusing specific tasks with broad work assignments or jobs. Examples of jobs might be to rewire a house, which would include several distinct tasks. Another example would be to rebuild an injection-molding machine that would also involve several distinct tasks. The primary problem of classifying broad activities as single tasks becomes especially obvious when an attempt is made to develop detailed work instructions. Writing a single, brief instruction that is both accurate and complete for such broad work assignments is impractical. If attempted, the development of a very general and (likely) flawed work instruction is virtually assured. Major job or work assignments must be broken down to their finer tasks before an effective analysis can be made.

3. **Inventory all tasks related to each job**

    Once the occupation inventory is completed, the more difficult effort remains of listing all the tasks performed within each job or major work assignment. This inventory should at least reflect all the hands-on work (as opposed to administrative duties) associated with each job or major work assignment. Once developed, this comprehensive task inventory will permit each of the tasks to be evaluated later to determine whether it is critical. Task analysis is a management technique, not an exact science. There are, however, several practical rules of thumb that can be invaluable to task inventory development teams.

- Such terms as operate and maintain, when used to describe a single task, often indicate that the work has been too broadly defined and should be broken down into several, more manageable tasks. Determine whether the work described is a skill or "a segment of work which requires a set of specific and distinct steps for its completion." The latter is our definition for the term "task."
- Activities that use the "-ing" form of the verb (stacking, moving, loading, cleaning) are usually general responsibilities rather than specific tasks. Tasks can be identified from such descriptions, however, by further asking, "What is being stacked, moved, loaded, or cleaned and where is this taking place?"
- Rarely would a task be comprised of a single step, such as "rotate the 7/8 wrench one half a turn clockwise" or "push the reject button." Rather, a task is almost always made up of a number of definite steps, each contributing to the completion of the task. (Tasks can be too narrowly defined, as well).
- The greater the number of individual steps, the greater the chance that more than one task is involved. For example, a task could theoretically contain more than forty individual steps, but practical experience shows that a given task will generally not exceed fifteen to twenty distinct steps.
- General responsibilities and relationships that are normally included in a position charter or job description are generally not tasks. They should not be listed as "tasks" if charters are referred to.

- The longer the time required to complete the work, the greater the chance that more than one task is involved. For example, ten to thirty minutes or perhaps an hour or more could be required to complete a given task. If a considerably greater amount of time is consistently necessary to complete the work, more than one task is likely involved.
- The greater the number of people required to complete the work, the greater the chance that more than one task is involved; for example, one to two workers versus three to five, etc.
- A maintenance-related work assignment will typically contain more total tasks than an operations or assembly-related occupation. The latter might contain relatively few tasks that are performed repeatedly.
- Tasks can be inventoried on a form such as the partially completed one in Figure 9.4 (pg. 187). This figure identifies eleven of the tasks that a Chief Grinding Operator might be expected to perform. Additional tasks would be listed on other copies of the same form.
- Front-line leaders and workers who are experienced or knowledgeable about work assignments are usually the best for identifying all tasks within that job. They can do this together as a team by brainstorming about the hands-on work related to that occupation, or by observing and talking with those who actually do the work. This provides an excellent opportunity to apply the principle of involvement by getting the expert experience and help of those who will be most affected—the work group. Remember, a team of people who are knowledgeable about the work being considered should always be made a part of every stage of task analysis.

4. **Identify the critical tasks**

   A question that comes up early in task analysis is, "Which tasks should we thoroughly analyze and describe?" Some organizations do them all. However, most organizations realize there are practical problems with this approach. For instance, the amount of time and effort required to analyze every task in the company may be formidable. Let's say, for example, that your company had 50 different occupations or work titles, with an average of only 20 specific tasks each. This means (allowing for duplication) there are probably more than 800 tasks to analyze and to keep up-to-date. Better results can be achieved in less time by applying the principle of the critical/vital few and concentrating on the critical tasks.

   - All tasks that are directly linked to the key competence of the organization would be appropriate to analyze.
   - All tasks with a history of loss, whether personal injury, property damage, quality loss or production loss, should be classified according to their criticality. To be predictive rather than reactive, it is also vital to include tasks having a potential for major loss, even if there is no history of such. To do this, the following questions should be asked:
     i. Can this task, if not done properly, result in major loss while being performed?
     ii. Can this task, if not done properly, result in major loss after having been performed?
     iii. How serious is the loss likely to be? What is the severity of injury, cost of damage or cost of quality or production loss likely to be? Are other persons or departments likely to be affected?
     iv. What is the expected probability of losses? Probability of loss is strongly influenced by how often the task is performed in the organization in a specific time period (frequency of exposure), and how likely it is to result in a loss each time it is done (probability).

Figure 9.4 (pg 187) gives an example of a Task Inventory Worksheet. There are many degrees of criticality and, in fact, every task worth doing is critical to some degree. Thus, a system that develops a scale of criticality is likely to result in fewer differences of opinion than one that merely classifies the task as critical or not critical. Determining the criticality of a task can be done using a risk evaluation approach.

Although some subjective judgment is still required by the team members, the fact that each factor is given due consideration results in a more consistent and logical classification of tasks according to criticality.

Severity (the first evaluation column) is derived from the costs of the losses being incurred or the loss most likely to be incurred as a result of wrong performance of the task. A scale of zero to six, such as the following, is suggested:

- 0 -No injury or illness or quality, production, environmental or other loss of more than ……
- 2 -Minor injury or illness without lost time; non-disruptive property damage; quality, production, environmental or other loss of …… to …….
- 4 -A lost-time injury or illness without permanent disability; disruptive property damage; quality, production, environmental or other loss of more than …… but not exceeding ……
- 6 -Permanent disability; loss of life or body part; extensive loss of structure, equipment, material; quality, production, environmental or other losses exceeding ……

These descriptions and evaluations of severity (including the dollar value), as well as the number of points on the scale, can be varied to suit different requirements.

Frequency of exposure (the second evaluation column) can be assessed from Figure 9.3, using a scale of one to three:

Number of Persons Performing tasks	Number of times a task is performed by each person		
	Less then daily	Few times per day	Many times per day
Few	1	1	2
Moderate	1	2	3
Many	2	3	3

Figure 9.3 Frequency Exposure

TASK INVENTORY WORKSHEET

Occupation or position	Department	Inventory Date(s)
Grinding Operator	Grinding	

| Tasks | General Loss Exposures | Risk Evaluation | | | | Program Needs | | | | | | |
List all task normally done or that might be done by a person in the occupation	Consider safety, health, environmental, quality problems etc. Consider people, equipment, materials and environmental interactions	Severity	Frequency	Probability	Critical Rating	Engineering	Work Instructions	Practice	Skill Training	Special Rules	I.H. Interview	Purchasing
Conduct grinding mill area pre-shift inspection	Substandard conditions can develop during prior shift	4	2	0	6			√	√			
Synchronize incline feed and exit ball mill belts	material overflow and spillage; poor delivery of material down line	4	2	0	6		√		√			
Start complete grinding circuit	The proper timing and sequence of start-up of equipment must take place or system will not function	4	1	0	5		√		√			
Start particle size monitor	If monitor is not brought on-line properly, grinding problems may not be detected and product quality will be compromised	6	2	1	9		√		√			
Bring rod mill dual drive system motors c-12 and c-14 on-line	if these motors are not started in proper sequence, the drive assembly could be severly damaged	4	3	1	8		√		√			
Change steel rods	Back injury from lifting worn rods from below spinning screen. Possible fall with major injury. Hand and finger injury. Poor grinding will overload ball mills	4	2	0	6	√	√					√
Charge ball mill with ore	Injury from mechanical scoop. Exposure to cyanide and lime. Injury from rotating screen. Poor material deed will cause clogs and inadequate separation of various ores	6	2	1	9		√		√		√	√
Routine rod mill shutdown	Poor grinding of remants, production interruption down-line	2	1	0	3				√			
Emergency rod mill Shutdown	Material spillage, equipment damage, down-line overflow and clogging	6	2	0	8		√		√			
Charge rod mill with ore	poor grinding of ore material, reduced motor efficiency, inadequate separation of products	2	2	0	4				√			
Hose down and clean up grinding area	Operation of high pressure water hoses around high voltage motors presents exposure to electrocution and motor damage	6	1	0	7			√		√		√

Figure 9.4 Task Inventory Worksheet

The probability of loss likely to occur whenever a particular task is performed (the third evaluation column) is influenced by the following factors:

- Hazardousness, i.e., how inherently dangerous is the task?
- Difficulty, i.e., how prone to quality, production or other problems is the task?
- Complexity of the task.
- The chance that there will be loss if the task is improperly performed.

These factors are not evaluated separately, but they should all be borne in mind. The key question is, "How likely is it that things will go wrong as a result of the performance of this task?"

Since, for the sake of simplicity, only the most likely loss is considered when evaluating severity, it follows that only the probability of that particular loss should be considered.

A scale from -1 to +1 is used as follows:

-1	= Low probability of loss
0	= Moderate probability of loss
+1	= High probability of loss

The points allotted to each of the three factors are then added to indicate a scale of criticality ranging from zero to ten. It is, in effect, an order of priority. Management may decide that all tasks allotted less than, say, three points will not be listed as critical tasks. On the other hand, it may be decided that tasks allotted eight or more points are the most critical tasks, requiring immediate attention.

The completed worksheet is shown in Figure 9.4. This worksheet also records the decision of whether work instructions or a set of task practices would best serve the overall purposes of this program activity. At times, this can be determined when the tasks are evaluated. At other times, further analysis of the tasks is required before making this decision.

One of the tasks that received a high criticality evaluation in the example is "Start Particle Size Monitor." It is used to illustrate the next step.
- Analysis and Identification
- Analyze the critical tasks

Break Tasks Down Into Steps

We could define a task step as one part of the total task where something happens to advance the work involved. Every task can be broken down into the steps required to do it, and there is usually a particular order to the steps that is best. It is this orderly sequence of steps that will eventually become the basis for the work instructions.

Identifying every step of a critical task is essential to the end result. When the task is first observed, write down everything the worker does. After each step of the task is identified, the team can go back and combine things or eliminate unnecessary detail. For example, the first five steps of the task "Start Particle Size Monitor" are properly identified as:

Step 1. Record each gauge reading
Step 2. Look for sand buildup in cyclone box
Step 3. Hose out air eliminator
Step 4. Close drain valve
Step 5. Open fresh water valve

When trying to do a good job, however, inexperienced team members are prone to include unnecessary detail as steps. Breaking a critical task down into each of its steps doesn't mean listing every tiny detail on the breakdown. These quickly become too difficult for the practical purpose of teaching a worker the steps to be remembered. Here is a list of task steps that can be recognized as being too fine a breakdown.

Step 1. Get proper form for gauge readings
Step 2. Study the gauge readings
Step 3. Record the gauge readings on the form
Step 4. Walk to the cyclone box
Step 5. Look for buildup
Step 6. Remove buildup if necessary
Step 7. Close cyclone box

It's obvious that this breakdown is much too detailed and it's not too difficult to visualize the final length if continued in this manner. The difficulty a worker would have in remembering such details makes the approach impractical. On the other hand, consider a breakdown that takes the opposite extreme and doesn't provide enough steps to be of significant value.

Step 1. Record gauges
Step 2. Ensure equipment is ready
Step 3. Turn on monitor
Step 4. Maintain the correct slurry level

As we look at this extremely general breakdown, it's obvious that many steps were missed that could involve significant loss exposures in any one or all of the areas of safety, quality and production.

To illustrate the most efficient way to do a task, the breakdown must include every key step that is inherent in doing the task correctly, but exclude those which will trivialize or overly burden the process.

The decision to consider any aspect of a task's performance as a distinct step can also follow the thinking used in classifying the task as being critical. "Could it result in a major loss if done incorrectly?"

Experience shows that many tasks will break down into ten to fifteen or twenty key steps. Certain tasks might justify a greater number of key steps. Each task must be evaluated on its own needs. The key to the prevention of losses from injury, property damage, quality problems or production losses is each team member's judgment in selecting the appropriate task steps.

Both approaches make good use of the management Principle of Involvement: "Meaningful involvement increases motivation and support." Participation is important in analysis by observation and discussion and in analysis by discussion alone. Even when staff specialists do the analyses, a vital key to success is the active involvement of front-line leaders and workers. Effective participation may well make the difference between failure and success in developing and implementing effective work instructions and practices.

Critical Task Analysis Worksheet

Plant/Division: Concentrator	Critical Task Analyzed: Start Particle Size Monitor	Signature: W. Livingstone	Function: Eng.	Date	
Department: Grinding	Date Completed/Revised:	Signature: R. Hogan	Function: Team Leader	Date	
Occupation: grinding Operator	Initial Approval: E. Bromley	Signature: R. Swinehart	Function: Team Leader	Date	

No.	Task Steps	Specific Loss Exposures (Safety, Quality, Environmental, Production)	Improvement Check Suggestions	Recommended control
1	Record each gauge's current reading (Particle Size Monitor)	Equipment damage, poor reading		Follow checklist
2	Look for sand build-up in cyclone box	Equipment failure will force coarse particles into system	Install alarm which warns of sand build-up	Clean any accumulation
3	Hose out air eliminator	Damage to air eliminator from sand		Clean any accumulation
4	Close drain valve	Water spills, electric shock		
5	Open fresh water valve	Inadequate flow of water will cause plug-ups		Clear air filter
6	Clear sensor pump	Hand injury from wrench slipping	Design/install special pump mount	Shut down before cleaning, use special cleaning tool
7	Check placement of main sensor	Poor reading		Replace if missing
8	Put safety system on automatic	Damage from low water pressure		
9	Clear sample screens in cyclone overflow box	Poor readings		Visually inspect. Clean any accumulation
10	Pull start button			
11	Raise water pressure to sixty(60) PSI	Automatic shut down of system		Record water pressure gauge, reading every thirty(30) minutes
12	Fill tank	Overflow, clogs, system shutdown		Listen for safety water to cycle off and on
13	Place sample screen in slurry	Inadequate vacuum	Change vacuum seals every 1000 hours of operations instead of 2000 hours	Look for normal vacuum of 17+ inches
14	Set intake flow valve at position five(5) for normal slurry level	Overflow or inadequate flow of slurry, slips and falls to surface		Allow 5 minutes to stabilize

Figure 9.5 Critical Task Worksheet

Pinpoint Loss Exposures

After breaking the critical task down into its steps, analyze each one to determine the loss exposures involved with that particular step. Every aspect of the task, including safety, quality and production, should be considered. Also consider losses to the area or environment where the task is being done and the possible long-term consequences of improper performance. This is another opportunity for employee participation in order to gain the benefits of their knowledge and experience.

When pinpointing these specific loss exposures, avoid describing them in general terms such as personal injury, poor quality, prolonged downtime, or increased costs. To be of real value, these entries must be specific enough (such as in the second column of Figure 9.5) to give team members sufficient insight when control measures are being considered. Carefully judge each of these four subsystems within the total system. Answer such questions as:

1. People
   a. What contacts are present that could cause injury, illness, stress or strain?
   b. Could the worker be caught in, on or between? Struck by? Fall from? Fall into?
   c. What practices are likely to downgrade safety, productivity or quality?
2. Equipment
   a. What hazards are presented by the tools, machines, vehicles or other equipment?
   b. What equipment emergencies are most likely to occur?
   c. How might the equipment cause loss of safety, productivity or quality?
3. Material
   a. What harmful exposures are presented by chemicals, raw materials or products?
   b. What are the specific problems involving materials handling?
   c. How might materials cause loss of safety, productivity or quality?
4. Environment
   a. What are the potential problems of housekeeping and order?
   b. What are the potential problems of sound, lighting, heat, cold, ventilation or radiation?
   c. Is there anything in the area that would be seriously affected if there were problems with the task?
   d. Has the external as well as the work environment been considered?

When things do go wrong, they result in losses. Identifying specific loss exposures is a key step in more effective loss prevention and control.

Make an Improvement Check

Making an improvement check is simply determining if the work being considered can be done in a better way. This, of course, raises the prospect of change.

The word **change** probably produces more anxiety than any other word in our vocabulary. This is curious indeed, because when change is introduced with structure, planning, innovation, employee involvement and team effort, change can be among the most exhilarating and profitable ventures imaginable! It permits modifications needed to keep pace with new processes, methods and materials or simply with better ways of doing things. In turn, this contributes to improvements in safety, quality, productivity and cost control, because the work can be performed in a more efficient manner. Task analysis and work instructions provide both the structure and the opportunity for these improvements to be made as a result of the efficiency check.

To conduct an improvement check, one need only ask the right questions and seek satisfactory answers. The old standby Who-Where-When-What-Why-How questions can be a good starting point. For instance, one can ask questions such as the following about each critical task:

- Who is best qualified to do it?
- Where is the best place to do it?
- When should it be done?
- What is the purpose of this task?
- Why is each step necessary?

- How does this task help create value to a customer?

Analyze the work in terms of major management goals (cost, production, environment, quality, safety). The interfaces of these four subsystems and four goals provide the following sixteen areas of questioning for a more thorough efficiency improvement check:

1. Cost-People: Could we control costs by having better trained people? By better utilization of people? Through enlarged responsibilities?
2. Cost-Equipment: Could we control costs by having different tools, machines or equipment? By using present equipment more effectively?
3. Cost-Material: Can less expensive or less scarce material be used? How can we reduce waste of material?
4. Cost-Environment: Can we save money through better housekeeping? Order? Layout? Lighting? Atmosphere?
5. Production-People: How can we reduce lost time? Increase manpower efficiency? Make it easier for people to be more productive?
6. Production-Equipment: How can we minimize damage and downtime? What tools, machines, and equipment can we provide to increase productivity?
7. Production-Material: How might materials be handled or transported more efficiently? What other materials might aid productivity?
8. Production-Environment: Can we improve production through better lighting, layout, cleanliness and order? Through better work climate or conditions?
9. Quality-People: What knowledge and skills are critical for quality performance? Could we improve quality through better selection, placement, training, cross-training, coaching and key point tipping?
10. Quality-Equipment: What tools, machines, and equipment could we provide to ensure optimum quality? Could we improve maintenance operations to get closer tolerances and better quality?
11. Quality-Material: What different materials might boost quality? Would it be helpful to make material quality checks earlier or more frequently?
12. Quality-Environment: Is quality or environment affected by dirt, dust or smoke? By solvents, vapors, mists, fumes or gases? By lighting, temperature or ventilation?
13. Safety-People: What are the potential hazards that could harm people? What are the critical needs for rules, for task instruction and for task observation?
14. Safety-Equipment: What are the potential hazards that could cause equipment damage, fire or explosion? How can we make better use of safety devices, protective equipment, preventive maintenance and pre-use equipment inspection?
15. Safety-Material: How can we eliminate or control exposure to hazardous materials? How can we improve training in safe handling practices? How can we best prevent waste and damage of raw materials and products?
16. Safety-Environment: How can we improve housekeeping (cleanliness and order) to control incident losses? What can we change in the work environment to improve safety?

The improvements from this step alone have often more than paid for all the time and effort invested in the entire task analysis process. In fact, for some organizations, the savings have exceeded the costs of the entire safety and health program for that period of time. The program coordinator who systematically ensures that this is being done, with proper records maintained, has taken a giant step in demonstrating the value of the safety and loss control program, both now and in the future. When it is considered that the primary purpose of work instructions is to guide training, it becomes even more important that they show the most efficient methods; otherwise, inefficiencies may be permanently entrenched in an organization.

Applying the Principle of Involvement will help to diminish anxiety caused by changes that result from the improvement check. It demonstrates that meaningful involvement increases motivation and support. In fact, many front-line leaders and workers find the improvement check to be the most rewarding part of the whole process of task analysis. It's a great opportunity to work together to…

- … make work easier and safer
- … reduce wasted time, space, energy and materials
- … improve quality and productivity
- … make the best use of tools, machines and equipment
- … make the best use of employees' knowledge, skills and abilities.

Here are seven major ways to make the improvements:

1. Eliminate: Challenge each task and step. Does it really have to be done? Eliminate unnecessary steps and activities that really do not contribute to the objective. Sometimes these are carryovers from earlier methods or problem solutions that no longer fit the situation. Eliminate or minimize exposures to injury or illness.
2. Combine: Combine task steps or even tasks so that one step or one task can accomplish several purposes.
3. Rearrange: Rearrange the sequence of the steps, the working area or the flow of work for greater safety and efficiency. Rearrange the sequence of tasks for process improvement.
4. Simplify: Simplify the job by providing appropriate aids, tools, instructions, information, feedback, etc.
5. Reduce: Develop a solution that will increase the life of the task—a better fitter to reduce clean-outs, a better lubricant to reduce how often it has to be done.
6. Substitute: Use a different substance, material, chemical, etc., that does not present the problem (i.e. less flammable, toxic, corrosive, etc.).
7. Relocate: Relocate the task so that it is done elsewhere in the process, or relocate where it is done (inside versus outside: shop versus on-site, etc.) for greater safety and efficiency. Increase people's desire to control losses by providing effective incentives and reinforcements.

The one common feature of all work environments is that they seem to be in a constant state of change. Some changes occur in a sudden or dramatic fashion and are easily noticed. Still other changes occur subtly or gradually, and their cumulative effects often go unnoticed. In the extensive research for his influential book some years ago, MORT Systems Safety Analysis, William G. Johnson discovered that unidentified change is a causative factor in most incidents. Examples may include changes to schedule, sequence of activities, personnel, methods, materials, tools, equipment, machinery, specifications, priorities, etc.

Develop Controls

Analyzing the work and potential problems, and making the improvement check, provide the information necessary to develop the required controls.

Ideas for controls will naturally have been generated throughout the improvement check and related discussions. Recording them on the worksheet becomes a fairly simple formality. Keep in mind that work instructions and practices should be directed primarily at the person or persons doing the task, by telling them what they are to do to avoid, eliminate or reduce the loss exposures.

Other control methods exist in addition to work instructions and practices, and might include such things as engineering changes, work rotation, personal protective equipment programs, and so forth. While these and other control methods are unquestionably valuable, they are not discussed in detail here, as the primary purpose of this chapter is to ensure that effective work instructions and practices are produced for the critical "hands-on" tasks that must be performed.

It should be noted that while many organizations call practices and work instructions by these names, other organizations might refer to both as work methods, standard operating procedures or other terms. What you call them is not important. What is important is to understand that some tasks require detailed work instructions, and others do not. The purpose of a task practice is to give people written guidelines for doing critical tasks in the best way.

Taking the time to develop work instructions and practices for the critical work activities will save a great deal of time in the long run. They provide carefully thought-out guidance, based on the best available knowledge, of how to do critical tasks in the most efficient way.

STANDARD WORK INSTRUCTION

TASK   OCCUPATION   DEPARTMENT

ORIGINATION DATE   DATE LAST UPDATE   LAST UPDATE REVIEWER

PRINT NAME AND SIGN RECEIVED BY/REVIEWED WITH   NAME OF REVIEWER   DATE RECEIVED

TASK PURPOSE AND IMPORTANCE

The particle size monitor analyzes the grind and density of the final grinding product. The trends are recorded on chart recorders. The result is a record of representative samples of the total day's grind.

The proper adjustment of the entire grinding and flotation process is dependent upon accurate sampling techniques. Errors and malfunctions can be responsible for many thousands of dollars of wasted ore, materials and efforts. Some of the equipment involved is easily damaged if not properly operated and regularly inspected.

The major steps are outlined in their proper order. Key points to remember follow each task step. All steps and key points must be followed in sequence to achieve maximum efficiency and avoid losses.

1. Record all instrument panel gauge readings. Use checklist.

2. Look for sand buildup in cyclone box and clean any accumulation before startup to avoid equipment damage and poor readings.

3. Hose out the air eliminator.

4. Close drain valve to avoid spillage and possible falls or electric shock.

5. Open main fresh water valve and clear water filter to assure adequate flow of water.

6. Shut down and clear sensor pumps. Use special cleaning tool to avoid disassembly of pump and possible hand injury.

7. Ensure that sensor is in place.

8. Put water system safety switch on automatic to avoid damage from low water pressure.

9. Visually inspect the sample screen in the cyclone overflow box and clean any accumulation to avoid poor readings.

10. Pull start/stop button on control box to start.

11. Ensure that water pressure is at least 60 psi to avoid automatic shutdown of system and record reading every 30 minutes to ensure that this pressure is maintained.

12. Allow tank to fill until the sensor section is full, at which point the safety water will automatically turn off. Listen for safety water to cycle on and off.

13. Place the sample screen in the slurry. The vacuum should rise to normal (17+ inches). Visually check.

14. Adjust sample intake flow valve for normal tank slurry level. Allow 5 minutes to stabilize to avoid overflow or starving the system.

Figure 9.6 Standard Work Instruction

Identify critical competencies

One of the world's largest personnel management organizations, the United States Office of Personnel Management (OPM), has identified the critical competencies of more than 400 Federal occupations, including trade and labor occupations.

OPM advises that competencies are defined simply and clearly and that they embody a single, readily identifiable characteristic. The competency should not be stated in a way that would confuse it with a task, as frequently happens when competency statements begin with a statement such as "ability to (perform a task)." It is also good practice to make the competency definitions behaviorally based, to the extent that an individual possessing that competency can be assessed through measurable behaviors. One way to do this is to incorporate action verbs into the competency definitions (except for definitions of knowledge areas).

Qualifiers such as "Thorough Knowledge, Considerable Skill, or Basic Understanding," are unnecessary. These qualifiers should not be part of the competency definition—they do not provide meaningful information to distinguish examples of performance clearly.

Based on the Task Inventory Worksheet (Figure 9.4), competencies were identified by each of the expert employees and rated individually with regard to their importance, the urgency of having that competency when entering the organization, and the distinguishing value of that competency.

As an example, Figure 9.7 may show the consensus ranking of the competencies for the Grinding Operator after the discussion by your organization's expert employees, and may list Industrial Equipment Operation, Problem Solving, Safety, and Technical Competence as the critical competencies for the job of Grinding Operator.

Within the organization, these competencies may have been defined as follows:

- Industrial Equipment Operation: Knowledge of principles and methods for operating industrial equipment.
- Problem-Solving: Troubleshoots, diagnoses, analyzes, and identifies system malfunctions to determine the source and cause of the problem.
- Safety: Knowledge of the concepts, principles and tools to identify, control, mitigate, and eliminate safety hazards in the use of the workplace, equipment, operations, and work processes.
- Technical Competence: Uses knowledge that is acquired through formal training or extensive on-the-job experience to perform one's job; uses machines, tools, or equipment effectively; uses computers and computer applications to analyze and communicate information in the appropriate format. Works with, understands, and evaluates technical information related to the job; advises others on technical issues.

It is also recommended to assess if—and if so, how—the person performing specific tasks, or a job, supports or has a role in assuring the key competence of the organization. If so, the task-specific translation of the key competence into a task-specific competency needs to be defined

TASK-COMPETENCIES INVENTORY WORKSHEET

Occupation or position	Department	Inventory Date(s)
Grinding Operator	Grinding	
Inventory Facilitator	**General Loss Exposures**	**Review Dates**
Mel Douglas	Elizabeth Bromley	

Tasks – List all task normally done or that might be done by a person in the occupation	Competencies											Hazards & Qualification		
	Attention to Detail	Industrial Equipment Operation	Mechanical Knowledge	Measurement and Instrumentation	Problem Solving	Perceptual Speed	Production and Processing	Safety	Technical Competence	Task specific translation of the Key Competence of the organization	Task specific translation of the Key Competence of the organization	Health & Work Area Hazards	Personal Protection Equipment	Job Qualification
Conduct grinding mill area pre-shift inspection	√													
Synchronize incline feed and exit ball mill belts		√			√	√	√	√						
Start complete grinding circuit	√		√	√	√			√	√					
Start particle size monitor	√	√	√	√	√	√	√	√	√					
Bring rod mill dual drive system motors c-12 and c-14 on-line		√			√			√	√					
Change steel rods		√	√		√			√	√					
Charge ball mill with ore	√	√		√	√		√		√					
Routine rod mill shutdown		√		√	√			√	√					
Emergency rod mill Shutdown		√			√	√		√						
Charge rod mill with ore	√	√		√	√		√		√					
Hose down and clean up grinding area	√	√					√	√						
Importance	4	5	3	3	5	2	3	5	5					
Need at Entry	3	5	3	4	5	3	3	5	5					
Distinguishing value	4	5	3	4	5	3	3	5	5					

Scales

How important is this competency for effective job performance?	When is this competency needed for effective job performance?	How valuable is this competency for distinguishing superior from barely acceptable employees?	Hazards	PPE	Qualification
1 = Not Important	1 = Must be acquired after the first 6 months	1 = Not Valuable	– Fume	– Helmet	– Regulatory Certification (e.g. OHSA)
2 = Somewhat Important		2 = Somewhat Valuable	– Burn	– Glasses	– Job Certificate
3 = Important	3 = Must be acquired within first 4-6 months	3 = Valuable	– Bacterial	– Gloves	– Test
4 = Very Important	4 = Must be acquired within first 3 months	4 = Very Valuable	– Noise	– Safety Shoes	– Observation
5 = Extremely Important	5 = Needed the first day	5 = Extremely Valuable	– Radiation	– Ear protection	– Training

Figure 9.7 Task Competencies worksheet

Put it to work

It is hard to find more practical leadership tools than work instructions and work practices. Here are seven key ways to put them to work.

- Employee orientation: One of the first things new employees want to know is what work they will be doing. Copies of work instructions and practices are useful for explaining this to them. Give them copies to study before starting proper task instruction.
- Proper task instruction: Work instructions and practices are of tremendous value in helping leaders meet their basic responsibility for teaching others how to do their tasks properly (correctly, quickly, conscientiously, safely).
- Planned task observation: Written work instructions and practices enable front-line leaders to systematically analyze how well worker performance meets the necessary standards.
- Personal contacts, coaching and tipping: Written work instructions and work practices are an abundant source of practical points for front-line leaders to emphasize in their personal contacts with workers, and in their vital leadership skills of coaching (the day-to-day actions designed to stimulate a subordinate to improve) and tipping (the organized process of giving employees helpful hints, suggestions, reminders or tips about key quality, production, cost, or safety points in their work).
- Safety talks: When everyone in the group performs the task or is directly affected by it, written work instructions and practices provide excellent information to emphasize in their team meetings (safety talks, toolbox meetings, tailgate sessions).
- Incident investigation: Written descriptions of the work help front-line leaders do a thorough job of investigating incidents and analyzing whether the work was being done as it should be, where the process went wrong, and what kinds of changes could lead to better control.
- Skill training: By showing specifically and systematically what the work is, written work instructions and work practices improve the efficiency and effectiveness of training programs for equipment operators and other skilled workers.
- It takes some time and effort to prepare work instructions and practices, but when they are put to work, the returns on the investment are highly profitable, in terms of:
- Greater efficiency, safety and productivity
- Better results in task instruction, task observation, coaching, tipping, safety talks, investigation and skill training
- Optimum protection of people, property, process, productivity and profitability

It is worth mentioning that information from the analysis of a critical task is often some of the best available for the purpose of composing specialized work rules for certain occupations, work areas or activities.

Here is an excerpt from a set of specialized work rules for electricians within Joe's organization. They were developed from an occupation and task inventory and through the analysis of related critical tasks.

Specialized Work Rules for Electricians

1. Only persons qualified (see qualification requirements) and familiar with the construction and operation of the apparatus, and the hazards involved, shall be allowed in those areas of open wiring, exposed and live switches, breakers, conductors, etc., as found in substations and generating rooms. Front-line supervisors shall be responsible for verifying which persons are qualified. Warning signs must be installed at the entrance of such areas.
2. Before starting work, worker shall make a thorough survey to determine all the hazards present, and to see that all necessary safeguards are provided to protect himself/herself, other workers and the equipment. It is not allowed to work on live circuits, live apparatus, or live wires, unless required.
3. For work that requires live circuits or working on high-voltage installations (whether live or not), a written and detailed description of each occurrence of work shall be proposed to the safety manager in advance for review and approval.

4. Before starting work, safeguards such as danger signs, roped-off space, etc., shall be used
5. In all cases where the work is hazardous and is being performed on or close to live conductors or apparatus, at least two workers shall work together. When it is necessary for one worker to leave for any reason, all such work shall be discontinued until both are again present.
6. It is the responsibility of the person to whom the instructions are given to account for all persons in his/her group before leaving the job at quitting time, for meals, or for any other reason.
7. Before starting work on live circuits or poles, rubber blankets or shields shall be placed over adjacent, intervening and ground wires or grounded structures for protection while working on selected wires.
8. Rubber mats or other suitable insulating material shall be used for protection while working on live circuits, or when operating high-tension switches.
9. While working on any wires, cables or apparatus, electricians should realize that, when there is voltage on a circuit, current can flow to ground, and therefore precautions shall be taken to keep their bodies properly insulated.

Update and maintain records

Well-maintained records of work instructions or practices are one of the best evidences to insurance carriers, government inspectors and courts of a well-established Safety Management System.

It is difficult to think of any tool with more potential payoff than well-developed and well-used work instructions and practices. Tools as valuable as these should not be allowed to become obsolete. Along with the original task inventories, each work instruction and practice should be reviewed for possible updating:

- at a stipulated period of time, usually based on criticality, annually being a common target.
- whenever a high-potential loss incident or serious loss occurs.
- whenever significant changes occur which can affect the tasks performance (such as materials used, process or design alterations, area changes, personnel changes and/or equipment changes).

Analyzing and describing the proper way to perform critical tasks is so vital to any organization that systematic documentation is a must. Since work instructions are developed to establish the one proper way to do a particular task, it is important that every area affected by them has an opportunity for input and final approval.

Conduct an individual competence-gap analysis

When analyzing needed skills, knowledge, or abilities related to a job, it is essential to know how the job is actually performed as opposed to how the job should be performed. The Task-Competencies Inventory will identify the competencies workers need to possess in order to do their jobs. It may also identify non-training problem areas that should be addressed in order to improve performance. The analysis results will help to determine which competencies need to be addressed and which should be included in a training program.

Under Competencies, indicate which competencies are required for each task. For this purpose, your organization needs to define the critical competencies for those critical jobs.

Under Hazards and Qualification, your organization needs to state the hazards associated with the tasks, the personal protection equipment required, and the qualification requirements for that critical job.

Under Health and Work Area Hazard, your organization needs to identify the hazards associated with the job, or those that may be encountered through the performance of the job. Special consideration must be given to the interactions of all work environment factors and the potential contacts with energy sources.

The possible effects of operations proximal or adjacent to the work must also be taken into account. Potential hazards include:

- Metal fume
- Flash burn
- Bacterial exposures
- Dermatitis
- Noise
- Radiation

Under Personal Protective Equipment, state the PPEs required due to the physical or health hazards associated with the job.

Under Job Qualification:

Regulatory Certification: Many occupations have training and certification requirements that are mandated by various regulatory agencies. These must be included in a list of Job Qualifications.

Your organization may also have a need for specific job certificates based on their own internal qualification programs. As a minimum, trainees should be designated as certified only after:

- The health and safety aspects and safe operating procedures have been learned.
- The trainee has practiced the job under supervision during non-production.
- The trainee has successfully performed the job under supervision during production.

Performance Observation is a good way to evaluate the performance and pinpoint whether or not the person performs in accordance with the standard work instructions and practices, or needs to participate in a training or certification program or successfully pass a test.

Tests can also be useful in analyzing the training needs of individuals. These may be knowledge tests (either verbal or written), performance tests, or both.

Training: Clearly define training needs by identifying the activity, skill and knowledge components of the work. Break the training needs down into specific training topics.

Example: Learning how to cut and thread pipe requires training in:

- What makes a good joint
- Purpose of threads
- Size and type of threads
- Length of threads
- Old and new fittings
- Use of tools

A training needs analysis is not a "once and done" process. Rather, it must evolve over time as the organization and its challenges change.

Once the Task-Competencies Inventory has been finalized, the persons assigned to the critical job need to be assessed in order to establish the competencies currently available. This can be done by:

- Surveys: These are usually either structured interviews or written questionnaires. Structured interviews are surveys in which a skilled interviewer finds out what knowledge and skills people possess (e.g. experience, accomplishments, completed training, certificates), and what they feel they need. These interviews yield systematic data that can be recorded, tabulated and analyzed objectively. In written questionnaires, employees can identify problems in their jobs, areas in which they wish they had more expertise, or their desire to upgrade their skills.
- Observation: Observation of the execution of tasks and the job, followed by discussion.
- Test: Knowledge tests (either verbal or written), and/or performance tests (including behavioral observation).

Develop a plan to bridge the competence gap

For each person that is (or will be) assigned to perform the critical tasks, an individual development plan should be developed in order to achieve the qualifications deemed necessary.

An individual development plan may need actions linked to the following topics:

- Objective:
    - Short-term objectives (one month, one to three months, three to six months)
    - Long-term objectives (six months and longer)
- Training:
    - Formal
    - On-the-job (mentoring and coaching)
- Certifications
- Tests

Each action should clearly specify a time-line, the resources (time, support, budget) made available, and the method of measuring in order to close the action.

Training and Tests

When training and/or tests are deemed necessary to qualify a person, the basis for selecting or developing tests and/or trainings can be derived from the competencies that were associated with the critical tasks.

Tests and trainings should have clear and specific objectives. Objectives are statements of intentions or desired outcomes, prepared in such a way that they form the basis for measuring results. They answer critical questions:

1. What is it that we must test or teach?
2. How will we know when the person has passed the test, or when the persons have learned it?

Objectives for a test or training on Correct Lockout Procedures might be as follows: The person that passes the test or completes the training will:

- Know the hazards and precautions associated with the tasks
- Be able to identify and explain correctly each of those conditions when equipment is to be locked out
- Be able to demonstrate and explain correctly where to place the appropriate locks and tags on each type of equipment
- Be able to demonstrate and explain correctly how to restrain parts of equipment to be locked out that could move, fall or slide, with chocks, blocks, chains, clamps or other approved restraining devices
- Be able to demonstrate and explain correctly how to clear unauthorized personnel from a designated area around the equipment being locked out
- Be able to demonstrate and explain correctly how to test the lockout to make certain that the power is off
- Be able to demonstrate and explain the proper procedure for storing and securing keys for the locks used to lock out equipment

Notice these characteristics of good objectives:

- They are stated in terms of what the tested or trained person must know and be able to do following the instruction.
- They use action verbs (describe, select, operate, etc.).
- By describing specific terminal behaviors (e.g. what the learner can do when the training ends), they make it easier to develop good lesson plans.
- They permit meaningful measurement of training results.

When developing tests or training, it is essential to break down the specific competencies (knowledge, skills and/or behavior) that need to be addressed in tests or in the training.

Figure 9.8 gives an example (partial) of the competencies for a tower crane driver

Competencies for Tower Crane Driver	knowledge	skill	behavior
The driver is able to take the appropriate preparations for working with the tower crane			
List the following elements in preparation of working with a towering crane:			
* understanding the lifting plan	Applicable		
* consultation with the supervisor	Applicable	Applicable	Applicable
* terrain inspection	Applicable	Applicable	
* choose personal protective equipment	Applicable	Applicable	
* inspection of the tower crane to confirm technical operability of undercarriage and structural components	Applicable	Applicable	
* check the operation of the mechanical, hydraulic, pneumatic	Applicable	Applicable	
* check the operation of the mechanical, hydraulic, pneumatic systems	Applicable	Applicable	
* check the operation of the electrical and electronic systems using the machine manual	Applicable	Applicable	
* check the hoisting equipment	Applicable	Applicable	
Describe that the objectives of the regulatory requirements for hoisting are:			
* avoid damage and injury	Applicable		
* avoid unsafe situations.	Applicable		
Identify malfunctions on tower cranes and take appropriate measures/actions	Applicable	Applicable	
The driver can take safety precautions when working with and on tower cranes.		Applicable	Applicable

Figure 9.8 Competence break down for a Tower Crane Driver

Eliminate non-critical elements from tests and course outlines, and apply proper sequence. Realize that trainees move from the simple to the complex, from the familiar to the unknown, and from the concrete to the abstract. Present questions and tasks through a series of steps of gradually increasing difficulty. Topics should be oriented and sequenced so that relevance to the job can be demonstrated when introduced into the course.

Use current literature, recognized scientific principles, the judgment of subject-matter experts, and regulatory requirements when developing the content. Review previously used material when appropriate.

Develop the tests and/or training program

When you have established the breakdown, you will have a good picture of what is needed to develop the test or training:

Tests:

- knowledge questions (open or closed questions)
- practical assignments (exercises, assignments, performance test)
- behavioral assessments/observations
- the practical assignment facilities (representing real situations)
- the answer model, scoring procedure and competence of the examiner
- Training:
- lesson plans, visual and/or audio aids, handouts and study materials, facilities tools, machines, equipment

Then you need to answer questions like these: Is a test or training program already available? If so, where? How feasible is it for our situation? Should we use outside examiners or instructors, our own instructors, or both? Will we need to train the examiners and trainers? What pertinent aids, materials, facilities, tools, machines and equipment do we have within the company? Which should we lease or purchase? Which should we develop ourselves?

Implement the actions of the plan

Now that the key competencies of the organization have been determined, the inventory of the critical tasks and associated competencies has been completed, and the individual competence development plans established, it is time to implement the actions in order to meet the competence requirements. Training, informal or formal, will often have been identified as one of the appropriate actions to bridge the competence gap.

Training delivery

Training success requires concentrating on the learners—on their needs; on their knowledge, skills and attitudes; on their job performance. If you resist the temptation toward instructor-centered training and remain learner-centered, you will have taken the biggest steps toward training success.

At the end of each day, the average person can remember:

- 10% of what they read that day
- 20% of what they heard
- 30% of what they saw
- 40% of what they heard and saw
- 70% of what they said as they talked
- 90% of what they said as they were doing something

Adults learn best by doing.

Adult Learning Principles

The following basic principles of learning are obvious when they are read. However, they are often ignored, especially in adult learning situations. Their application will make training less frustrating and more productive for everyone concerned.

Principle of Readiness: When people are ready and have sound reasons for learning, they profit from teaching and make progress in learning. You help to create this readiness by letting learners know how important the training is, why they should take it, and the benefits it should bring them (such as growth, recognition, easier work, variety, challenge, safer work and increased potential). Helping to create the desire to learn helps people learn.

Principle of Association: It is easier to learn something new if it is built upon something we already know. In training or teaching, it is best to proceed from the known to the new, to start with simple steps (based on what the learner already understands or can do) and gradually build up to the new and more difficult tasks or ideas. Make full use of comparison and contrast, of relationships and association of ideas.

Principle of Involvement: For significant learning to occur, learners must be actively involved in the learning process. The more senses involved (hearing, seeing, tasting, smelling, feeling), the more effective the learning. The more fully the learners participate in the learning process, the more effectively they learn. The good instructor gets the learners to do the repeating, the practicing, and the learning by doing. The good instructor uses learner involvement tools such as hands-on training, question and answer, group discussion, audiovisual aids, case problems, role playing, simulations, quizzes and application exercises.

Principle of Repetition: Repetition aids learning, retention and recall. Conversely, long disuse tends to cause learned responses to weaken and be forgotten. Application and practice are essential. Accuracy should be stressed before speed, to avoid learning a wrong habit that must later be "unlearned." The more often people use what they have learned, the better they can understand or perform it.

Principle of Reinforcement: The more a response leads to satisfaction, the more likely it is to be learned and repeated. For best results in a teaching/learning situation, accentuate the positive (praise, reward, recognition, success). Also, breaking complex tasks down into simple steps allows the successful learning of one step to help motivate learning the next one. When learning is pleasant and beneficial, people more readily retain what they have learned, and are more likely to want to learn more. Successful learning stimulates more learning.

The effective instructor facilitates learning by creating a warm, participative, positive learning climate. He or she uses feedback to satisfy learners' needs to know that they are doing things correctly and that they are making progress.

Leader/instructor guidelines

You can learn to instruct, but for almost everyone it is something that must be learned. Giving instructions, teaching or training effectively are not necessarily "doing what comes naturally." A person may know how to do a job very well, but not know the best way to help someone else learn to do it. Instructing requires preparation, practice, and patience; knowledge of the principles of learning; knowledge of the job to be taught; and application of these guidelines:

- Base training on needs. If no needs exist, there is no reason to train. You can determine needs by checking the requirements of the job (work objectives, job/task analyses and position descriptions are valuable here) and comparing them with the person's job performance. You might also ask the employees what they think they need to learn.

- Take the learner's viewpoint. You get best results when you put yourself in the learner's shoes and orient the instruction to the learner's viewpoint. Keep in mind the learner's goals, abilities, needs, personality and feelings. Keep the instruction at the learner's level.

- Maximize motivation. You can lead a person to knowledge, but you can't make that person learn unless he or she is motivated. You can help bring out people's motivation by working with them to set meaningful goals; by showing personal interest in them; by providing proper incentives for learning and performance; by setting a good example, being a good role model; by using the positive power of praise, reward and recognition; by training effectively.

- Expect ups and downs. Typical learning curves show that learning often occurs in spurts. It may advance quite rapidly for a while, then level off a bit, then increase again, and so on. Occasionally, there may be a slippage to a lower level of knowledge or skill than the learner already has shown. Both instructor and learner should be prepared to expect these varying rates of progress. Sometimes it may be necessary to find the causes of the slowdown, such as changes of motivation or effort, temporary stress or fatigue, or the training method, and take corrective action.

- Recognize individual differences. Nearly everyone agrees that each person is unique, but may overlook the importance of the differences. Some of the important differences in training are intelligence, desire to learn, knowledge, aptitudes, interests, motives, attitudes, emotions and learning ability. Trainers should keep these factors in mind and fit the training to the individual.

- Don't expect the same method to work equally well with all people, or all employees to learn to perform at the level of the best worker. Good instruction can help the person develop his or her aptitudes to the highest degree, but that potential may not be the same as someone else's.

- Give frequent feedback. People usually don't like to play ball unless they know the score. Similarly, learners need to know how they are doing. In fact, some experimental studies have shown that providing systematic knowledge of progress may speed up the learning process by as much as 50 percent. You can give feedback in many ways, such as test results, checklists, charts, graphs and credit for work well done.

- Remember follow-up. You must follow up to make sure the training has been effective. This involves special attention until you are certain that the person has learned and is performing properly. This follow-up should be unobtrusive, patient and helpful—not critical—and can be tapered off to normal supervision when you are sure the person is performing well. Long-range follow-up, an important part of good leadership, may show the need for refresher training.

Special Issues Involved in Different Training Delivery Techniques

There are many techniques used in delivery of safety, health, and environmental training. Three broad categories of delivery techniques are described below: traditional classroom training, on-the-job training (OJT), and advanced technology training. Following the description of each category, advantages and special issues that trainers must consider when selecting and utilizing the various delivery technique categories are presented.

Classroom training

Traditional training typically occurs in a classroom setting, but may include a wide array of techniques, including lecture, demonstration, discussion, practice, or assignment of projects.

Advantages:

- meets many regulatory requirements.
- can include more than one person.
- most trainers are familiar with the techniques.

Special considerations:

- Traditional techniques may not be the most effective way to communicate specific information to a particular group of workers.
- If training includes demonstration or practice, the equipment used must be similar to (if not the same as) that to be used in the actual workplace. Otherwise, irrelevant or erroneous information may be taught.
- Trainees may not readily see the applicability of classroom training to their work setting.

On-the-job training (OJT)

OJT is training done in the actual workplace, ranging from short training sessions (sometimes called toolbox or tailgate training) to long-term, formalized apprenticeship programs.

Advantages:
- Saves time and money because employees do not have to travel to a distant training location.
- Can use actual equipment present in the workplace. For example, the available brand(s) of respirators or other personal protective equipment can be demonstrated and used in practice.
- Training is immediately relevant and applicable to the trainee's work.

Special considerations:
- Record-keeping: This kind of training must be properly documented, e.g. date, attendees' names, and training topics.
- Training objectives: If not considered during training development, objectives may be left to the discretion of the team leader.
- Location: While the workplace can be an excellent place to hold training, care should be taken to ensure that learning can occur. The work area should be quiet enough that the trainer can be heard. If materials are to be read during the training, there should be adequate lighting.
- Care should also be taken that OJT does not create a safety risk for the trainee or workers in the surrounding work environment.

Advanced technology training

Advanced technology training includes the myriad alternative training delivery techniques that involve advanced technologies, e.g. distance learning (e-learning), computer-based training (CBT), video conferencing, and simulation or virtual reality.

Advantages:
- Can allow training of persons from different facilities simultaneously. This can allow for sharing of experiences, which can greatly enhance learning.
- Training can be self-paced and offered at any time of the day or night, and may not require the presence of an instructor.
- Record-keeping can be automated.
- Some of these techniques are especially useful for refresher training.

Special considerations:
- Mechanisms for trainee feedback need to be assured. In the case of distance learning, trainee questions and concerns may be posed and responded to via email, chat rooms, or site facilitators.
- The cost for setup of these techniques can be high.
- Required hardware and software must be available.
- Trainees must be comfortable with, and knowledgeable about how to use, the technology; e.g., they must have the requisite computer skills before training begins.
- The trainer must have adequate technical support.
- There should be a technically feasible backup mechanism to deliver the training if the selected method is not effective.
- Generally ineffective for training that requires hands-on experience, e.g. forklift training. Although virtual training is available to overcome this problem, it is very expensive at the present time.
- Generic or packaged programs may be a poor fit for workers at different work sites or organizations with specific job tasks.

Evaluation and Improvement

Improvement

As with all management systems, on a regular and systematic basis, all components of the competence management system (addressed in this chapter) need to be monitored, measured and reviewed on their effectiveness, and, if possible, improved.

Continual improvement linked to training starts with an evaluation to determine:

(1) the degree to which the objectives were met, and (2) how the program can be improved. Evaluation can be done at any of three stages: input, throughput or output. In terms of input, the costs of training can be assessed, either in comparison with other programs or against a budgeted figure. Throughput is usually assessed in terms of the number of people trained in a given period of time. Output assessment is harder, but more valuable. It involves four criteria:

1. **Reaction:** Measuring the emotional responses of participants in the program. This typically is done with anonymous questionnaires immediately following the program. This feedback should let you know how the learners have received the program, and whether or not they feel they have learned things of value for job performance.
2. **Knowledge:** Measuring the knowledge gained by the participants. This usually involves before-and-after tests, oriented to the training objectives.
3. **Behavior:** Measuring the skills developed by the training activities. This may involve proficiency tests, direct observation of participants' performance, and/or self-reports of skill improvements.
4. **Results:** Measuring the organizational effects of training. This is done by direct calculation of changes in incident losses, waste, increased quality, productivity and cost effectiveness, employee retention, fewer customer complaints, etc.

Evaluations enable orderly analysis of factors that helped training effectiveness, factors that hindered it, and the program improvements to be made. Knowledge, behavior and results can be assessed before, during and after the training program, and again at follow-up dates. The basic purpose is to find out whether, and to what degree, positive changes occurred—practical, significant changes influenced by the training.

Everyday reality puts much of the responsibility for such measurement and follow-up squarely on the shoulders of front-line leaders, the ones best able to evaluate on-the-job applications of knowledge and skills. Here are five simple, practical post-training actions for meeting this responsibility:

1. **Post-training discussions:** As soon as feasible after the training, have at least one discussion with the person on the training about what was learned, and about plans for putting the learning to work.
2. **Job assignments:** Make practical assignments that enable the individual to apply what was learned. For maximum benefit, such assignments should be given soon after the training.
3. **Performance observation:** During both informal and planned performance observations, note evidence of changed behavior related to the training. Contact newly trained people frequently to answer questions and review key points of proper performance. Gradually taper off to the normal amount of contact.
4. **Performance feedback:** During performance discussions and coaching contacts, include specific references to newly acquired knowledge and skills. Use constructive coaching and positive behavior reinforcement.
5. **Record and Report:** Keep records of each person's progress and submit reports to higher management. Recommend improvements and/or further use of the training program.

Records aid evaluation and follow-up. You should keep track of who has had various skill training, and who still needs it. You should also keep training records on each worker. Good records not only are a sign of good management, but also can be invaluable in incident investigation, in the handling of grievances and arbitration cases, and in court cases.

Refresher training should also be an ongoing part of training follow-up activities. You should encourage employees to improve and update their knowledge and proficiency. In addition to your informal updating, there should be regular formal refresher training. A good rule of thumb is to have refresher training amounting to a minimum of one-half the time of the original training, at least every three years. Successful completion of this retraining should be a condition for maintaining certification or licensing.

Certificates: Where appropriate, issue a company license or permit. Among the reasons for licensing are that it:

- shows learners that the company is really interested in proper performance.
- serves as evidence that the holder has met specified requirements—a symbol of status.
- motivates continuing attention to proper performance, for maintaining license.
- deters unqualified people from operating expensive, critical equipment.
- facilitates periodic review of qualifications, refresher training and re-issuance of right to operate.
- increases job pride by requiring operators to maintain a high level of proficiency in order to maintain or upgrade the license or permit.

acquiring the knowledge and skills they need for proper performance is of prime importance. Effective training means that:

- Your group will be more efficient.
- Incidents will be eliminated or at least reduced.
- A properly trained employee knows the job hazards and what to do about them.
- Employee morale and teamwork will improve. Your own and your employees' "job satisfaction" will increase.
- Your own work will be made easier. Less time will be spent correcting mistakes and less oversight of job performance will be required.
- The work force will be more flexible. Employees trained in all phases of their work may readily be transferred from job to job within the group.
- You can meet legal requirements for certain types of training.

Front-line leadership in learning

In your capacity as a front-line leader you have a tremendous impact on the learning environment. The training you do may range from the common situation of giving on-the-job instruction, to serving as a discussion leader or instructor in formal training programs.

Training benefits

Among the many skills required of you as a front-line leader, the ability to lead your team in

Key Point Summary

1. Organizations create value by meeting the environmental, social, and economic needs of the world. In order to do this, the organization must be a creative and learning entity.

2. Learning organizations benefit from an organized competence management system to help meet their sustainable business development goals.

3. A comprehensive and systematic identification and examination of tasks (task analysis) to identify training and competence needs is a best practice for building a competence management system.

4. The output of a task analysis process can be used for many purposes; for example, identifying training needs, developing procedures and practices, identifying the need for and developing specialized work rules, and conducting individual competence gap analysis.

5. Understanding adult learning principles is fundamental to the development and implementation of an effective training process.

Personal Planning

6. Does my organization have a systematic and effective training process? Why or why not?

7. Have we implemented a task analysis process that is used properly and provides the benefits outlined in this chapter?

8. How confident am I that my people are sufficiently trained in all aspects of their responsibilities?

9. What do we need to do to strengthen our task analysis and/or training process?

Y – Model for Action Planning

Present Situation

Desired Situation

Need for Change

Present Situation

Stop Responsibility Target Date

CHANGE MANAGEMENT

Chapter 10

CHANGE MANAGEMENT

> **CHAPTER OBJECTIVES**
>
> 1. To demonstrate the critical need for a change management process in any organization.
> 2. To present best practices for developing, implementing, and managing a proper change management process.
> 3. To present various types of change and demonstrate how a change management process can and should be applied to each.

A Hard Lesson Learned

Part of the process in Joe's plant requires the use of methanol, a highly flammable substance. It is stored in a 3000-gallon tank just outside one of the production buildings.

On one particularly warm day, three workers were assigned to remove part of a structure around the methanol tank. With no specific instructions on how to proceed and no written procedures in place, the workers chose to use an oxy-acetylene torch to cut the structure in pieces.

The work went as expected for a couple hours, but as the increasing temperature warmed the methanol inside the tank, vapors formed and vented through a flame arrestor on top of the tank. An invisible vapor cloud formed around the tank and was ignited by the sparks from the cutting operation. The three workers were burned in the resulting fire, but were able to escape serious injury. However, the fire outside flashed into the flame arrestor, which was designed to prevent the contents of the tank from being ignited by a fire outside. The flame arrestor was badly corroded and failed to function. The fire reached the methanol and an explosion occurred. The tank was destroyed.

The investigation into the incident revealed several contributing causes. One of the primary immediate causes was that the flame arrestor was badly corroded, allowing the flames into the tank. There were two basic causes identified for the inadequate state of the flame arrestor. First, this critical safety device had not been inspected in several years. It was not on any inspection checklist. Second, it was determined that the plates in the flame arrestor were made of aluminum, a material that is readily corroded by methanol. When the tank was originally installed, it was used to hold a different chemical, for which the aluminum plates in the flame arrestor would have been effective. However, when the change was made to use the tank for methanol, there was no MOC process applied and the organization failed to understand the risk presented by incompatibility of aluminum and methanol. Had an effective MOC been conducted, the problem could have been identified and a different flame arrestor installed.

This happened when Joe was the operations manager. He resolved that such an incident would not occur again and set about to improve the organization's change management process. Joe relied on the following information to help him.

Introduction

It is a fact of life that things change. Change can be specific and acute, or can be more vague and drawn out. It can be far-reaching in its implications. Whatever form it takes, it is a challenge to the status quo, and a business that is going to sustain itself needs to be able to recognize, understand and effectively manage change.

Change management happens in a range of areas. This chapter will cover the common areas and discuss challenges in implementation and the process of measuring success. Although change affects all business concerns, this chapter will focus on the health and safety aspects of undetected or unmanaged change and offer guidance on how change can be effectively managed.

Why is Change Management Important?

There are a number of factors that drive changes in a business. External and internal pressures gradually cause a business's risk exposure to increase. It is often the case that that change in exposure is not recognized until an event occurs which alerts the management to the issue. There are good examples of this. The Deep Water Horizon disaster caused many companies to reconsider their exposure to major accidents, often with worrying results. The demographic shift towards retired people in the populations of developed economies has been known about for a long time, but is not until managers begin to see skills gaps appearing, making doing business more difficult and more expensive, that action is taken. Gaps in skill and proficiency can have a negative impact on quality, production, morale, etc., but can result in incidents as well. As in everything, being prepared is more cost-effective, and so an ability to anticipate change and plan for it is an essential skill for leaders at all levels of the organization.

Change management provides a process for determining where change could occur, and mechanisms for understanding the nature and implications of that change. This allows change to be effectively controlled, and opportunities to be identified.

It is important to recognize that managed change has a lifecycle and its risk profile changes over that lifecycle. The lifecycle is made up of a move from the pre-change "current situation" to a post-change "desired situation" through a "transition" period. Generally, we are looking for the desired situation to be at a lower level of risk than the current situation, although in some business situations a greater level of risk may be accepted, where the risks are greater but there is no adverse impact on risks to people and the environment. Of course unmanaged change will generally see a relentless increase in risk. In large part, improved health and safety performance relies on continual efforts to reduce risks.

The figure 10.1 below shows a typical risk profile for a change. Note how the risk may peak during transition because of the potential absence of risk controls, and/or transitioning to new risk controls during this period. Alternative temporary risk controls may be needed to manage this peak risk.

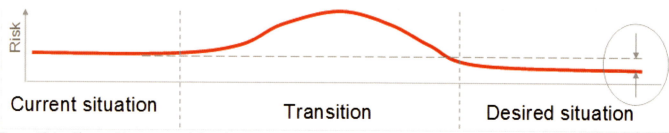

Figure 10.1 - Change Management Lifecycle

As a result, businesses need to understand the risks before and after the change and the associated risk benefit. But they also need to be mindful of the transition risks and the means for managing them. In engineering change, this may be simply a case of turning off equipment before making the change, but in organizational change this is often not possible, and transition risks can be substantial.

What is the Focus of Management of Change?

The aim of a management of change system is:

> **To ensure that a proper level of review(s) is applied to prevent adverse effects from changes. Change management ensures that the future of the business and its personnel is not compromised by inadequate identification, evaluation, control, and monitoring of hazards related to change.**

Typical expectations of such a system are as follows:

- All changes shall be identified and defined as to their scope and nature.
- All changes shall be subject to proper hazard identification and risk assessment.
- All changes shall be subject to endorsement by the proper level of authority.
- The MOC process shall identify and consider suitable and sufficient information to support the process.
- MOC shall ensure that the change is reflected in all relevant documents.
- MOC shall ensure that the change is effectively communicated to affected personnel.
- The MOC process shall be continually monitored, action tracked , and improved to ensure ongoing adequacy, proper implementation, and compliance with the system.

The types of change that may be included in a typical MOC system are:

- **Facilities and process-related change:** Typically, facilities (equipment) and process (parameters and technology) changes relate directly to the need to change, or modify the asset, equipment, tools, chemicals used, etc.
- **Organizational related change:** Typically these involve changes or modifications to the organizational structure and size, manning, personnel, use of employees vs. contractors, etc.
- **Procedure-related change:** Changes initiated here typically affect both document control and records management systems, in both electronic and hard copy formats.

The model for effectively implementing MOC is described in figure 10.2 below. MOC is, in essence, a risk management activity, so the model follows the same basic approach as defined in standards such as ISO31000 and in the Risk Management chapter of this book.

Figure 10.2 - The Management of Change Model

The steps in the model are described as follows:

Initiate/Identify Change: Businesses require a mechanism that allows for changes to be initiated or triggered. The need for change may arise in several different forms including strategic decisions, risk assessments, employee suggestions, management reviews, assurance findings, technology advances, incident investigations, and any of the steps in the lifecycle of a business's hardware assets (design, construct, commission, operate, maintain, modify, decommission, abandon).

Since this is the beginning of the MOC process, formal documentation of this process begins here as well, with appropriate initiation of change and change approval templates, checklists, etc., all managed in an appropriate change management case filing/recording system.

Screen: The screening determines whether the identified change has the potential to impact the current HSE and business environment, and whether or not it shall proceed. This initial screening should be guided by a suitable checklist and done by competent personnel, such as an MOC Screening Team.

Initial Preparation: This is the initial development of the change in order to determine how the change shall be implemented through the application of conceptual design, feasibility studies, and/or other activities to prepare for an informed assessment of the associated risks. Such initial development shall be documented.

Risk Assessment: Suitable risk assessment of the change is required to determine opportunities to reduce overall risk, introduce controls over risks requiring them and those that cannot be reduced further, and to maximize the originally intended benefits of the change in the first place:

- During the implementation of the action plan designed to achieve the change (see discussion of Transition Risks below).
- Once the change has been implemented/ achieved (the end-state of the original proposed change).
- After the change has been in place or for a defined, reasonable time period during the life of the change.

Chapter 10   215

Plan: Final planning takes place considering the initial preparation stage and the action plans developed, while incorporating the results of the risk assessment(s) conducted above. This includes detailed design and planning for the transition and operational phases of the change.

Implementation and Operation: Once the change is approved, the formally approved change will be implemented. Implementation includes the activities of communication, consultation, and training in preparation for the change, the transition phase, and the post-transition activities such as documentation updates.

After implementation, the change needs to be tested to ensure it meets the expectations set at the screening and approval stage. This is to facilitate the approval of the change for operation and is generally through the application of a pre-startup safety review. In the case of organizational changes, this process is an ongoing activity; as such changes become live with immediate effect.

Monitor and Review: The purpose of this stage is to confirm that the MOC system has been applied properly and that the change has been implemented in a suitable manner and according to plan. Lessons that can be learned from the process should be collated into a knowledge management system, and changes or improvements made to the implemented change and the MOC system itself as necessary.

Closeout: The closeout process formally draws a line under the change; in other words the "change" becomes permanent. A closeout checklist should be applied to ensure that all relevant documentation has been updated, all relevant training carried out, and all relevant MOC documentation collated and archived.

Application of MOC

The application of MOC is a challenge for any business. There is often a problem with the bureaucratic burden that comes with the records that need to be maintained, and this depends a lot on the design of the overall system. Many organizations have a range of MOC procedures covering the various aspects of the change, all sitting under an umbrella Change Management Philosophy that defines the overarching principles and responsibilities. A one-size-fits-all approach is rarely successful, as it is inefficient—there is more discussion on this subject later in this paper.

Logging changes is vital for maintaining an overview of the amount of change occurring on the site and tracking the status of each request. Logs are also important for maintaining the audit trail associated with the change, and for identifying the interactions between changes. Logs generally require some form of computer-based database to maintain and control them, although the best-implemented systems often still use paper-based processes for managing the actual change requests, rather than being fully electronic systems.

Generally, businesses recognize the need for at least one MOC Coordinator to administer the system, maintain change logs, report on the status of changes and audit the system to ensure compliance. This is often a challenge for businesses, but regular monthly auditing of a selection of change requests is critical for the good functioning of the system. Another role for the MOC Coordinator is to enforce the closeout criteria for change requests. This requires that a set of criteria are defined to describe what constitutes completion and generally includes finalization of documentation, archiving of records, formal handover of the change into operation, and, in some cases, verification that the change has delivered the necessary benefit.

Given that an MOC often involves a large number of people, there are inevitable bottlenecks that appear in the process. These are generally related to the flow of information and the process of approval. It is not unusual for managers to meet monthly to review and approve MOC requests, but this may not be sufficient where a backlog is developing. Devolving some aspects of the approval process may be possible, but only where risks can be managed. Identifying inefficiencies and resolving them is an ongoing process in keeping the MOC system working well. Monitoring the performance of the MOC system requires an understanding of what success looks like. It is not uncommon for businesses to have no clear idea how many change requests they should expect within a given period, and as a result it is difficult to determine whether compliance with the system is being properly completed. The closeout status of change requests within acceptable time frames is a key measure. If there are delays in closeout, management should investigate why this is and take appropriate action. Given that MOC is a risk management process, the tracking of actions arising from the MOC process is important, and the status is a key measure of performance.

> *Case Study: Temporary EMOC*
>
> *A company discovered a leak on a medium-pressure steam system and decided to apply a temporary clamp rather than shut down the steam system. The clamp was manufactured and installed by a specialist vendor, but in the process of installation the clamp failed, killing the technician and causing a much larger steam leak requiring shutdown of the system.*
>
> *It became clear that the vendor had not designed, manufactured or installed the clamp correctly. When, prior to the change, the company had asked for details of the clamp, they had been told that the design was proprietary and the information could not be disclosed. The company accepted this because of the pressure to install the clamp and restore production. This was in contravention of its MOC process.*
>
> *Lesson: The system is there for a purpose and must be applied correctly.*

Recording Changes

It is essential that changes be properly documented. The process of making a change means that decisions have to be made, and this requires that a range of people are engaged. Documentation ensures that people understand the decisions that were taken and, importantly, the basis and assumptions made during that process. The documentation trail allows businesses to learn from the positive and negative implications of changes and, critically, can demonstrate that they acted with due diligence.

Engineering Management of Change (EMOC)

EMOC requires the application of appropriate capabilities to ensure that performance of equipment and systems remains appropriate in terms of its functionality, availability, reliability and resilience. The attributes of a good EMOC system include thorough, multi-disciplined engineering review processes, robust application of appropriate risk assessment methods, clear links to project management processes, and well-defined criteria for acceptance. As discussed later in this section, it may be desirable to have a range of different EMOC procedures and associated forms for different types of engineering change to ensure it can be efficiently applied. However, all of the different procedures have to meet the objectives set at the beginning of this document.

In defining what constitutes an engineering change, it is often easier to define what is not a change. The most obvious example of this is the "like for like replacement," where a component is changed for one that is exactly the same. It is important that it is "exactly the same," as even a small deviation from the original specification is critical. As such, part of the MOC process needs to capture changes to part numbers, even for consumable items, and subject that change to an engineering review to confirm the new part conforms to the desired specification.

Where this debate between what is a change and what is not a change becomes a bit blurred is where repairs are made to equipment. Different companies have different views on this, but a pragmatic approach is to accept that if a repair is made using an approved procedure and returns the equipment item to the same level of performance, then it need not go through a full MOC process as long as it is properly documented. However, if the repair changes the nature of the equipment item—e.g., the material of construction is upgraded—then that should result in an MOC process.

Temporary Changes

Temporary changes offer a challenge to MOC systems. Often they are required to be put in place at short notice, such as in an emergency situation, and because they are temporary there is often a desire to shortcut the MOC process, trading thoroughness of the process for limited exposure. It is critical that the business recognize that temporary changes generally mean they are living with a higher risk exposure, and understand what constitutes "temporary." It is not uncommon for temporary changes to be put in place "until the next opportunity to remove it." This opportunity can be years away and the risk exposure inevitably increases over that time. Best practice suggests that a clear timeframe should be put in place, generally six months, beyond which the change is considered permanent and subject to the full rigor of the EMOC system. This means it will be subject to thorough engineering review and proper risk assessment, and be included in maintenance and inspection programs.

Temporary changes can be subject to short-cut EMOC approaches where the risks associated with them are mostly understood, and robust controls are in place to manage associated risks. Examples of these include placing clamps on process plants and putting overrides or inhibitors into a process control system.

Another area that needs careful thought by management is the relationship with engineering projects. It is vital that the EMOC system does not become an OPEX project management system (PMS) by default. This can often happen where the PMS is weak or ill defined. EMOC should be considered a check on the effectiveness of the PMS, purely considering the safety implications of the change, and leaving the commercial and performance aspects of the design to the PMS. It is the author's experience that where the two processes become one, the safety concerns become swamped by the concerns about funding the project. Good practice is that the two processes run in parallel, managed by different teams and touching at project stage gates where the question "Are there any issues from the MOC process?" is dealt with.

With regard to CAPEX projects, the EMOC system is deployed differently. It can be used as a mechanism for managing the interfaces between the existing facility and the new one. It can also be used as a "placeholder" for the new facility, documenting that this substantial change is being made, but referencing the project's processes to effectively manage associated risks. Clear bridging requirements between the operational EMOC system and the project's management processes are needed to ensure that risks are being effectively managed, and by whom.

Another challenge for EMOC is the availability of information where changes involve proprietary systems. Examples of these include software-based systems, novel technology and licensed processes. The challenge in these situations is that there may be insufficient access to information or insufficient knowledge within the company about the equipment to be able to confirm that risks have been effectively managed. This poses problems that need addressing when putting in place the contractual relationships with the vendors, and may require the use of independent experts to provide assurance to both parties that risk is managed.

> **Case Study: Reorganization OMOC**
>
> During the merger of two major oil companies it was decided to rationalize the onshore support organization but leave the offshore production facilities as they were.
>
> The change team assessed the impact of the onshore reorganization on the offshore teams as minor. A senior manager visited each of the offshore facilities to talk to each of the shifts and explain that the situation.
>
> Over the following months safety performance and productivity offshore dramatically deteriorated.
>
> An investigation discovered that the offshore personnel felt disconnected from their support networks onshore as people they had relationships with were moved. Furthermore this feeling of disconnection resulted in concern that there were secret plans to sell the offshore facilities. This was exacerbated by a lack of regular communication and consultation from the change team who felt they had sent a clear message at the beginning of the change processes.
>
> Lesson: Organizational changes had all sorts of unforeseen impacts and continual consultation is essential.

Organizational Management of Change (OMOC)

OMOC covers changes to individuals and their movement between roles, and changes to organizational structures. Appropriate change management processes have to be put in place.

The impact of organizational change on health and safety is not as readily apparent as the impact of engineering change, but can be equally important.

For those changes involving the movement of people from position to position, the OMOC system typically consists of mapping the capability profile of the new position with the capability of the proposed individual. Where there are gaps, then additional training and mentoring may be required to support that person until they have the requisite capability. In some cases this may require redefining the position to focus it on the individual's particular skills. This is generally an efficient process and is conducted between the relevant line manager and the human resources department.

Where changes are made to organizational structures, the process becomes a lot more involved. Generally, a specific team needs to be put in place to redesign the organization and manage the change. The team will involve a range of specialists from different parts of the organization and sometime from stakeholders such as workforce unions.
Organizational change is generally a very disruptive process, and it is not unusual for businesses to underestimate, and thus inadequately manage, the effects.

As OMOC involves changes affecting people, a different change model is often deployed. This is shown in figure 10.3.

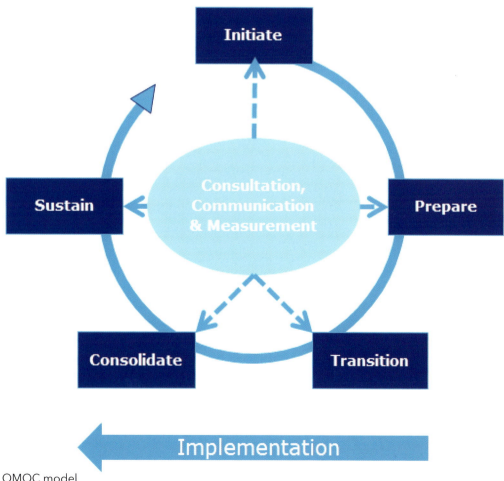

Figure 10.3 - OMOC model

Initiate: This is where it is identified that a change is needed, and what it is expected to achieve. This step defines how the change is initiated and by whom. It is also common to start consulting some key individuals and consider benefits and risks of the change. However, it is often the case that the change has a degree of secrecy about it at this time, and so consultation is restricted.

Prepare: It is necessary to understand the implications of the change. This is generally achieved through the suitable application of a detailed risk assessment of the implementation process and the post-change situation. However, it is important to understand the "givens" and "non-negotiables"—the things that we cannot change or that define the boundaries of the change process. A structured organizational design process should be employed, considering task mapping (who does what), spans of control (how many people report to the next level of management) and separation (disciplinary, organizational and geographical). All of this information is used to plan for the implementation of the change, develop assurance processes to monitor its progress, and ensure that success criteria are defined. The use of "go/no-go" decision points, with appropriate criteria, will allow stages in the change process, and optional aspects, to be effectively managed.

Transition: This involves effectively managing the implementation and applying the structures and processes put in place to manage the transition. This may include temporary measures, such as procedures, agency staff or outsourcing, to make the transition a success. Critically, this will include providing mechanisms for capturing corporate knowledge that may otherwise be lost in the transition. Training programs will need to be in place to ensure skill levels are maintained in the transition. A risk register, started during the prepare phase, should be continuously updated with new issues to ensure that no exposures are unrecognized or unmanaged.

Consolidate: After the change, there is a need to get back to normal and allow the management systems to be updated to reflect the new organization. It is also a time for the careful removal of temporary measures. There is also a process of beginning to reflect on whether the new organization is meeting the defined expectations, although it may be a bit early to draw conclusions. However, the most critical aspect of the consolidation phase is the decision to stop changing—it is common for management to continue to tweak the organization after the change has occurred, but this causes uncertainty and drift.

Sustain: This is where the organization starts building its own culture and the new processes become "the way we do things around here." This basically means building resilience into the organization by putting in place systems to manage succession and knowledge retention. It also about driving the organization to meet its potential through measurement and benchmarked against industry peers, and through thoroughly understanding the new risk profile for the organization to facilitate decision-making. Ultimately it is preparing the organization for the next change.

Consultation and Communication: This is about ensuring that everyone knows what is going on and has their views considered. This requires regular, clear communication throughout the change to all stakeholders, and the nature and form of that communication needs to be carefully considered—who communicates and how they do it is critical to getting the message across. While communication may sometimes be one-way, consultation is two-way and there need to be simple, effective tools for gathering queries and providing feedback. And it is essential that the relevant authorities be communicated with where necessary to maintain legal consents and licenses.

Measurement: Throughout the change process, it is important to measure progress and effectiveness of the change. Key Performance Indicators need to be defined and monitored in line with the change plan, and audits need to be completed by suitably competent and independent people to confirm that critical activities are being conducted correctly. Another very important measurement is of the perceptions of individuals within the organization—do they believe the change has being managed properly, and has it improved their situation? Ultimately, management has to review the performance of the change and its outcome.

Procedural MOC (PMOC)

PMOC is generally thought to be managed through document control systems, and while this is true, there are some challenges with managing procedural change. These include:

- ISO9000 quality systems usually provide a mechanism for managing the change to controlled documents, but don't cover a technical review of the contents of the procedure.
- Risk management and human error is often considered informally.
- Responsibilities and accountabilities need to be carefully defined as performance standards in terms of who, what, when or how often, and what is expected as the deliverable from the action.
- Validation of the procedure with the end users often yields great benefits. This may be through involving them in shaping and risk-assessment of the procedure, simulation of the procedural steps, and dry runs.
- Changes to procedures are triggered from all sorts of sources, and PMOC is often a follow-on change from EMOC or OMOC activities. As such it can often be forgotten or ignored.
- Communication of the procedure is critical to its successful implementation.

Procedures need to be properly designed to ensure they provide clear guidance and value to the users. The model in figure 10.4 shows the three main aspects of a good procedure.

Figure 10.4 - Aspects of well designed procedures

This includes its having clear boundaries defined by relevant codes and standards, specifying the performance standards on individuals applying the procedure, and effectively managing the risks associated with the activities described in the procedure by explaining them, the associated controls, and the expected behavior of the users. Confirming that these three aspects are in place is a key aspect of PMOC.

The Relationship Between Changes

Changes can have complex relationships among each other. It is important that the MOC system have mechanisms for identifying these relationships and for understanding their implications. This is often the role of the MOC Coordinator—to monitor the change logs for these interactions.

Change Within Change

Sometimes change-within-change can occur in the following ways:
- Subsequent to the originally proposed change, such that there is a "change to the change" or the MOC Plan.
- Within the originally proposed change, which may be within another change, and so on. In other words, a component or stage, or sub-component or sub-stage, embedded in the MOC plan requires modifying.

Either of these two situations may be the result of intentional or unintentional, foreseen or unforeseen, circumstances.

Concurrent Change

Change that is concurrent can also be referred to as simultaneous change.

If known/intentional, it must be reflected in the MOC Plan.

Unintentional concurrent change represents the introduction of potentially new hazards into the MOC process

Management needs to Identify such change through the ongoing change monitoring process,
- Evaluate it, and
- Manage it as necessary.

This will also necessitate the reviewing and likely updating of the MOC Plan.

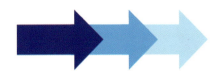

Follow-On Change

Follow-on change is simply change that happens in sequence, and like the other types of change can be either intentional or unintentional.
- If follow-on change is intentional and known from the beginning, it shall be reflected in the MOC Plan.
- Unintentional follow-on change may reflect the fact that additional activities were not initially anticipated.
- This should result in a revised and updated MOC Plan.

Follow-on changes often require that the immediately preceding change activity be done before the next activity can be done. This simply means that some aspects of an MOC Plan cannot be done concurrently.

Cumulative Change

Cumulative Change is most likely the result of many minor changes occurring over time.

Can be hard to recognize, representing a "slow drift" in OPU conditions.

- For example, an increase in feed rates, which is done gradually over several years, could have a large impact on the existing HSE controls in place.
- The unchanged HSE controls may not be able to handle the cumulative increase in feed rates over time.

Management should:

- Look at the big picture.
- Ensure that there are monitoring and review activities which periodically look at the cumulative effects of changes over time

Tool Box: Sample MOC Procedures and Forms

The following forms and procedures are meant as examples only, and may or may not be appropriate or applicable to your organization. For more information pertinent to Change Management, see the chapter on Risk Management.

Change Management Process

Process Flow Chart

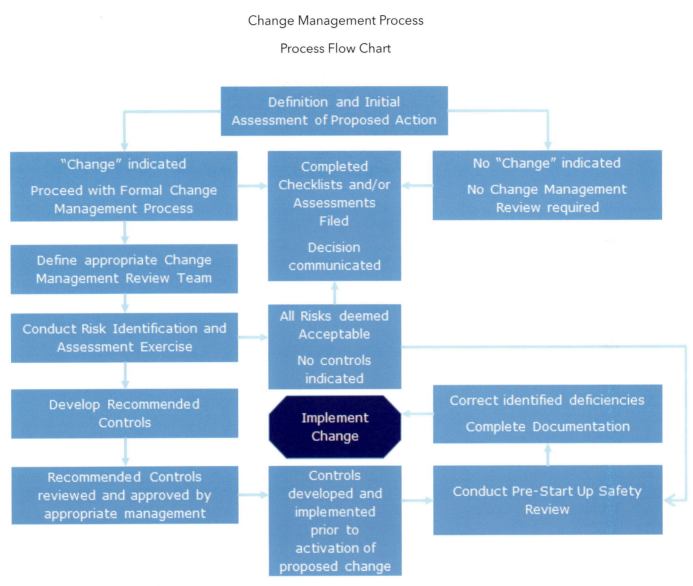

Figure 10.5 - Process Flow Chart

Change Management Process

Process Flowchart Details

The Change Management Process Flowchart provides a quick reference for the effective implementation of the process requirements. The following information provides the details of each step in the process.

1. **Definition and Initial Assessment of Proposed Action**

    When an action is proposed that is not already permitted under Standard Operating Procedures or other management policies, processes and standards, the manager of the unit in which the proposed action originates will undertake an initial assessment to determine if the action requires formal application of the Change Management Process. "Manager" in this context refers to front-line supervisors as well as middle and senior managers. This initial assessment is to be conducted using the Preliminary Assessment of Proposed Actions checklist. The completed checklist is to be reviewed, and the resulting decision approved by the immediate superior of the person conducting the initial assessment. Copies of the completed checklists are to be maintained (hard copy or electronic) by the persons signing the document. An electronic copy is to be sent to the EH&S and Engineering Managers, and filed in the common drive under MOC documentation.

2. **No Change Indicated—No Change Management Review Required**

    If it is determined that the proposed action does not constitute a "change" as defined in the process, then no further action is required until the point at which a Pre-Startup Safety Review will be completed.

    A Pre-Startup Safety Review is required in all cases of change and "replacement in kind" activities.

3. **Change Indicated—Proceed with Formal Change Management Process**

    If it is determined that the definition of a "change" has been met, then the person who reviewed and approved the initial assessment shall institute a formal Change Management Review.

4. **Define Appropriate Change Management Review Team**

    The responsible person, as defined in item 3 above, will appoint a team of three to five persons to conduct the risk identification, assessment and control activity. These persons will have direct knowledge of and responsibility for the proposed change. They will be trained in the proper application of risk assessment technology.

    PLEASE NOTE: The time required to complete the Change Management Process should be commensurate with the complexity, risks and costs of the proposed change. Some smaller, simpler changes may require only an hour or two to review. Major changes may require days. It is not intended that this process be unnecessarily burdensome, and the most senior manager/leader involved, usually the person who reviews the preliminary checklist, will determine the resources required to effectively and efficiently carry out each application.

5. **Conduct Risk Identification and Assessment Exercise**

    The review team will conduct a structured risk identification and assessment exercise, utilizing the approved risk criteria and risk matrix to prioritize each exposure. All potential participants in such an exercise will receive training in the application of these tools. The time spent on the exercise will be commensurate with the complexity and projected cost of the change.

6. All Risks Deemed Acceptable No Controls Indicated

If the risk assessment exercise determines that all identified risks meet the defined criteria for acceptable risk, and that no additional controls are necessary, then the risk assessment exercise documentation will be completed, the team will justify its decision in writing, the documentation will be filed with both the EHS Manager and the Engineering Manager, and all stakeholders and participants in the change will be notified. The change can be implemented.

7. Develop Recommended Controls

Should the risk assessment exercise determine that additional controls are necessary, the team will proceed to develop a list of appropriate, recommended controls, considering the types of controls in the following order of effectiveness:
- Elimination of Risk
- Substitution of Materials or Processes
- Engineering Controls
- Administrative Controls
- Work Practice Controls
- Personal Protective Equipment

Recommended controls should address, at a minimum, the following issues:
- Design of Guards and Barriers
- Noise Control
- Safety Devices (Limit Switches, Gauges, Relief Valves, Warning Devices, etc.)
- Interaction with Immediate Environment
- Required Changes to SOP's and Work Instructions
- Required Training (Target Audience, Objectives, Content, Methodology, etc.)
- Work Schedule Changes
- Communications Processes
- Leadership Responsibilities
- Control Monitoring Methods

8. Recommended Controls Reviewed and Approved by Appropriate Management—Responsibilities Assigned

The recommendations of the change review team will be reviewed by an appropriate level of management, and approved or modified as necessary. "Appropriate" is defined as a department manager or higher in whose area of responsibility the proposed change is occurring. Upon agreement on the controls to be employed, specific responsibilities for the development and implementation of those controls will be assigned, and target dates established. There will also be agreement on a means of monitoring progress toward these objectives. Documentation of this review and approval process will be maintained and filed in the common directory under MOC Documentation.

9. Controls Developed and Implemented Prior to Activation of Proposed Change

All agreed controls will be implemented prior to activating the change. The means of monitoring progress on these controls (required in item eight above) will be routinely employed throughout the life of the change/project to ensure this objective is met. Should any agreed control not be in place by the appointed time (change/project initiation), it will be the responsibility of the senior manager to either delay initiation, determine and implement alternative controls, or approve initiation in the absence of a specific control. Documentation of these decisions will be maintained and filed on the common drive under MOC Documentation.

10. Conduct Pre-Startup Safety Review

The change management review team, along with the HSE Manager and representatives of the operators/end users of the change, will conduct a final review prior to initiation to determine that all appropriate controls are in place and that there are no as yet unidentified risks. The approved Pre-Startup Safety Review Checklist will be used to guide this activity.

The time required for this review will be commensurate with the level of risk the change presents and its cost. A "go/no go" decision will be taken by the group. Documentation of this review and the decision of the team will be maintained and filed on the common drive under MOC Documentation.

11. Correct Identified Deficiencies Complete Documentation–Communicate Implementation Schedule

Any additional controls or modifications to the implementation plan that are developed during the Pre-Startup Safety Review must be completed prior to initiation. Any exception to this requirement must be approved in writing by the senior manager of the facility. All documentation must be complete and filed appropriately. Affected persons must be notified that the change/project is being initiated.

12. Implement Change–Monitor Controls

The change can now be implemented. In the case of a major project that has been under development, the new or modified process or equipment can be started. The process for monitoring the effectiveness of controls that was developed under item seven above will be in force and persons assigned responsibility for its management, including front-line supervision in the area(s) affected, will follow approved record-keeping and documentation procedures.

Change Management Process

Preliminary Assessment of Proposed Actions

Purpose: This brief checklist is to be used to help determine if a proposed action meets the definition of "change" as employed in this process, and whether or not it requires a formal Change Management review. A front-line supervisor or higher level of management in whose area of responsibility the proposed action originates must complete the initial assessment. It must be reviewed and approved by the initial assessor's immediate superior.

1. Briefly describe the proposed action. What is it you wish to do?

2. Does the proposed action involve a physical change; that is, a change to equipment, parts, materials, etc. **that does not require a design change?** Examples: replacement of a part, replacement of a piece of equipment, etc. if the answer to this question is YES, consider question three. If the answer is NO, proceed to question four.

3. If so, does the replacement equipment, part or material have exactly the same attributes and characteristics as that being replaced?
   - Is the replacement part/equipment/material being purchased from the same supplier as the original?
   - Is the replacement part/equipment/material designated by the same model number or name as the original?
   - Does the replacement part/equipment/material look the same as the original?
   - Does the replacement part/equipment operate in exactly the same way as the original?
   - Will the replacement part/equipment fit in the physical environment exactly the same as the original?
   - In the case of a material purchase, does the replacement material have the same chemical formulation and properties as the original?

If the answer to all of these questions is YES, then the proposed action is considered a "replacement in kind" and no formal application of the Change Management Process is required. If the answer to any of these questions is NO, proceed with the rest of this checklist.

4. Does this proposed action require a design change; that is, a modification to plant structure or equipment? If so, then a formal application of the Change Management Process is required.

5. Indicate which of the following areas the proposed action will affect.

    ___ Standard Operating Procedures (SOP's) or Work Instructions

    ___ Processing Conditions (Schedules, Traffic, Targets, etc.)

    ___ Operating Parameters (Speeds, Pressures, Temps, etc.)

    ___ Reporting Relationships (Organization Structure, Responsibilities)

    ___ Company Policies, Procedures and Systems (HR, IT, Finance, etc.

If *any* of these items are checked, a formal application of the Change Management Process is required.

6. Are there any additional circumstances or conditions regarding this proposed action that you believe justify the formal application of the Change Management Process?

7. Does this proposed action require the formal application of the Change Management Process?

    YES _____   NO _____

    Briefly explain your decision.

Copies of this record are to be maintained by the parties signing below. Electronic copies are to be sent to the EH&S Manager and the Engineering Manager and filed in the common drive under MOC Documentation.

_____   _____
Initial Assessor   Date

_____
Title

_____   _____
Reviewer   Date

_____
Title

Change Management Process

Change Management Risk Identification Checklist

This checklist is to be used to guide the risk/loss exposure identification exercise as required in the Change Management Process. Consideration must be given to initial risks or exposures during the implementation of the change, as well as residual risks or exposures that remain present after the change and for the life cycle of the change.

Category	Item	Y	N	Explanation
Operator/End-User Exposures	Does this change have the potential to cause harm to the operator or end-user of the change? - Injury - Illness - Undue Stress - Decline in Morale - Decreased Quality of Work Life - Diminished Perception of the Company			
	Does this change have the potential to eliminate or alleviate any of these exposures to operators and/or end-users?			
Persons in Proximity to the Change	Does this change have the potential to cause harm to other persons working in close proximity to the change? - Injury - Illness - Undue Stress - Decline in Morale - Decreased Quality of Work Life - Diminished Perception of the Company			
	Does this change have the potential to eliminate or alleviate any of these exposures to persons working in close proximity to the change?			

Category	Item	Y	N	Explanation
Customers	Does this change have the potential to cause harm to our organization's customers? - Injury - Illness - Undue Stress - Diminished Perception of the Company - Economic Loss			
	Does this change have the potential to eliminate or alleviate any of these exposures to customers?			
Shareholders	Does this change have the potential to cause harm to our shareholders? - Economic Loss - Loss of Community Good Will - Loss of Confidence in the Company			
	Does this change have the potential to eliminate or alleviate any of these exposures to shareholders?			
Community	Does this change have the potential to harm members of the surrounding community? - Injury - Illness - Undue Stress - Diminished Perception of the Company - Diminished Quality of Life - Economic Loss			
	Does this change have the potential to eliminate or alleviate any of these exposures to the community?			
Contractors and/or Visitors	Does this change have the potential to harm contractor personnel or visitors? - Injury - Illness - Undue Stress - Diminished Perception of the Company - Diminished Quality of Work Life - Economic Loss			
	Does this change have the potential to eliminate or alleviate any of these exposures to our contractors and visitors?			

Category	Item	Y	N	Explanation
Damage	Does this change have the potential to cause damage to equipment, structures, facilities, vehicles, or other property in any of the following categories?			
	Company Property			
	Contractors' Property			
	Visitors' Property			
	Community or Public Property			
	Does this change have the potential to eliminate or alleviate exposures to property damage in any of these categories?			
Downtime and/or Production Loss	Does this change have the potential to interrupt or diminish production capability other than that time approved and planned to implement the change?			
	Does this change have the potential to improve through-put and/or available production time?			
Product Quality	Does this change have the potential to damage or diminish the quality of products?			
	Does this change have the potential to improve product quality?			
Raw Materials	Does this change have the potential to damage raw materials, catalysts, or other materials required by the process?			
	Does this change have the potential to eliminate or alleviate these exposures?			
Supply and Distribution	Does this change have the potential to interrupt supply and/or distribution lines?			
	Does this change have the potential to improve either supply or distribution processes?			

Category	Item	Y	N	Explanation
Stakeholder Relationships	Does this change have the potential to negatively impact the organization's relationships with stakeholders? • Suppliers • Customers • Contractors • Community • Regulators • Media • Shareholders			
	Does this change have the potential to improve relationships with stakeholders?			
Environmental	Does this change have the potential to result in environmental harm in any of the following areas? • Ground Water • Air • Flora • Fauna • Soil			
	Does this change have the potential to improve our environmental performance?			
HSEQ Impacts	Does this change have the potential to impact, either negatively or positively, any of the following: (Consideration must be given to the potential impact of these exposures both inside and outside the plant property.)			
	Amount of working space available?			
	Traffic patterns (pedestrian and vehicle)			
	Noise levels			
	Air quality and/or flow			
	Temperatures in the working environment			
	Lighting effectiveness			
	Required body position			
	Repetitive motion requirements			

Category	Item	Y	N	Explanation
HSEQ Impacts	Lifting			
	Routine or Monotonous Tasks			
	Operator interface with process controls			
	Work/rest cycles			
	Biological exposures (natural cultures, flora, fauna, etc.)			
	Occupational Health Monitoring requirements			
	Personal Protective Equipment requirements			
	Rules and Work Permits			
	Content of work instructions, task procedures or SOP's			
	Physical capability requirements			
	Training requirements			
	Job skills requirements			
	Manning levels			
	Individual responsibilities and performance standards			
	Reporting relationships			
	Documentation requirements			
	Required raw materials			
	Required chemical substances such as catalysts, solvents, etc.			
	Chemical substances produced by the process such as gasses, fumes, vapors, etc.			
	Maintenance procedures			
	Access points for maintenance and inspection			
	Inspection requirements and schedules	Y	N	

Category	Item	Y	N	Explanation
HSEQ Impacts	Task or behavior observation requirements			
	Level and sophistication of required process control and monitoring technology			
	Process monitoring procedures			
	Through-put			
	Emergency procedures, equipment and/or training			
	Routine communications activities such as orientations, task instruction, and safety meetings			
	Contractor selection and monitoring criteria			
	Purchasing specifications and requirements			
	Emissions and/or effluent monitoring requirements			
	Security requirements			
	IT support requirements			
	Required access to process and equipment expertise			
	Systems auditing requirements			
	Insurance requirements			

Change Management Process

Change Management Review Team Worksheets

Description of Proposed Change:

Review Team Members and Titles: Signatures (Upon Completion)

_____   _____

_____   _____

_____   _____

_____   _____

_____   _____

Authorizing Manager and Title:

_____   _____

Date of Initiation: _____

Projected Duration of Exercise: _____

Actual Duration of Exercise and Concluding Date: _____

Management Authorization:

_____   _____
Name   Title

The following worksheets are to be used to record the work of the review team. A Department Manager or higher, with responsibility for the area in which the change is occurring, will review and approve the completed work. Electronic copies of the completed sheets will be filed with both the EHS Manager and the Engineering Manager. They will also be filed on the common drive under MOC Documentation.

STEP 1: The team will gather or arrange access to all pertinent information required to conduct a systematic and comprehensive risk assessment. Such information may include:

- Blueprints
- Engineering documents and P&ID's
- Materials substances inventories
- Task procedures, work instructions, and/or SOP"s
- Purchasing guidelines and specifications
- Vendor-supplied information
- Operator expertise
- Management process flow charts
- Specialized expertise

STEP 2: The team will systematically apply the approved risk identification checklist and record all identified risks or exposures to people, property, process, product, workflow, and the environment. All findings and decisions shall be recorded in writing.

STEP 3: The team will consider each identified risk or exposure individually and, using the approved risk criteria and risk matrix, assess the level of risk in each. Consideration must be given to probability of occurrence, loss severity potential, and, where appropriate, the frequency of the exposure. All risk rankings will be recorded on the worksheets included with this package. Should the team determine that all risks presented by the proposed change fall within acceptable limits as defined by the approved risk criteria and matrix, and that no controls are required, it will submit its work to the appropriate management for review and approval or modification. Should the management authority determine, the team might be required to reconsider its work. If the management authority accepts this initial recommendation of the team, then the proper documentation will be completed and submitted to both the EHS Manager and the Engineering Manager. It will also be filed in the common drive under MOC Documentation.

STEP 4: The team will consider each identified risk or exposure, according to the priority established in Step 3, and develop a recommended control or controls for each of the exposures. This completes the first responsibility of the team, and the results of their work will be submitted to appropriate management for review and approval or modification. The types of controls employed should be considered in this order:

- Engineering controls
- Administrative controls
- Work Practice controls
- Personal protective equipment

Recommended controls should address, at a minimum, the following issues:

- Design of guards and barriers
- Noise control
- Safety devices (limit switches, gauges, relief valves, warning devices, etc.)
- Interaction with immediate environment
- Required changes to SOP's and work instructions
- Required training (target audience, objectives, content, methodology, etc.)
- Work schedule changes
- Communications processes
- Leadership responsibilities
- Control monitoring methods

STEP 5: Should the appropriate management authority decide it is necessary, the team will revisit and modify controls to meet acceptable criteria and resubmit their work for approval. Should the appropriate management authority accept and support the controls recommended by the team, that management authority will develop an action plan designed to effectively implement the controls and make specific assignments accordingly. These assignments will be recorded on the team's worksheets and filed as required. It will be the management authority's responsibility to follow up on these assignments to determine their proper and timely progress.

STEP 6: When all controls are in place and the change ready for implementation, the Change Management Review Team, along with the HSE Manager and appropriate representatives of the operators/end users of the change, will conduct a Pre-Startup Safety Review using the approved "Pre-Startup Safety Review Checklist." Based on this review, a "go/ no go" decision will be taken by the group. In the case of a "no go" decision, perceived problems will be discussed and remedial actions determined. These remedial actions must be completed prior to approving start-up. The management authority referred to in earlier steps of this document has final approval. In the case of a "go" decision, the change will be implemented, the proper documentation completed and filed, and all affected parties notified.

STEP 7: The team will remain in place for an appropriate period to monitor the effectiveness of the controls in the early stages of the change. Some teams may need only a few hours to determine that the change has been successfully and safely implemented. Longer monitoring periods will be required for more complex changes. In no case should a team remain in place in a monitoring role for more than two weeks after the initiation of the change. Should a team identify unacceptable, residual risk during this monitoring period, they will report the situation in writing to the appropriate management authority and participate in the determination of required modifications to the control plan. Other means of routine monitoring, such as planned inspections and supervisor observations, should be sufficient at this point. Upon satisfactory completion of their work, the team will sign the cover to this document and be disbanded.

Key Point Summary

1. Change is inevitable in any organization or process. Change introduces new risks that must be managed. A systematic and comprehensive change management system is critical for any organization.

2. Change may take many forms.

    a. Engineering changes such as replacing or modifying equipment, redesigning a process, or building infrastructure.

    b. Procedural changes such as task procedures, administrative procedures, or new documentation requirements.

    c. Organizational changes such as reorganization, introduction of a new manager, and acquisition or divestiture.

3. All forms of change should be considered and accommodated in a change management process.

4. Risk identification and assessment is the cornerstone of a change management process.

5. Temporary changes must be covered by the change management process.

Personal Planning

1. Does my organization have a change management process?

2. Do all appropriate persons know and understand the requirements of the change management process?

3. What kinds of changes have occurred in my area of responsibility in the last six months? Have we applied the change management process in each of them appropriately?

4. What do we need to do to strengthen our change management process?

Y – Model for Action Planning

Present Situation

Desired Situation

Need for Change

Present Situation

| Stop | Responsibility | Target Date |

PLANNED INSPECTIONS

Chapter 11

PLANNED INSPECTIONS

> **CHAPTER OBJECTIVES**
>
> 1. To present best practices for developing and implementing a robust planned inspection process.
> 2. To prompt the reader to consider planned inspections in a broader context; that is, as a means to identify all existing and potential loss exposures.
> 3. To introduce a unique understanding of housekeeping, including a definition of order that has the potential to produce dramatic improvement when properly applied.
> 4. To encourage continual improvement in a fundamental health and safety element.

The Leadership Team Drives Improvement

To emphasize the importance of the organization's sustainability initiative, Henry decides to meet with each direct report to discuss a plan to meet corporate goals. One of the first requirements of the initiative was a Health and Safety audit/assessment of each site to measure current Health and Safety performance and identify opportunities for improvement. The leadership team believes that better utilization of resources will help ensure meeting the corporate goal of achieving sustainable performance.

The assessment had been completed for Joe's site so he and Henry begin discussing the results. They reach an agreement on what they believe are the critical areas to be addressed and begin planning how Joe's site will meet these issues. One area of particular concern is the quality of workplace inspections currently being done. Following Joe's less than ideal experience with trying to implement new inspection processes earlier in his tenure, he wants to be very careful to do it right this time.

Following discussions with Henry, Joe calls a meeting with his direct reports. The general findings of the health and safety assessment are discussed and the critical issue with workplace inspections is highlighted. A number of the managers believe that training for those doing the inspections will be a positive step forward. One manager believes that the quality of the inspections should be measured. Her experience convinces her that things that are measured get more attention than things that aren't. In the end, everyone agrees that a project team should be formed, one that includes a diagonal slice of those working at the site.

Shortly after the meeting, Joe discussed the report in more detail with Lisa and Carlos. They decided to form a project team of six members with representatives from the Joint Health and Safety Committee, one senior manager, and employee volunteers. It was also agreed that training for those doing inspections was an important part of improving performance in the inspection area. Therefore, one of the outputs from the project team was to develop a training package for inspectors. Lisa and Carlos would act as advisors to the team. Carlos had been identified as a candidate for advancement in the company, and since his operational results were known throughout the site, his views would be respected.

Lisa suggested that a key part of this effort would be to ensure that all inspections be risk-based. Carlos asked for clarification, and she explained that first, there are inspections required by regulations. Those compliance inspections have to be done and are outside the scope of this project. Other inspections should be risk-based, i.e. making the inspections, frequency and what to look for commensurate with the risks in different areas of the site. This would maximize resources so they are concentrated where risks are the greatest. She mentioned that the current inspection system had evolved over time and there was likely an opportunity to improve inspection performance.

A notice was sent to all on-site about the purpose of the planned inspection project team, and volunteers were requested. Members were selected based upon their skills, objectivity, ability to work with others on the team, and amount of time available to devote to the project.

The resulting team was thoroughly briefed on the purpose, scope, and objectives of the improvement initiative, and identified critical activities they believed could make a difference. A couple of people who had been doing inspections reinforced the need for more comprehensive training. They said they had simply been given a checklist and told to inspect certain areas or equipment and turn in a report. There was no training provided. The decision was taken to make training a priority.

Lisa and Carlos assumed the role as primary trainers, and all persons with inspection responsibilities were scheduled to attend a one-day course. Joe opened each session with words of support and commitment. The course content was based on the following material.

Inspections take a lot of time and resources. All organizations must conduct certain regulatory-required inspections. In addition, there are general workplace inspections (wall-to-wall, "look at everything" kinds of inspections). Some organizations conduct dedicated housekeeping inspections. There are pre-use inspections on mobile and materials handling equipment, food processing equipment, and other types of critical equipment. There are preventive and predictive maintenance inspections, insurance-related inspections, fire and emergency systems inspections, etc. When you add up the time and resources required, inspections can be a significant investment. Any organization simply must maximize the value of their inspection processes and understand that inspections are not only health and safety tools. They should be seen as tools to improve overall organization performance.

All persons in the organization should understand the need for a rigorous inspection regimen, and the basics of how such a regimen should work. This begins with understanding the specific reasons and expected benefits from workplace inspections. Among those benefits are:

- Properly done, inspections can identify and highlight positive aspects of the workplace. Often, inspections are viewed as only being focused on things that are wrong and need to be corrected; however, they provide the opportunity for the organization, through inspectors, to reinforce the positive aspects of the work environment and employee behavior.
- Proper inspections identify potential problems. The key word here is potential. Effective inspections can help keep substandard acts, practices, and conditions from becoming incidents.
- Effective inspections can identify equipment deficiencies. Such deficiencies may be health and safety issues, but may be quality or production issues as well.
- Traditionally, inspections were focused on workplace conditions. They also provide the opportunity to identify substandard or at-risk behaviors.
- All organizations should have a robust change management process, as described elsewhere in this book.

> Well-managed inspections provide a measure of leadership performance and provide a way for leaders to demonstrate their commitment to ensuring a safe, healthy work environment, as well as a tool to improve overall organizational performance.

- Pare a second opportunity to catch the effects of change that may have been missed in the change management process. All inspectors should keep this question in their minds while conducting inspections: "Has anything changed out here since the last inspection, and what are the potential negative effects of that change?"
- Each inspection provides the opportunity to check the effectiveness of corrective and preventive actions implemented as a result of previous inspections.

These informal inspections are important, but our focus here is on planned inspections; that is, inspections that are structured and intentional.

There are two general categories of workplace inspections.

Informal Inspections

It is important to emphasize that all employees can contribute to the improvement of workplace conditions simply by developing a better awareness and use of their senses to help identify issues that need to be addressed, those that are substandard and those that deserve recognition. This category of inspections could also be called casual. There are no checklists applied, no set-aside time, and no formal report generated. The informal inspection simply asks all stakeholders to keep their eyes and ears open and report issues they identify as they go about their daily work. There should be a bit of structure, that is, continual promotion of the process and means provided for stakeholders to report issues.

The means to report might be a brief card made available to everyone in break areas or other convenient points. Some organizations use alert cards or a combination of incident and substandard condition report forms to identify areas for improvement. Employees are encouraged to fill them out when they see something that needs attention. This allows them to capture something while it is fresh in their minds and when leadership might not be available. Things change between structured inspections, and employees on the floor are most likely to notice those changes. One of the keys for this to continue working is communication. It is important to respond to each and every card or form, even if nothing can be done. People had rather hear "no," and the reasons for it, than to hear nothing at all.

Planned Inspections

The following are types of planned inspections.
- General safety and health
- Housekeeping
- Pre-use equipment checks
- Preventive maintenance
- Special systems

While some of these types may be partially included in a general safety and health inspection, the focus of each is unique enough to examine them independently.

General Health and Safety Inspections

A general inspection is a structured, planned tour of a predetermined area by an individual or a team. Time is dedicated and the objectives of the inspection are respected. Inspectors look at anything and everything to search out loss exposures. A formal report is generated.

The following are considerations in the development of an effective general inspection process.

- How often should inspections be done?
- What specific things or aspects of the area/equipment should be inspected?
- Who should conduct them?
- Why and how should we use inspection teams?
- How should we design our checklists?
- What role should senior leadership play in the inspection process?

Frequency and What to Inspect

The frequency of inspections, and what specific things to inspect, should be based upon the risks in each area of the site. The information developed through the risk identification and assessment processes described in the chapter on Risk Management would be a very good place to start. In addition, the four inventories referenced in the chapter on Emergency Preparedness and Response would be a good source of information. The organization can use this information to identify and develop a schedule of inspections and an appropriate checklist for each area or piece of equipment.

The general inspection process should be comprehensive. All areas, structures, or equipment owned or used by the organization should be included. Certainly, all areas where hands-on work is done (operating and maintenance) would top the list. However, the organization should be careful to include items such as parking lots, storage areas, offices, break rooms, restrooms, fencing, outdoor lighting, roadways, etc. Off-site storage areas owned or leased should be inspected. Any abandoned or inactive property should be included.

Figure 11.1 below identifies categories of items that should be included in any inspection process. It is not intended to be a complete list. Each organization should design its own such list.

GENERAL PHYSICAL CONDITIONS

1. Electrical fixtures: wiring, cords, grounds and connections.
2. Mechanical power transmission: condition and guarding.
3. Machine guarding: nip points, cutting and shear edges, presses, rotating parts and gear devices.
4. Walking and working surfaces: guarding and condition.
5. Compressed gas cylinders: segregation in storage, weather protection and restraints.
6. Flammable: storage, ventilation and working supply.
7. Exits: marking, visibility, lighting and unobstructed access.
8. Deluge showers and eye baths: flow, temperature and drainage.
9. Ladders and climbing devices: condition, storage and proper use.
10. Hand tools: condition, storage and proper use.
11. Materials handling equipment and lifting devices: condition, proper use and storage.
12. Scrap and refuse: accumulation, removal, storage and disposal.
13. Aisle ways and storage stacks: accessibility, marking, adequate dimensions.
14. Stacking and storage: location, segregation, stability, damage, and protection.

Figure 11.1: Key Points for Inspection

FIRE PREVENTION AND CONTROL

1. **Fire detection and alarm systems:** installation, adequacy of coverage and service testing.
2. **Sprinkler systems:** clearance for type storage, adequacy of pressure and flow volume of water or chemical supply and maintenance.
3. **Fire evacuation:** exit route maps, personnel training and emergency drills.
4. **Portable extinguishers:** correct type and mounting, locating signs and guides, unrestricted accessibility and maintenance of serviceability.
5. **Fire prevention:** adequacy of housekeeping, waste disposal and flammable materials work.
6. **Fire containment:** fire control doors and seals, ventilation controls.
7. **Fire notification:** telephone and alternate systems for notification of fire team and outside services.
8. **Fire services:** hose outlets, valves and other supply adequate, compatible with local fire unit equipment and tested for serviceability.
9. **Fire equipment:** color coding, signs and access, compliance with governmental standards.

ENVIRONMENTAL HEALTH

1. **Caustic, corrosive and toxic materials:** container labels, storage, disposal and spill clean-up.
2. **Ventilation:** of toxic fumes, vapors, mists, smoke and gases.
3. **Noise exposure:** measurement and controls.
4. **Radiation exposure:** measurement and controls.
5. **Temperature extremes:** measurement and controls.
6. **Hazardous substances:** information to affected employees.
7. **Illumination:** surveys and controls.
8. **Human factors engineering:** surveys and controls.
9. **Personal protective equipment:** selection, location and compliance.

Figure 11.1 (continued): Key Points for Inspection

Who should conduct inspections?

Best practice is that front-line supervisors and other appropriate line leaders should be held accountable for ensuring inspections are conducted; however, the inspection activity is a great opportunity to engage a variety of stakeholders in the health and safety process. As you will see below, we are going to advocate a team approach to these types of inspection. Although line leaders may be accountable, they should use the expertise and insight of their people in this activity. Engaging people in inspection teams does not require extensive training, but all persons in an organization should have a basic understanding of acceptable and substandard conditions. The need for some hazard recognition training is apparent. One simple means of accomplishing this objective is to take pictures around the site of standard and substandard conditions, acts or practices and use them in safety meetings. As each picture is presented to the group, they could be asked if there are any problems or issues they see, and if so, what they are, what their potential is, and what should be done about them. The presentation could be made into a game or contest to add interest. Doing something like this on a routine and repetitive basis could prepare employees to participate on inspection teams.

Another technique used by some organizations is cross-inspection. An inspection team from one area may go to a different area of the site, one with which they are not necessarily very familiar. The advantage to this activity is that different eyes see different things. The old saying that "familiarity breeds contempt" may well be true. Employees in a specific area can live with exposures so long that the exposures become part of the normal working conditions or routine and, as such, their risk potential is not fully appreciated. People who do not work in that area routinely may well see and challenge conditions that the usual residents would not. In addition, it is sometimes valuable for persons who have little or no familiarity with an area to have the opportunity to ask the proverbial "dumb question" or questions that no one intimately familiar with the area would think to ask, but may result in an epiphany.

Care should be taken that cross-inspection does not become a situation where groups see the opportunity to take a measure of revenge for perceived negative inspections by rival groups.

The use of teams for general inspections can be a powerful tool. Teams provide more eyes and more experience focused on an area. What one person misses, another sees, simply due to their varied knowledge and experience. They also provide the opportunity to engage stakeholders in the health and safety process.

Inspection Checklists

Checklists should be specific to each area being inspected. A generic checklist for an entire site, especially a large site with varied types of exposures, is not sufficient. The checklist should not be used as the inspection report; that is, with inspectors simply checking that an item has been inspected and/or writing in good, fair, or poor, or checking acceptable/unacceptable.

The Role of Senior Leadership

Periodic engagement of senior leaders in the inspection process is evidence of commitment and stresses the importance of the investment of time. Middle and senior leaders should actually participate on inspection teams from time to time. They should review inspection reports and provide feedback to inspectors. In most organizations, middle and senior leaders engage in tours as a separate activity in addition to the actual inspections. They consult with their health and safety resources to identify areas or items on which to concentrate, and they engage the workforce in related discussions as they tour. A sample tour checklist is found at the end of this chapter.

Steps in General Inspections

Getting maximum value out of the inspection process largely depends on conducting inspections in an organized way. The following are general steps that will be discussed in some detail:

- Prepare
- Inspect
- Determine basic causes
- Develop appropriate remedial actions
- Take follow-up actions

Prepare

This step in the inspection activity involves ensuring that all areas of the particular work area to be inspected are identified, and that no area is overlooked. This may not be an issue unless the inspection team is doing the inspection in another area of the site (cross-inspection).

Part of preparing involves looking at the previous inspection report(s) to identify items/areas that need to be rechecked. These should be added to the current inspection checklist and evaluated to make sure adequate controls were put into place and are working. This review also offers the opportunity for inspectors to identify issues that routinely and repetitively appear on inspection reports. The fact that these issues may continue to appear means that the basic or root causes of the problem have not been identified and corrected.

Another consideration in this step is deciding what should be taken by the inspector(s) to the area to be inspected. A list of inspection equipment and supplies could include:

- Checklist and clipboard
- Clear plastic bag to cover clipboard to protect from weather
- Flashlight
- Mirror for looking behind equipment, etc.
- Camera to document conditions and items (intrinsically safe may be necessary)
- Caution tape
- Danger/Do Not Operate tags
- Personal protective equipment and appropriate clothing
- Writing materials
- Tape measure and appropriate test instruments

Inspect

The inspection should be intentional, comprehensive, and focused.

The area-specific checklist should be used to ensure the thoroughness of the inspection. The checklist should be a guide, but inspectors should be practiced in assessing situations not covered on the checklist.
Inspectors should go everywhere and look at everything. This type of inspection cannot be done simply by walking the beaten path. Exposures are not always obvious, and they can hide very easily. Inspectors should go under, over, around, through, and behind to find them. Doors should be opened and covers removed. Many operating sites have storage areas that are not used routinely, where exposures can hide. Remember, go everywhere and look at everything. If it is deemed unsafe for the inspection team to enter such areas, then persons who are specially trained and equipped to do so should conduct that part of the inspection.

When problems are found, a concise description of the issues should be recorded, with the exact locations. Photographs may aid in the description. This detail is needed since other people may need to locate the item. Maintenance and repair personnel should not have to spend time looking for an exposure, but should be guided by the notes on the report.

GO EVERYWHERE

A large manufacturing complex is located in the downtown area of a major city, close by a deep water harbor. There are many older buildings in the complex.

An inspection team was conducting a general inspection of the research and development building, the oldest in the operation. The team went into the basement of the building where they observed a door through which none of them had ever entered. There was an old padlock on the door that was rusted to the point of being unusable.

The team had been trained to go everywhere and look at everything. Although they were very hesitant to do so, they had maintenance cut the padlock from the door and entered.

Inside they found drums of unknown content. The drums were not properly labeled. The only markings were a project number and a date. The date was forty years in the past.

It was then necessary to have the drums removed by a hazardous waste contractor.

The contents of the drums were eventually determined to be rather benign, but they could have been a carcinogen or explosive. No one knew they were there.

Go everywhere, look at everything!

Risk assessment should be applied to items identified on inspections as a means of prioritizing the items for attention. This enables the organization to address the highest potential risks first. The organization may choose to use its standard risk matrix for this purpose, or a simpler system, such the hazard classification system described below.

Class A Hazard *(Major)* – A condition or practice likely to cause permanent disability, loss of life or body part and/or extensive loss of structure, equipment or material.

Class B Hazard *(Serious)* – A condition or practice likely to cause serious injury or illness, resulting in temporary disability or property damage that is disruptive but not extensive.

Class C Hazard *(Minor)* – A condition or practice likely to cause minor, non-disabling injury or illness or non-disruptive property damage.

The organization should define minimum time frames in which each hazard class must be addressed.

Regardless of the risk assessment system used, the assignment of risk level should be done by the inspection team, which has access to the necessary information to make an informed decision. Such assessment should not be done exclusively by the health and safety function, the maintenance function, or a third party external to the inspection team.

Any unnecessary items identified on the inspection should be removed to an appropriate place (disposal, spare parts, storage, etc.).

Determine Basic or Root Causes

One of the most frustrating issues for some organizations in regards to inspections is that the same problems or exposures keep appearing on numerous subsequent inspections. When the same or very similar problems keep recurring, it is often because the organization has addressed the immediate problem, but has failed to identify and fix the basic causes behind it. The vast majority of the items the inspection team will identify in a report will fit into the potential immediate cause category; that is, they will likely be substandard conditions and/or substandard behaviors. As discussed in the chapter on Basic Concepts of Safety and Health Management Systems, these conditions and behaviors are symptoms of deeper problems. Unless those deeper problems are effectively addressed, the symptoms will likely recur.

One of the most valuable contributions inspectors can make to their organizations is to constantly and consistently look for basic or root causes to the problems they identify.

Developing Remedial Actions

Identifying the immediate and basic/root causes is only part of the work required. Remedial actions to control the causes must be developed and implemented. A leader can make a better decision on a proposed action if certain critical factors are looked at systematically. Six of them are:

- The potential severity of loss
- The probability of a loss occurrence
- The cost of control
- The likely degree of control
- Control alternatives

By carefully considering the above, inspectors and supervisors can evaluate the different control alternatives and be better prepared to support the control measure(s) recommended.

Do your health and safety efforts have to be economically practical? Yes! No one would recommend spending $5,000 to solve a $5.00 problem. Cost/benefit analysis is always appropriate.

Taking Follow Up Actions

Potential follow up actions include:

- Ensuring commendations for improvements or best practices noted
- Writing work orders to correct issues related to physical plant
- Monitoring resources to ensure sufficient attention

- Verifying timely actions based on risk level
- Monitoring progress of action items
- Verifying adequacy of controls that are implemented
- Final review and sign off.

Please note that work orders do not solve every problem. If the identified exposure involves substandard or at-risk behaviors, other mechanisms will be necessary.

Writing the Inspection Report

A standard inspection report template is recommended. The report is a different document than the checklist and one format is useful throughout the organization. Standardization makes inspection report analysis and evaluation much easier. A sample report form is found in Figure 11.2.

An inspection team identifies a puddle of oil in a walkway as a slip hazard. It is recorded and immediately cleaned up. The team may believe they have solved the problem, when the reason for the existence of the puddle has not been determined. A following inspection again identifies a puddle of oil in the same spot as the original and again the oil is cleaned up without further evaluation. It is entirely possible that the oil spot will continue to develop and that someone will slip and be injured.

A prudent inspection team would deal with the problem in a very different way. Yes, it would be recorded in the report and immediately cleaned up; however, the team would ask some very important questions.

Why is this oil spot here? Perhaps the team surveys the area, looking for the origin of the oil. They find a leak in a small pump. Oil is dripping, running across the floor, and pooling in the walkway. They record on the inspection report that there is a leak in the pump. Once again, they pursue the basic causes for the leak.

Why is the pump leaking? Not being experts on the pump, the team asks maintenance to determine the cause of the leak. Maintenance finds that the seals in the pump are improper. The team records that there are improper seals in the pump and asks another why question.

Why do we have the wrong seals in the pump? The maintenance person tells the team that there is only one type of seal in storage and they are used for everything. Purchasing only buys the one type. The team visits the stores area and verifies that, indeed, there is only one type of seal available and it is not necessarily the proper seal for all uses. They record that there are insufficient supplies of proper seals and ask another why question.

Why do we only have one type of seal in storage? The team visits purchasing and are told that purchasing has never been provided any specifications for seals. They buy whatever is available.

The existence of the oil puddle, the leak in the pump, the improper seals in the pump, and the lack of proper seals in storage are all substandard conditions or symptoms. It is proper to address them all, but if this and similar problems are to be prevented in the future, the inspection must deal with the basic or root cause behind them. In this case, that basic cause is a flaw in the purchasing system.

If that flaw is properly addressed, it will be less likely that the wrong seals are purchased, less likely that the wrong seals will be installed in pumps, less likely that pumps will leak, and less likely that oil puddles will be a continuing problem.

		INSPECTION REPORT		DEPARTMENT
				Machine Shop

INSPECTOR(S)	AREA INSPECTED	REVIEWER
Bob Mettner, Paula St. John	Plant #2	John Sharp

ITEM NUMBER	HAZARD CLASS	TYPE OF REPORT (INITIAL, FOLLOW-UP, FINAL)	DATE(S)	QUALITY SCORE
		~~Initial~~ Final	~~8/9~~ 8/31	86%

ITEMS DETECTED - ACTIONS TAKEN - DATES

ITEM NUMBER	HAZARD CLASS	ITEMS DETECTED - ACTIONS TAKEN - DATES
*①	A	6/10, guard missing, cutting head machine #2046. N.E. corner Bay #2 bldg.
*2	C	B6/16, door at south end Bldg. 2 warped, hard to open. WO issued to carpenter shop. Work scheduled for 7-22.
✗	B	7/8, heavy accumulation of oil and trash under main motor in Bldg. 2 pump house. Cleaned out Aug. 20, discussion with workers all turns, permanent signs protected.
4	B	Two pallets of chemical 265 in yard, Column B14. Directions warn against outside storage. Reported to R. Jones, area leader. Pallets moved to inside storage Aug. 6.
5	A	Major building column P32 is receiving severe damage from bulldozer operation cellar Bldg. 4. WO issued for concrete barricade base Aug. 12, meeting held with all operators on major damage.
✗	A	Seven leaks in natural gas line between columns A1 and A2 in north bay, Bldg. 2. <u>Strong odor of gas in entire area</u>. G. Sutter, area foreman, roped area off. Gas dept. called. Leaks repaired Aug. 6.
✗	C	Sharp edge on latch - tool shanty door Bldg. 2. Maintenance worker filed surface Aug. 7.
⑧		Compressed air pipe N. side of truck door, E. end press shop damaged. Guard or relocation could prevent major loss. WO issued 8-9 for permanent striped metal guard, hazard striped board wired to pipe Aug. 10.
9		Two empty whiskey bottles found in empty locker #15, washroom Bldg. 1 Plant protection notification Aug. 6, request area leader to permit observation before discussing.

NOTATIONS:
* Indicates item detected previously   O - around a number indicates intermediate action   X - over a number indicates item corrected

Figure 11.2: Sample Inspection Report

There is likely a direct correlation between the quality of the inspection and the quality of the report submitted. Therefore, a quality measurement of inspection reports would help ensure consistency and provide a tool for coaching for improvement. The basis for this type of measurement can be found in the chapter Reviewing Performance. Once inspectors are properly trained, a coaching process based on this type of measurement can help ensure the sustainability of the process. Figure 11.3 provides an example of how the quality measurement of inspection reports can be done.

Inspection Reporting Scoring Worksheet

FACTOR	POSSIBLE	AWARDED	COMMENTS
Thoroughness of Inspection	20	16	visitor area not inspected
Hazards Accurately Classified	10	10	well done
Clear Description and Location of Each Item	10	10	well done
Effectiveness of Remedial Actions	20	12	need more communication with operators
Clear Responsibility for Remedial Actions	15	13	assign follow-up Dept. 600
Follow-Up Data Recorded	15	15	OK
Timeliness of Report	10	10	OK
TOTAL	100	86	Good job overall

Figure 11.3: Example of Quality Measurement Technique

Housekeeping Inspections

The legendary Henry Ford was once asked, "What would you do if you were called upon to take charge of a business that had failed?" His response was, "No business I know of ever went to the wall without first accumulating a vast pile of dirt. The dirt and all that goes with it, untidy thinking and methods, helped to cause that failure. The first thing I would do would be to clean that business up."

Since dirt and disorder are enemies of safety, quality, environment, productivity and cost-effectiveness, housekeeping evaluations are a vital part of inspections. Some organizations separate housekeeping inspections from the general inspection. Others simply include housekeeping as part of the general inspection. That's fine, as long as inspectors understand what housekeeping really means and how it should be evaluated. Housekeeping includes both cleanliness and order. They are not the same. Many leaders and safety professionals feel these are so important that they agree that the First Law of Good Work is to be 'clean and orderly.'

" A place in order when there are no unnecessary things about and when all necessary things are in their proper places. "No" in this sentence means none! - Not any! Not even one!"

Harry Meyers

Two key questions that inspectors should ask about items they are not sure of are:
- Is this item necessary? and
- Is it in its proper place?

These tie in with this tried, tested, proven and practical definition of order:

Order means more than cleanliness. It means more than neat. It means that things are where they ought to be for maximum productivity, quality, safety and cost control.

Our friend Lisa once asked a group of employees, "Can an area be clean, but not in order?" After getting a variety of answers she explained that cleanliness is a janitorial function, while order is a leadership activity. She used the following example: If a visitor was to come into one of our work areas and was asked to clean it up, it is likely that they could do that. However, they wouldn't be able to put it in order. They wouldn't know what items are necessary to complete the work done in that area. Figure 11.4 illustrates.

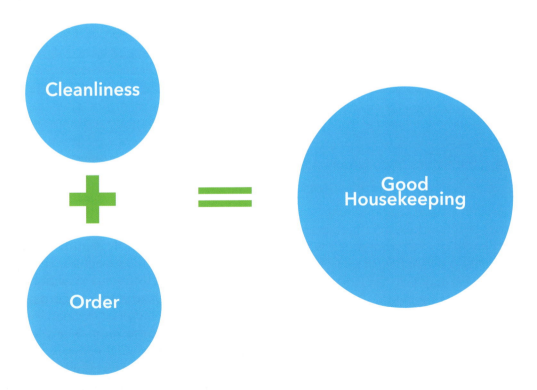

Figure 11.4: Housekeeping

Similarly, any one of us could probably do a decent job of cleaning up an operating room; however, it would take a medical professional to put it in order.

For those of you familiar with the Five S system, this thinking will be very familiar.

There are many opportunities provided by this approach to housekeeping.

Opportunities:

- Cluttered and poorly arranged areas cleaned up
- Untidy and dangerous piling of materials alleviated
- Items that are excessive, obsolete or no longer needed removed
- Blocked aisle ways cleared
- Material stuffed in corners, on overcrowded shelves, in overflowing bins and containers removed
- Tools and equipment returned to tool rooms, racks, cribs or chests organized and available, instead of being left in work areas
- Broken containers and damaged material discarded or repaired
- Gathering dirt and rust from disuse cleaned up
- Excessive quantities of items redistributed
- Waste, scrap and excess materials that congest work areas removed
- Spills, leaks and hazardous materials creating safety and health hazards alleviated

Benefits:

- Eliminates accidental injury and fire causes
- Prevents wasted energy
- Maintains greatest use of precious space
- Keeps stores' inventory at a minimum
- Helps control property damage and waste
- Guarantees good work area appearance
- Encourages better work habits
- Impresses customers, and others such as potential customers, visitors and regulators
- Reflects a well-run area

Order is the first step in doing anything right; if you cannot manage the order of your department, you cannot manage your department.

Pre-Use Equipment Checks

Many types of equipment have parts, items, or systems that should be checked regularly at the start of the shift, or prior to use, by the operator. The steps needed to ensure that these checks are carried out successfully include the following:

- Systematic identification of the equipment requiring such checks
- Development of checklists of items to be inspected, customized to each piece of equipment
- Development of specific requirements (what is to be inspected, who is to be held accountable, when or how often should the inspections be done)
- Definition of actions to take when substandard conditions are uncovered
- Establishment of a follow-up system to ensure corrective actions are completed in a timely manner

Mobile and materials handling equipment such as forklifts, cranes, front-end loaders, trenching equipment, railroad switch engines, tugs, mine haul trucks and shovels are among equipment usually covered by pre-use inspection requirements. In the food industry, sanitation and food safety requirements include pre-use inspections on process equipment. Lifting equipment such as slings and chains require inspection. Some organizations include all company vehicles, even passenger cars to be pre use inspected. In the United States, Department of Transportation regulations require both pre and post-use inspections on covered vehicles. The organization should conduct a systematic survey of all applicable regulations to determine what equipment is required to undergo pre-use inspections. In addition, the organization should set its own internal standards for these inspections, based on the output of the risk assessment process. An inventory or list of this equipment should be kept up to date and included in all training of persons responsible.

The second step is the development of checklists specific to the equipment being inspected. A generic checklist for all equipment is not sufficient. All responsible persons should be trained in the content and use of the checklist.

The organization should develop written requirements that detail what types of inspections are required, who is to be held accountable for conducting them, and when or how often the inspections are to be done. This helps avoid confusion and provides a performance expectation against which performance can be measured.

The organization's corrective and preventive action system should define specific actions to be taken when problems are detected in pre and post-use inspections.

A robust follow-up system must be in place to ensure that the system continues to function properly. This system should include a periodic audit of the process.

All persons required to conduct pre and post-use inspections should be trained in all aspects of the process. Just because an individual is a trained operator, it should not be assumed they know how to perform proper inspections.

Preventive Maintenance Inspections

Preventive maintenance may be defined as predetermined work performed without prior knowledge of a defect.

The aim of such inspections is to keep equipment and machinery in an efficient condition, thereby preventing an undesired failure.
Most organizations have robust preventive maintenance inspection systems based on the following data:

- Historical failure, past accidents/breakdowns
- Risk assessments
- Planned general inspections
- Regulatory requirements
- Other identification systems

The types of work that typically occur in a preventive maintenance program include:

- Lubrication
- Adjustment
- Condition monitoring, such as noise and vibration
- Integrity tests, non-destructive testing

Most organizations use software programs to manage this type of system. A best practice involves evaluating breakdowns and incidents, their frequency and repetitive causes, to determine the effectiveness of the preventive maintenance system.

Special Systems Inspections

Special systems inspections involve equipment that provides protection, detection, alarms and response for safety, health and environmental hazards. This equipment is inspected periodically and in accordance with statutory requirements as a minimum. These items may be incorporated into other inspections, for example fire extinguishers and eye baths and showers. Others may be incorporated into a preventive maintenance inspection. In some cases, contractors with special knowledge are used to inspect this category of equipment on a pre-determined frequency.

Examples of items falling within this category are:

- Flood alert/alarm systems
- Radiation monitoring equipment
- Pressure relief systems
- Blowdown systems
- Fire, smoke, heat and gas detectors
- Fire pumps
- Fire suppression systems
- Fire extinguishers
- Rescue air packs
- Eye baths and showers
- Shutdown systems
- Grounding (earthing) systems
- Lifejackets/life belts
- Rescue boats/craft
- Flame arrestors
- Master controls for emergency shutdown
- Other components and systems
- Spill response equipment/materials

Management Actions to Support an Inspection Process

There are certain functions that support a robust inspection process that can only be done effectively by senior and middle leadership.

The following are examples:

- Budget resources. Inspectors need time and equipment to do inspections effectively. Some corrective actions cost little in time or material; others can be quite expensive. These resources must be provided in the programming of operating activities. If resources are not provided, people assume that the upper manager really has little concern for inspections—or for safety.
- Set performance expectations. State how often inspections of each type are to be performed, who is to inspect, what reports are required and how often follow-up is expected.
- Set objectives related to inspections. Help subordinates in completing inspection plans, checklists, report forms, etc. by setting these as objectives with middle and line supervisors or leaders, and by reviewing them as they are completed.
- Provide adequate leadership in employee training. Make sure that those involved are trained in hazard recognition and appropriate inspection methods, techniques and records keeping.
- Monitor the status of the inspection program. Have responsible leaders give periodic input on inspections performed, numbers of items in each hazards classification found, and numbers of remedial actions completed in the period.
- Program audits. Have periodic audits of program compliance made by members of leadership, and conduct an audit review meeting to discuss the results and actions to be taken.
- Make safety and health tours. Tours by senior and middle leaders provide visible evidence of interest, involvement and commitment. As used here, tour means a walk-through specifically to observe critical or especially important safety and health items and talk to employees. They are not in-depth inspections.

Management Tour Checklist

Manager: _____ Date: _____

Department : _____

Area Covered : _____

Item	Notes
1. Look for opportunities to reinforce positive behaviors or actions on both a group and individual level.	
2. Are there new employees in the area? Speak to them and welcome them to your organization. Ask them for feedback on the quality and thoroughness of their work area orientation.	
3. Ask employees about any near-misses or substandard conditions of which they may be aware.	
4. Is there new or modified equipment in the area? Ask operators about the status of the equipment. Is it operating properly? Are there any noted problems? Check to see if proper MOC and pre-start up safety reviews were completed.	
5. Has there been any recent training for area personnel? Ask them for feedback on the quality and thoroughness of the training. Are there any outstanding concerns?	
6. Ask employees if there are any substandard conditions in the area that have not been appropriately and effectively addressed.	
7. Ask if there have been changes to the work area, equipment, procedures, scheduling, personnel, etc. Confirm that the MOC process was applied properly in all such cases.	
8. Check the status of housekeeping in the area.	

Corrective and Preventive Action Plan

Deficiency	Action	Responsible	Target Date	Completion Date	Notes

Figure 11.4: Example of Management Tour Checklist

Conclusion:

The inspection process is an opportunity for the manager to find and correct problems before losses occur. An effective inspection program requires detailed planning, careful observation of facilities and activities, clear communication on findings and follow-up to make sure that all remedial actions are completed and effective. But the many benefits make it a most worthwhile investment.

WAYS TO MOTIVATE GOOD INSPECTION METHODS

- Measure quality of reports
- Develop or motivate development of inspection guides for each area
- Train inspectors properly (include inspection guide)
- Clearly show and tell inspectors how they will be evaluated
- Recognize good inspectors
- Rotate coordination of inspection program through senior management. Assignment should be for short duration
- Have motivational contact by senior management prior to inspection
- Communicate performance ratings to all levels not less than quarterly
- Complete and maintain critical parts inventory. Establish file for each area
- Use photography in positive way

Figure 11.5: Ways to Motivate Improved Inspections

After several months, the hard work of Joe, Lisa, Carlos and the project team became apparent. Although not perfect, the inspectors are better prepared. They know where to look and what to look for. As a result of inspectors classifying hazards and better defining substandard conditions, maintenance personnel are able to make better use of their time. Housekeeping improvement is noticeable with less clutter and this presents a better visual image to all at the site. Pre-use inspections improve, resulting in an improvement in equipment reliability and availability. New items are added to the special systems inspection checklist, giving an added degree of protection. Lastly, the management team begins making tours with a purpose. Lisa helps them focus their attention on specific issues and they spend much of their time talking to people about specific issues.

Joe is pleased with the progress and keeps Henry current on their journey of continual improvement, part of the corporate sustainability initiative.

Key Point Summary

1. Planned inspections of the workplace are perhaps the most traditional tool organizations have used for identifying exposures or hazards.

2. General safety and health inspections are systematic, comprehensive, physical assessments of the workplace. They should be performed on a regular basis and cover all operating and maintenance areas in their entirety at least every two months. Typically, a team inspection is best and provides a good opportunity for employee engagement.

3. A hazard classification system should be used to prioritize exposures identified through the inspection process and provide leadership with guidance on appropriate response.

4. Housekeeping is a proper focus of inspections. Housekeeping doesn't focus on cleanliness alone, but includes equal consideration of orderliness according to the following definition: "A place is in order when there are no unnecessary things about and all necessary things are in their proper place. No in this sentence means none, not any, not even one!"

5. Pre-use equipment inspections, especially on mobile and materials-handling equipment, are critical to control of exposures related to these high-hazard items.

6. Special systems inspections are those performed on things such as fire detection and suppression systems, alarm systems, chemical control systems, emergency shut-down systems, emergency power and lighting, etc. The site must ensure that all required inspections of this type have been identified, accountability assigned to appropriate persons and frequency established.

Personal Planning

1. What responsibilities do I have for our inspection process?

2. How effectively do I carry out those responsibilities?

3. What are the strengths of our inspection process? Opportunities for improvement?

Y – Model for Action Planning

Present Situation

Desired Situation

Need for Change

Present Situation

Stop   Responsibility   Target Date

EMERGENCY PREPAREDNESS AND RESPONSE

Chapter 12

EMERGENCY PREPAREDNESS AND RESPONSE

CHAPTER OBJECTIVES

1. To present best practices for managing an organization's emergency response activity.
2. To emphasize the importance of using a risk management approach to developing the organization's emergency plan.
3. To present the primary components of a comprehensive emergency plan.
4. To provide practical tools for assessing your organization's emergency plan.

He takes his concerns to Joe and Lisa. They agree that the emergency plan is weak and has not been effectively implemented. Joe asks Lisa to research emergency preparedness tools and techniques and produce a report of her recommendations.

One month later, Lisa's report reaches Joe's desk. It is based on the information provided in this chapter.

Carlos is Concerned

Carlos routinely conducts health and safety meetings with his work-group. During one particularly engaging discussion, an employee admits he does not know what to do in certain emergency situations. Other members of the group, emboldened by this individual's openness, begin to express their concerns about emergency issues. Carlos takes notes, but decides to meet one-on-one with some of the more vocal team members and get more detailed responses.

During the next couple of days, Carlos gets a lot of information from discussions with six members of his work-group. He identifies some common concerns including, a lack of refresher training in emergency response, a lack of frequent drills, inadequate postings of emergency instructions, lack of knowledge of where to find emergency-related information, and a lack of qualified first responders on the floor.

Emergency Planing Failure

On 22 December, 2008, at 1:00AM, a dam at a power generation plant near Knoxville, TN in the US, burst. The following paragraph quotes the newspaper story.

"The 40-acre pond was used by the Tennessee Valley Authority to hold a slurry of ash generated by the coal-burning Kingston Steam Plant in Harriman, about 50 miles west of Knoxville. The dam gave way just before 1:00AM, burying a road and railroad tracks leading to the plant under several feet of dark gray mud."
A very disturbing point is discovered in the following statement by a resident of the affected area.

"But what upsets me is they didn't have a plan in place. Why hadn't anybody thought, "What happens if this thing bursts?"

Emergency Response Failure

In April of 2010, the Macondo Well incident in the Gulf of Mexico resulted in the deaths of several workers and an environmental event with devastating impact across a wide area of the US. The official government investigation into the incident revealed significant flaws in emergency preparedness and response. Emergency alarms and shutdown systems failed to function. Emergency equipment was damaged or destroyed in the initial explosion, and backup power could not be started.

Emergency Planing and Response Failure

A tsunami on 11 March 2001, damaged the Fukushima nuclear power plant in Japan. The investigation revealed several flaws in emergency planning and preparedness. Theoretical physicist Robert Rosner, founding director of the Energy Policy Institute at the University of Chicago, summarized a portion those findings as follows:

- There was no provision for tsunami risks in the design basis of the Fukushima reactors (the worst cases for which the design should allow).
- Plant staff was not prepared with detailed emergency procedures, and specifically was not prepared for a loss of plant power situation.
- Staff was also not prepared for loss of cooling and took some actions initially that made things worse rather than better.

Commenting on the poor performance of the on-site team sent by Tokyo regulators, Rosner said that because there were no detailed emergency plans, the regulators were just as confused as everybody else about what was going on and were, therefore, almost completely ineffective.

Introduction

These examples are extreme events and it is unlikely that any one organization is going to experience an incident on a similar scale. However, similar situations have occurred in many organizations and there are a lot of lessons to be learned from these events. Regardless of the scale of potential events facing any organization, there are fundamental aspects of emergency preparedness and response plans that should be considered inviolate.

Lessons Learned

On the subject of dealing with emergency planning failures, the US Federal Emergency Management Agency (FEMA) website states the following:

In order to deal effectively with any planning failure, it is first necessary to understand how and why they typically occur.

The primary, relevant failures are:
- A failure to learn;
- A failure to adapt; and
- A failure to anticipate.

Flaws causing emergency planning failures include:
- Lack of imagination;
- Faulty assumptions;
- Analysis paralysis;
- A desire to protect the status quo;
- "Turf" battles;
- Complacency;
- Lack of risk awareness;
- Ignoring all warnings;
- Executive mindset to avoid change;
- A "group-think" mentality that seemingly forces us to move with the crowd;
- A failure to act on valid warnings; and
- The belief that government will somehow protect us all from every danger.

To plan effectively, we must replace assumptions with facts, anticipate the future, adapt to the present, and learn from the past. In addition, we must develop leaders while conserving and making the best use of all resources, including funds. In recent years, we have thrown emergency preparedness funds at states, counties, and cities without having an overall plan or effective accountability. In brief, we have been experiencing a series of planning failures.

Education and coaching in effective emergency planning needs to be a top priority for our emergency managers, as well as other leaders in government. If we cannot learn to successfully plan for emergencies, then we should anticipate more disaster response failures similar to what we have seen in recent years.

This information is based on FEMA's experience with emergencies occurring in the public sector and managed by governmental organizations; however, emergency management failure analysis in the private sector produces similar findings.

The examples given in the Introduction sub-heading of this chapter are evidence that many organizations are not adept at developing and effectively maintaining systematic and comprehensive emergency plans. The overall objective of this chapter is to provide information on how your organization can avoid all-too-common pitfalls in your emergency preparedness and response program.

Developing a Plan

The process used to develop the emergency plan is the same as that presented in the chapter on Risk Management: identify the possibilities, assess the risk in each possibility, and develop a plan for each possibility determined to require controls.

Identification of Potential Emergencies

In order to properly identify potential emergencies, a systematic and comprehensive approach must be taken. Management systems auditors within our organization (DNV GL) have frequently found emergency plans that address only a very limited number of situations and which do not cover all appropriate, potential emergency needs. Such plans sometimes only deal with fire and weather emergencies, including evacuation and shelter in place plans. Some organizations are very focused and proficient at addressing potential emergencies involving their specific hazardous materials, but do not necessarily

Figure 12.1: PEME: Four Subsystems of Loss

consider situations that other organizations might routinely address. Because the hazards presented by chemical substances usually have a higher profile, they may be sufficiently addressed in the plan while other potential situations are not.

A good guideline in the development of a comprehensive emergency plan is for the organization to understand and use the four categories of loss potential as illustrated in Figure 12.1 above.

Known by the acronym PEME, these four categories serve to remind the organization to consider all possibilities when identifying risks or threats.

All locations or units, even within the same organization, have unique exposures and, therefore, require site-specific emergency plans. Plans generated at the corporate level generally are insufficient for site application and should be used only as templates. Each individual location in an organization should develop a site-specific listing or inventory of the specific components in each category present at the site. Although examination of each individual component would reveal many emergency response needs, it is the interaction of these components that must be closely evaluated. Each individual component in each of the categories should be compared with the other components in other categories to identify emergency response needs. For instance, there might be a simple task to change a light bulb. Under normal circumstances, this task would not be perceived as requiring any special emergency response need. However, if the light bulb is on a tower seventy-five feet above ground level, the potential exists for the person performing the task to become incapacitated. This would constitute a specific emergency need, that being, high-rise rescue to include providing first aid in an aloft position.

Using Inventories

Each site should develop four inventories; that is, systematic and comprehensive listings related to each of the PEME components.

Task Inventory

This involves a complete task listing of all work performed by each category of employee. The task listing can then be used to identify potential response needs such as rescue.

Equipment Inventory

The next inventory is a complete listing of all equipment. The equipment list can be analyzed to identify the potential for violent or unexpected failures that could result in incidents.

Materials Inventory

The third inventory is a complete listing of all materials on-site. Chemical substances used in the process or produced by the process, as well as raw materials, should be listed. This listing should include also the maximum amount of each substance that can be on-site at any given time. It is also important to examine the means by which employees or the public can be exposed to hazardous materials. Each material, by itself or in concert with other materials, can produce emergency situations that must be considered in the plan.

Environment or Areas Inventory

The final inventory is the environment or areas list. This is a list of where the work is performed. A task performed in one area may not be perceived as requiring special attention, while the same task performed in another area could become critical. A routine welding task in a maintenance shop may not be perceived as requiring any special emergency planning. However, if the task must be performed in a confined space, a confined space entry procedure, to include special rescue procedures, would be indicated.

Once again, it is the interaction of the four components that presents a special challenge to the identification of emergency needs, but which must be carefully considered if the identification of emergency needs is to be sufficient for use in developing the plan.

Management of Change

Changes in process, administration, or equipment can create health and safety risks. The chapter on Change Management provides more detailed insight and advice on this issue. At this point, it should simply be pointed out that the impact of change on the emergency needs of the organization must be considered and accommodated. The change management process should link to the identification, assessment, control, and monitoring aspects of emergency preparedness. Both permanent and temporary changes must be included.

Types of Potential Emergency Situations

In Figure 12.2 below, you will find a list of general types of emergencies to be considered in the identification of needs process.

- Fire
- Bomb threats
- Disruption of computer system
- Damaged public relations
- Death of a senior manager
- Earthquake
- Weather events
- Flood
- Loss of public utilities
- Espionage
- Kidnapping
- Off-site emergencies
- Product tampering
- Civil unrest
- Sabotage
- Supply chain disruption
- Workplace violence
- Incident involved in disposal of a hazardous substance
- Transportation emergencies
- Truck fleet shut-down by regulator
- Terrorism
- Hazardous material releases

Figure 12.2: Categories of Potential Emergency Situations

Employee Engagement

It is a best practice to involve employees at all levels of the organization in this process. Not only is it possible they will have unique insight into potential situations, engaging them at the outset goes a long way toward obtaining their ownership of the resulting plan and their commitment to apply it appropriately.

Using Risk Assessment

There are obviously a myriad of possible emergency situations that could occur in any specific operation. It would not normally be a good use of resources for any one operation to try to address all possible emergency situations. When systematic identification has been accomplished and a comprehensive list has been developed, the organization should employ its risk assessment process to determine which of these possible situations should be addressed in its plan.

An effective risk assessment process is described in the chapter on Risk Management and will not be repeated here. A risk matrix, supported by risk criteria defined by the individual organization, can be a good tool for assessing emergency needs.

In any case, each organization must determine for itself which specific emergency needs should be addressed in its plan.

Developing a Comprehensive Emergency Plan: Potential Content

From the lease of the top five floors in a high-rise building in a major city to a mining operation in the desert, emergency plans can be simple or complex based on the needs of the organization. The following are examples of items or actions to be described in a comprehensive plan. The specific content of individual plans will be determined by the identified emergency needs. Some of the items in the list below may be contained in documents outside the emergency plan itself, such as a Business Continuity Plan.

Reporting an Emergency

All employees of the site should know how to report each type of emergency. Reporting instructions, even if they are as simple as dialing a central number, should be spelled out in the plan. This includes the location of appropriate alarms and their proper operation. A call list specific to types of emergencies should be provided.

Proper Response

All employees of the site should know the proper response to each type of emergency. If evacuation is indicated, employees must know where to exit, where to muster, head-count procedures, etc. If shelter-in-place is indicated, employees must know where shelters are located.

Emergency Management Responsibilities

Certain qualified persons should be identified as having key roles in managing all types of emergencies. Incident commanders must be identified in the plan, and their identities known to employees. Persons who have specific responsibilities for activities such as hazardous materials control, security, work shut-down, liaison with community responders and authorities, media representatives, emergency team leaders, etc., should be identified in the plan, and their identities known to employees.

Regulatory Agency Notification Procedures

The plan should include clear, specific identification of persons responsible for notifying required regulatory agencies, and the procedures they are to use. It is critical that these persons be thoroughly trained in the procedures.

Certain emergency situations will result in representatives of regulatory agencies being present on the property. There should be written procedures identifying the person or persons who are to be responsible for hosting them, and for how they should interface.

Designation of Primary and Secondary Control Centers

A control center is a central place where the necessary personnel can gather in safety to manage an emergency. The center should be carefully chosen based on its proximity to major exposures and its accessibility. The center should be equipped with supplies crucial to emergency management, such as:

- Blueprints
- P&ID's
- Chemical Substances Inventory and Safety Data Sheets
- Access to electronic data
- Access to primary and backup communication
- Personal protective equipment
- Survival equipment

A secondary control center is important in case the primary center is involved in the emergency itself or inaccessible. Some organizations arrange with outside entities such as local hotels or businesses to locate their secondary control centers off-site.

Lists of Equipment and Supplies Necessary to Respond

The organization should prepare a list of all emergency response equipment and supplies and their location. Best practice is that the organization should conduct a systematic and comprehensive assessment of emergency equipment and supply needs at least every three years. This assessment is not for the purpose of ensuring that all identified equipment or supplies are on-hand. It is for the purpose of making sure that all equipment and supplies required by potential emergencies have been identified and supplied appropriately.

Emergency equipment and supplies should be on inspection checklists so that their condition, appropriateness, accessibility, and storage are checked regularly.

In some cases, it may be necessary for specialized emergency equipment, not regularly owned or maintained by either the organization or community responders, to be used in rescue. Such was the case on the evening of July 17, 1981. at the newly constructed Hyatt Regency Hotel in Kansas City, Missouri. Part of the structure collapsed, resulting in 114 fatalities and 219 injuries. Heavy steel beams trapped many people, and rescuers were prevented from getting to them because they could not move the collapsed beams. There was significant delay in providing medical attention. Cranes were eventually obtained and used to move the steel beams. As result of this event, the fire department of Kansas City identified cranes that are owned in the city and the surrounding area. Contact was made with the owners, and an agreement was created that they would respond to an event if called upon by the fire department.

The organization should ensure that all equipment and supplies not maintained on the property are conveniently available.

List of Internal and External Emergency Response Teams

The plan should identify all emergency response teams and specify their roles and how they are to interact. Leaders of each team should be identified, along with all available contact information.

Training Requirements

The plan should identify all training needs for employees, incident commanders, organizational leadership, etc. Both initial and refresher training should be defined along with requirements for when and how often such training must be conducted. The chapter on Task Competencies, Analysis and Training provides detailed guidance on how the organization might identify training needs and ensure that proper training is carried out.

The organization's orientation or induction process should include a significant component on emergency response. The general orientation should provide information on the overall plan for the operation. A job-specific orientation, usually provided by the employee's immediate supervisor, should include information on specific emergency response required in the employee's department or work area.

Best practice is that annual refresher training is provided to all employees.

Work Shutdown Procedures

Some work processes and equipment can become dangerous when left unattended in operating condition. The plan should define how work processes and equipment are to be shut down or made safe in the event that an evacuation is necessary.

In some operations, emergency shutdown might be a simple as activating a button or switch. Other operations might require a series of steps to bring the process down to an acceptable level of operation before evacuating operators.

Drill Schedule

The plan should specify what types of drills are to be conducted, persons responsible for managing the drills, and a timetable.

Training in emergency procedures is essential, and is typically provided beginning in the employee orientation or induction process and continuing on a regular basis. However, the effects of initial or even refresher training can be relatively short-lived unless supported with some periodic reinforcement.

Drills help ensure that, when an actual emergency occurs, people respond in proper ways and do not revert to overreaction, panic, or emotional responses.

The frequency with which drills should be conducted should be based on the relative probability of a specific type of event. For example, most organizations have fire and weather exposures and would conduct some type of drill related to those exposures at least every six months, perhaps quarterly. Other emergency situations might be drilled annually.

Lessons Learned System

A lessons learned system is critical to the sustainability of the emergency management activity. The emergency plan should define how such a system is to work and designate persons responsible for the system.

Following a drill or actual emergency, representatives of all responding entities involved, including employees, should conduct a lessons learned session. This is a structured evaluation of the effectiveness and timeliness of the response, identification of problems or deficiencies, and development of corrective and preventive actions.

The 11 September 2001, attacks in the US revealed a serious deficiency in many organizations' emergency plans. Although it could legitimately be argued that no organization could have foreseen such an event and planned for it, many organizations realized afterward that they had no plans in place to respond to a national emergency. They became concerned about issues such as how to account for persons traveling on behalf of the organization, arranging alternative travel and/or accommodations for traveling personnel, communicating with all facilities or entities within the organization, making decisions on short-term business continuity, etc. Commercial resources have since been developed, providing emergency management services to organizations for some of these concerns.

An organization can always learn from experience, and should take the opportunity to do so in an organized way.

Procedures for Communication with the Community

The community is a critical stakeholder in any organization. Certain types of emergency situations can quickly raise questions and concerns. The plan should specify who is responsible for coordinating communication with the community, media, and local government representatives, and establish procedures by which information will be managed.

Emergencies in some types of industries have the potential to require shelter-in-place or evacuation procedures for the surrounding community. In a case where such eventualities must be considered, it is important that the organization establishes a plan of action with the community and ensures that all neighbors know how to respond. Traffic patterns for ease of evacuation should be established. Neighbors should know how to ensure their property is safe before leaving; that is, making sure gas is turned off and all ignition sources made safe. They should be instructed on what supplies to bring with them, such as medications. They should be reminded to ensure the safety of pets. The organization could develop and provide the residents with a checklist of items and actions to consider in the need to evacuate. Residents with special needs, such as the wheelchair-bound or persons restricted to bed, should be identified and made known to agencies that would be needed to evacuate persons with special needs.

Residents who are evacuated or sheltered should be provided with convenient phone and/or e-mail contact information where up-to-date information on the status of the emergency can be obtained. The organization should establish pre-existing procedures for using local media to keep the public informed.

Procedures for shelter-in-place and instructions on how to protect the health and safety of family members should be established and communicated.

All-clear and re-entry procedures should be established for residents.

Internal Communications

Employees will have their own questions and concerns. Failure to provide information in a timely manner can result in employees developing their own explanations of what is happening and increase their concerns for their own safety. The plan should establish procedures for how such information is to be provided and specify the responsible person(s). Communication procedures with headquarters and other organizational entities should be developed.

Notification of Personal Emergency Contacts

The organization should maintain records on all employees that list primary and secondary contact information. The emergency plan should identify person(s) responsible for making notification in case of injury or illness, and those persons should be trained in how to handle these delicate conversations, both in person and by phone.

Notification to Other Interested Parties

Procedures for notification of insurance carriers, legal advisors, and similar entities should be defined in the plan.

Control of Energy Sources

The plan should contain documents such as drawings, blueprints, or P&ID's that include the specific location of valves, switches, or other devices that control energy sources such as electricity, gas, and water. In addition, these devices should be color-coded and labeled for ease of location and identification. Responsible persons should be designated to operate these devices, and trained on the conditions under which their operation is required.

First Aid and Medical Response Requirements

All persons who are qualified as first aid or medical responders should be identified in the plan. Their work locations and contact information should be included. The names, locations, and contact information for these persons should be posted and/or made immediately available to all employees.

Some exposures require specialized first aid and medical procedures. These exposures must be identified in the initial activity discussed earlier in this chapter. The necessary supplies and specialized training for these exposures must be ensured.

Organized Outside Help and Mutual Aid

Procedures for working with persons or entities who might respond to an emergency from outside the organization should be established.

The organization should consider a proactive approach to fire, hazardous materials, and medical responders who would be called on in an emergency. Many organizations have established a regular process of communication with these entities. The process includes activities such as annual meetings and tours of the organization's facilities. Representatives of potential emergency responders are invited to a presentation on the manufacturing processes, health and safety risks, hazardous materials data, etc. A tour helps familiarize these persons with the physical layout of facilities, primary and secondary access points, etc. They are provided with copies of the organization's chemical substances inventory and plant layout. Physicians and hospitals are made aware of the types of exposures in the organization and specific injuries or illnesses they should expect. These meetings might also include mock drills to practice the plan. Such activities help ensure a more prompt and proper response to any emergency.

Mutual aid agreements should be included in the plan for quick reference. A mutual aid agreement is typically a written document of understanding that details the circumstances under which private organizations would provide aid and assistance to other private organizations, and the types of aid and assistance they will provide. Most often, private organizations are not going to provide fire-fighting, rescue, or hazardous materials control assistance to their neighbors. However, they may be willing to lend equipment, expertise, emergency management space, temporary storage space, and other assistance. There are exceptions, of course. In some areas where there are a number of similar industries, such as petrochemical operations, in close proximity, organizations may actually be willing to assist with on-site emergency response. Mine rescue teams are well-known for their willingness and ability to insert themselves into emergencies outside their own company.

Back-Up Communication Arrangements

In case of failure of primary communications technology, there should be provision made for secondary means of maintaining contact with all appropriate parties.

All Clear and Re-entry Procedure

The plan should define the circumstances under which the emergency is declared to be over and how all employees are to be notified they can return to work. A person or persons should be designated to communicate this information.

Stress Counseling

Consideration should be given to the potential need for counseling following particularly traumatic events. Employees and responders may well need resources to help them deal with the psychological and emotional issues that can result from such events. The organization should identify available counseling resources and develop working relationships that enable quick response.

The Impact of Modern Technology

The availability of mobile phones, tablets, etc., has created a relatively new issue that must be managed by an organization. Not only can the use of these devices on the job create risk and contribute to incidents, it can also prove problematic in managing the release of information following an incident or emergency. Most of these devices have cameras. When allowed to be carried on the job, this makes it very easy for anyone to take unauthorized pictures and communicate them, along with comments, outside the organization. Such actions create and support the rumor mill and can cast the organization in a less than favorable light.

The organization should carefully consider how the potential for unauthorized information could be controlled. Guidelines should be included in the emergency plan.

Emergency Response Teams

Some organizations may determine a need to develop specialized emergency response teams based on specific emergency potentials. Organizations that perform a lot of work at height may decide to develop a team dedicated to high work rescue. Others, based on fire potential, may decide to train and equip an internal fire brigade. Still other organizations, because of their chemical storage requirements, may develop teams to respond to releases or spills. Mines, especially underground operations, have long invested in development and training of rescue teams. However, it may be completely appropriate for any organization, outside of legal requirements, to decide that such teams put their people at unnecessary and unacceptable risk and, therefore, decline to use them.

Should any organization determine the need for specialized emergency response teams, the guidelines in Figure 12.3 can be helpful.

> **GUIDELINES FOR SELECTING RESPONSE TEAM MEMBERS**
>
> 1. Members should be physically capable to perform response duties.
> 2. A leader should be designated for each response team.
> 3. Training objectives should be identified and conducted to ensure proper response.
> 4. Necessary equipment must be provided and maintained to include PPE.
> 5. There should be enough response team members to ensure full coverage allowing for sickness and vacations on all shifts.
> 6. Drills should be scheduled and conducted with documentation of results and actions taken to address weaknesses in the response.
> 7. Team members should be familiar with procedures to shut-down operations to minimized severity.

Figure 12.3: Guidelines for Selecting Emergency Response Team Members

Business Continuity Planning

The scope of this book is health and safety. Business continuity planning is concerned with much more than health and safety, but there are certainly health and safety issues that should be addressed in a business continuity plan. For example:

- How any physical facilities that may have been damaged in an emergency are to be restored to an acceptable state so that the health and safety of cleanup and restoration personnel is protected.
- Procedures for evaluating the health and safety risks of the site to determine under what conditions employees may return.
- How the health and safety impacts of a specific emergency on all stakeholders is to be assessed and controlled.
- The roles of health and safety staff in managing the aftermath of an emergency.

Crisis Management

A crisis is defined as an emergency situation that escalates to the point where the survival of the organization is threatened. While all of the advice in this chapter is applicable to such a situation, it is vital that the organization develop a crisis management plan (in addition to, or as a part of, the emergency plan) to include any special needs for these extreme situations.

A crisis management plan would include many of the same activities listed previously, but would also include development and training of a crisis management team. Members of such a team would typically consist of senior leadership in operations, legal, human resources, sales and customer relations, public relations, etc.

Tool Box: Emergency Plan Assessment

The following is a brief checklist that can be used to perform a high-level assessment of your organization's emergency preparedness plan. This is not to be considered a complete or comprehensive assessment.

Assessment Checklist

1. Do we have a written document, signed by the senior manager, assigning responsibility for administering the emergency preparedness and response activity?
2. Have we assigned departmental or sectional coordinators to administer the emergency plan in their areas of responsibility?
3. Have we conducted risk identification and assessment to identify the probable emergency situations for which our specific operation should prepare?
4. Did the risk identification and assessment activity include consideration of off-site emergencies as well as emergency potential presented by neighboring industries or activities?
5. Was a comprehensive emergency response plan developed to address all emergency situations identified as probable for our operation?
6. Were representatives of all stakeholders (leadership, employees at all levels, the community, emergency response resources, etc.) have been engaged in the development of the plan?
7. Does the plan include, at a minimum:
    a. Procedures for reporting all types of emergencies?
    b. Designation of roles and responsibilities for emergency response?
    c. Training requirements for all personnel, based on their roles and responsibilities?
    d. Consideration for the protection of people including shelter-in-place and evacuation procedures?
    e. Systematic shutdown of hazardous operations?
    f. The management of hazardous materials?
    g. Communication with and protection of the surrounding community?
    h. Information management?
    i. Procedures for interaction with emergency responders?
8. Does the emergency plan establish an appropriate schedule for drills in all types of emergency situations?
9. Do documentation and interviews confirm the drill schedule is being met and is appropriate to maintain a high level of confidence in knowledge and skill?
10. Does the plan establish requirements for emergency lighting and power resources?
11. Does documentation confirm that all emergency lighting and power are tested on a regular basis and maintained in proper operating condition?
12. Have all master control valves and switches for energy sources (electricity, water, gas, etc.) have been both color-coded and labeled for ease of identification?

Figure 12.4: Assessment Checklist

Tool Box: Relationship of the Emergency Plan to other Health and Safety Activities

Every element or activity in an organization's health and safety management system has a synergistic relationship with all other elements. They do not operate in isolation, and their interaction can have both positive and negative effects. The organization's emergency plan has implications for other elements. The information below can be used to help the organization understand those implications and take advantage of the opportunity to keep all elements in balance.

Knowledge and Skills Training

A review of the emergency plan should be conducted to identify training needs.

Purchasing

Specifications should be developed to guide the purchase of emergency equipment to ensure it meets the specific needs of the organization.

Preventive Maintenance

All emergency equipment must be inspected and tested regularly to ensure that it maintains operating condition.

Specialized Work Permit System

When a piece of emergency equipment is taken out of service for maintenance or is unavailable for any reason, a work permit that identifies and ensures readiness of backup systems should be issued.

Task Analysis

Tasks that must be performed during emergency situations should be assessed, and those deemed critical should be thoroughly analyzed, and procedures developed.

Task and Behavior Observations

Observations of both critical tasks and critical behaviors during drills are important to identify and correct deficiencies, as well as to provide the opportunity for positive behavior reinforcement.

Personal Protective Equipment

Potential emergency situations may well demand that specialized PPE such as self-contained breathing devices or chemical handling suits be provided. These also require training in proper use.

Planned Inspections

Inspection checklists should include critical emergency equipment and supplies.

Change Management

Any change in equipment, structures, procedures, process, or administration has the potential to affect the emergency plan. The change management process should trigger a review of the emergency plan.

Carlos is Confident

A few months after expressing his group's concerns, Carlos has seen significant improvement in the organization's emergency preparedness activity. There has been a thorough review and revision of the emergency plan, based on systematic risk assessment. Training in the updated plan has been completed for all employees. Drills in various aspects of the plan are being conducted monthly. A member of senior leadership has been designated as the person responsible for ensuring effective management of the plan. A lessons-learned system has been put in place and the health and safety committee now has the responsibility to audit the plan annually.

Carlos has just concluded a meeting with his team in which they expressed greater confidence in their understanding of how the plan is to work. He visits with Joe to discuss progress.

"I really want to thank you for what the organization has done with our emergency preparedness plan in the last few months. My people are feeling better about it, too."

"You know, Carlos, it was your initiative that started it all and I thank you for doing that. Can I ask, what drove your concern?" asked Joe.

"Well, I guess the feedback from my team was the most immediate thing, but I also have a past personal experience that has made emergency preparedness more important for me in the last few years. You see, before I moved here and took this job, my brother and I worked together at a manufacturing plant in our hometown. One day, he was seriously injured when he got trapped in rotating equipment. No one on the floor knew what to do, the plant manager was away, and there was no one who took charge. It took a lot longer to get emergency services to him than it should. He was permanently disabled and his family has really suffered because of it. I have always believed that, if help had come sooner, he might not be in that situation today. After his injury, the company did take some steps to improve their plan, but it was too late for him. I just didn't want that to happen here."

"You did the right thing. I am going to recommend to Harry that all our plant locations take similar steps to what we have done here. Would you be willing to talk to him with me? It would be more powerful coming from someone with your experience and first-hand knowledge of what's going on out on the floor."

"Sure. I think our health and safety progress is a good thing for the company and I'd like to see our influence continue."

"Okay. I'll set it up and let you know. And, thanks again! I feel confident that we are properly prepared."

"So do I. By the way, can you come to my team meeting next Wednesday and thank them for starting this discussion? We meet at eight a.m."

"Will do. See you at Tom's birthday party this afternoon."

Key Point Summary

1. A proper emergency plan is based on systematic, comprehensive identification of exposures that would require emergency response.
2. The Risk Management chapter can help you understand how risk management thinking and technology can improve your organization's emergency planning.
3. A comprehensive emergency plan should address things such as:
    a. How to report an emergency
    b. How to respond to notification of emergency situations
    c. Emergency management responsibilities
    d. Regulatory notification procedures
    e. Designation of control centers
    f. Lists of equipment and supplies necessary to respond to emergency situations
    g. Lists and contact information for both internal and external emergency response teams
    h. Training requirements
    i. Work shut-down procedures
    j. Required drills and schedule
    k. A lessons learned system
    l. Communication procedures with all stakeholders
    m. Control of energy sources
    n. Medical response requirements
    o. Organized outside help and mutual aid agreements
    p. All clear and re-entry procedures
    q. Stress counseling requirements
4. Comprehensive Business Continuity Plans, while not specifically focused on health and safety, are critical to the sustainability of the organization.

Personal Planning

1. Is my organization's emergency plan based on a systematic, comprehensive assessment of needs?
2. Is my organization's emergency plan comprehensive? Does it address all potential emergency situations? Does it contain provisions for the items listed in this chapter?
3. Do I understand my organization's emergency plan and what my responsibilities are?
4. Do the people with whom I work understand their responsibilities and how to respond to all emergency situations?
5. Do we hold sufficient drills to enable proper response?
6. Do we conduct lessons learned sessions following any emergency or drill?
7. What should we do to improve our emergency planning and response activity?

Y – Model for Action Planning

Present Situation

Desired Situation

Need for Change

Present Situation

Stop Responsibility Target Date

LEARNING FROM EVENTS

Chapter 13

LEARNING FROM EVENTS

> **CHAPTER OBJECTIVES**
>
> 1. To provide advice on the design of an effective incident investigation or learning from events process.
> 2. To provide guidance on developing a proper culture around reporting and investigation of incidents.
> 3. To introduce practical tools to be used to improve reporting and investigation.
> 4. To help develop investigative skills at all levels of leadership.
> 5. To help individuals and organizations benefit from the valuable learning that events, both positive and negative, can provide.

Lisa Expresses Concern

Lisa has been the safety and health manager for the plant for a short time. She has been busy with compliance issues, but is also spending time developing a report for Joe, the plant manager, on ideas for improving the safety and health management system. Among those ideas are some concerns about the quality of incident investigation reports she is seeing. They are cursory, at best, and often stop with identifying unsafe acts or conditions. She meets Joe in the hall and has a brief conversation.

"Joe, I would like to set a time for us to meet and discuss some ideas I have for improving our safety and health management system."

"Good, Lisa. It's time we focused more on improvement than the fire-fighting we've been doing. I know you have been trying to lead us in a more positive direction and I apologize that I haven't paid as much attention as I should. You know these new initiatives and growth targets have taken precedent."

"I know. There are several things I would like to talk about. We don't have time right now, but I do want to bring a specific issue to your attention. Our incident rates are pretty good and showing improvement, but when they do occur, the investigations we are getting are not very good. I am concerned that we are really not investigating and solving problems, just reporting. I would like to set some things in motion to improve in that department."

"You're right. I have noticed the same thing in the reports I have reviewed, but I don't know what to do about it. We provided training a couple years ago."

"Training is part of the problem, but there are some more things I think we need to do. I would like to set up a team to review our entire investigation process and bring it up to current best practice."

"I can support that. Go ahead and choose your team. I would like to be on it by the way."

"Great! Meanwhile, here is some information on best practices for investigation programs I think you will find interesting and helpful to our project. I would like to discuss it with you at our meeting."

"Sounds good. How about Friday afternoon around 2 p.m.?

"See you then!"

Introduction

Incident investigation is a problem-solving process. We intuitively understand the need to examine incidents to identify their basic causes and take proper actions to prevent recurrence, and to minimize risk from similar events. This problem-solving process can also be applied to quality problems, environmental events, production problems, morale problems, etc.

The title of this chapter is Learning from Events. The use of these words is intentional, to promote the idea that the same general approach used for effective investigations can also be used to evaluate successes, identify the factors that drove those successes, and use that information in the design and implementation of future projects.

Developing Your Investigation Process

Some organizations have no formal, written investigation procedure. They have a report form and perhaps some guidance on how it should be completed, but nothing that details how an investigation and related activities should be carried out. The report form itself does not constitute an investigation procedure. A comprehensive investigation procedure should contain:

1. Specific explanation of the types of incidents that must be reported (injuries, illnesses, property damage, process loss, product loss, contamination, releases, spills, customer complaints, defects, etc.). Effective investigation processes cover all types of loss and near-loss events.

2. Clear instructions on how these various types of events should be reported.

3. Provision of risk assessment criteria and tools used to determine the appropriate level of investigation required for each individual event. The level of investigation attention given to each individual event should be based on the potential in that event, not on its actual outcome. Most organizations use some type of risk criteria/risk matrix to assess risk in given situations. Those tools can be used to determine the potential of incidents so that proper decisions can be taken on how much effort should be devoted to investigation of individual events.

4. Roles and responsibilities for investigation activities should be defined.

5. Terms such as major injury, major loss, high-potential loss, and high-potential near-miss should be defined. These can be related to the use of the risk assessment criteria mentioned in item three above.

6. The required training for all potential investigators should be specified.

7. Proper methods for gathering information (evidence) should be defined. The organization should determine how witness interviews should be conducted, how photographs

and other documentation should be handled, identify and secure resources for technical examination of tangible evidence, and define how records pertinent to investigations should be secured and assessed.

8. Optional, available resources for information interpretation should be defined. There are numerous root or basic cause analysis tools available. The organization should identify those most appropriate for their needs and provide training in their application. Because each of these tools has both strengths and weaknesses, the organization might want to secure more than one such resource to ensure that all potential analysis needs are covered.

9. A "call tree" or notification process for various types/levels of incidents should be clearly defined, such that all appropriate persons are notified and can respond in a timely manner.

10. A proper corrective and preventive action system, tracking and close-out mechanism should be defined. Most organizations have such systems in place and just need to ensure that they are effectively used for incident investigation purposes.

11. Established report formats and proper routing of all reports should be clear. A standard report form is important to enable for enabling consistency and promoting ease of analysis of incident data.

12. A "lessons-learned" distribution system should be prescribed. It is vital that lessons learned from events be shared in a timely way with all appropriate parts of the organization.

13. There should be defined processes for working with outside and regulatory investigators. In cases where external investigators become necessary, the organization should have pre-determined guidelines for interaction between parties, and responsibility assigned for that interaction.

14. There should be a clear control-of-information process. This would likely be the same process as that defined in the organization's emergency plan, and would help ensure that only appropriate and accurate information is made available to the public.

Developing a Proper Reporting and Investigating Culture

Fundamental Concepts

There are some fundamental concepts that all persons in the organization need to understand if they are to also understand the criticality of reporting and investigating incidents. There are two models which were presented in a previous chapter, but which also have relevance here.

The Incident Ratio Study, Figure 13.1 below, illustrates the need for the organization to pay attention to all loss and potential loss events, not just those that result in significant loss.

The Serious or Major Injury at the top of the pyramid will most certainly be examined in the investigation process. The ten Minor Injuries at the second level include both medical aid (reportable or recordable injuries) and first aid injuries. Some organizations may tend to ignore the lesser of these events, assuming they are not deserving of investigation efforts. Remember, however, best practice is that the determining factor on the extent of investigation is not actual outcome, but potential. Some first aid injuries have the potential, under slightly different circumstances, to recur as serious events and, therefore, deserve detailed investigation.

Property damage incidents, in which there are no injuries involved, do not have the same drivers to investigate as do injury events. There is no emotional aspect to them and there are no regulatory requirements for conducting such investigations. However, many, if not most, property damage incidents have the potential to harm people as well. If an organization experiences incidents in which structures such as roll-up doors and pallets of material are struck and damaged by mobile equipment, the only factor that kept those events from resulting in injury to persons is the fact that no person happened to be standing at the precise spot where the damage occurred. The causes of the incident would still be the same. Only the outcome would be different. Because of their potential to cause injury, many property damage incidents should be thoroughly investigated. There is also an economic reason why these events should be investigated, which will be discussed shortly.

The 600 events illustrated at the base of the pyramid are sometimes called near misses. Some of these events deserve thorough investigation, based on their potential. Remember, the extent of any investigation is determined by potential, not actual outcome. There is a basic principle of management, the Pareto Principle, which states, "The majority (80%) of any group of effects is produced by a relatively small (20%) number of causes." Studies tell us that about 20% of near misses have the potential to result in a serious injury.

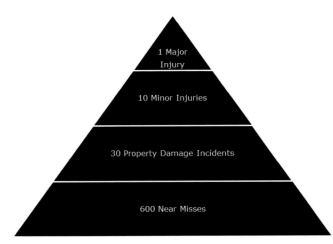

Figure 13.1: Incident Ratio Study

Figure 13.2 below illustrates the economic argument for investigation of property damage incidents. Safety has always been a human thing; that is, our first obligation is to take care of our people and prevent injuries and illnesses. However, we should not apologize for talking about the economic aspects of incidents as well. Although the cost of injury incidents is typically a significant cost of doing business for most organizations, the uninsured cost of property damage and process interruption is much greater, typically five to fifty times greater. If the organization is involved in highly labor-intensive work, the cost of property damage and process interruption may be toward the lower end of the scale. If the organization were involved in highly capital-intensive work, such cost would be toward the upper end of the scale. For example, a meat processing operation will employ a lot of people as butchers. They will work with relatively inexpensive equipment in a labor-intensive environment. Injury events in such environments can be expensive, while damage to the equipment may not be as significant, and damaged knives and other hand tools can be quickly and easily replaced. On the other hand, an operation that uses expensive process equipment to produce chemical products may not expose a lot of people to the hazards of the operation, but damage to the equipment would result in extensive repair and replacement costs, and downtime could be significant.

A third and extremely important concept that needs to permeate the organization at all levels is that incident investigation is a problem-solving exercise, not a blame-fixing, fault-finding exercise. The culture around reporting and investigating incidents must be one in which the investigative effort is directed at determining the basic or root causes and developing effective corrective and preventive actions to prevent recurrence.

This is not to say that individuals should not be held accountable for violations of rules or procedures that may lead to incidents. However, discipline should not be the objective of an investigation. If, in the process of a proper investigation, it is determined that an individual or individuals willingly violated rules or procedures, it may be appropriate to take disciplinary action. Such action is taken, not because the persons involved had an incident, but because they violated requirements.

The Costs of Accidents at Work
ILCI Cost Studies

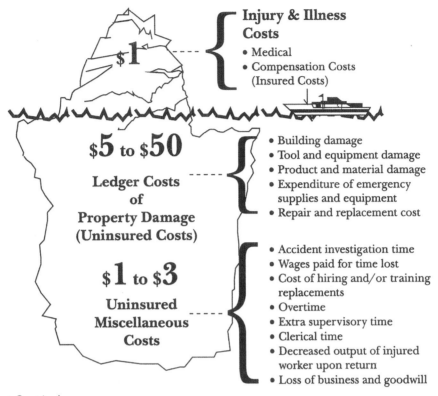

Figure 13.2: Incident Cost Iceberg

Investigators must understand that proper investigation is not necessarily an easy process. Investigations rarely follow a linear pattern of gathering information, doing cause analysis, and developing corrective and preventive actions. Most often, they involve the formation of hypotheses, collection of information, proving or disproving hypotheses, gathering more information, etc. It is a process in which layers of the proverbial onion are gradually peeled back, revealing new information, which leads to new questions and more peeling, until the core of the onion is reached.

Practical Actions

There are several things organizational leadership should do to ensure a proper culture around incident reporting and investigation.

1. All employees should be trained in, and have a basic understanding of:
    a. The concepts of loss causation and control described in the previous sections of this book.
    b. The overall investigation process. They need to understand what is happening and why.
2. All potential investigators should be trained in how to conduct a proper investigation. Training in how to complete the investigation report form does not meet the intent of this recommendation. Such training should include:
    a. How to respond to an incident and get a good investigation started promptly.

b. How to gather evidence or information, including how to conduct witness interviews, how to protect a scene, how to preserve evidence, etc.
   c. How to conduct proper cause analysis.
   d. How to develop appropriate remedial actions.
   e. How to monitor follow-up actions.

Proper handling of an investigation goes a long way toward supporting a positive culture.

3. When appropriate, employee representatives can be an asset to an investigation team. Inclusion of employees on teams facilitates insight into critical information and provides the opportunity for those employees to accurately communicate the progress and findings of the investigation.
4. Within the guidelines for control of information, stakeholders should be kept informed of progress.
5. Follow-up is critical. If stakeholders do not see proper actions taken as a result of an investigation, they begin to legitimately question whether their efforts to report are taken seriously.

Improving Near-Miss Reporting

Near misses are more numerous than actual loss events. They offer more opportunity to learn from and prevent injuries and illnesses, and the causes and potential of near-misses are exactly the same as those o actual loss events. It is vital that the organization develop effective means of capturing as many near-misses as possible, realizing that no organization captures them all.

There are two practical techniques that may help improve near-miss reporting.

Incident Recall Interviews

Private, one-on-one, confidential interviews with all employees in which they are asked to try to recall near-miss incidents that have not been reported can be effective, if the culture in the organization is a positive one.

In this scenario, supervisors conduct brief interviews with each of their direct reports. There are two very important guarantees that must be made if these interviews are to be productive. First, all information is confidential, and no names will be associated with the information in any way. Second, and probably most important, based on the information provided in the interview only, no disciplinary action will be taken against the individual or any other employee. These guarantees must be agreed upon at the highest levels of the organization and consistently employed; otherwise the effort loses its integrity and potentially destroys organizational culture.

Once the guarantees are clear, the supervisor or interviewer simply walks the individual through their workday, providing the opportunity for them to recall events in a structured way. Information is collected and risk assessment is conducted to determine which of the recalled events deserve a complete investigation.

Incident Imaging

This is risk assessment at the working face. Supervisors or other leaders simply ask employees to imagine what could go wrong in their work area. This can be done in a group setting, such as a safety or team meeting. When workers are prompted to simply imagine, all the barriers to reporting are removed, as the events reported have not yet happened, but could. The process can result in quite an extensive list of things that could happen. Leaders will quickly understand that most of the items contributed in the discussion have actually happened. Once again, risk assessment is conducted to determine which of the events on the list deserve a complete investigation.

Understanding Loss Causation

The Loss Causation Model, Figure 13.3 below and introduced earlier, provides a simple means of understanding loss causation. It also provides a visual guide to the steps in an investigation.

The investigation process follows the model from right to left. It proceeds from identifying all losses associated with the event being investigated, to identifying all the contacts which resulted in the losses, to identifying immediate causes (substandard acts or practices and substandard conditions), to identifying the basic, root, or underlying causes, to understanding the role that the management system played in loss causation and potential control.

The same process can be effective as a tool for learning from successes. In that case, the model would prompt the user to identify the specific positive outcomes of the event or project being evaluated, the specific events which resulted in those outcomes, the acts or conditions which contributed to success, the basic causes which prompted the acts or conditions, and the role that the management system played in providing the culture, resources, planning, etc.

"Many accident investigations make the same mistake in defining causes. They identify the widget that broke or malfunctioned, then locate the person most closely connected with the technical failure; the engineer who miscalculated an analysis, the operator who missed signals or pulled the wrong switches, the supervisor who failed to listen, or the manager who made bad decisions. When causal chains are limited to technical flaws and individual failures, the ensuing responses aimed at preventing a similar event in the future are equally limited: They aim to fix the technical problem and replace or retrain the individual responsible. Such corrections lead to a misguided and potentially disastrous belief that the underlying problem has been solved."

The Columbia Accident Investigation Board, 2003

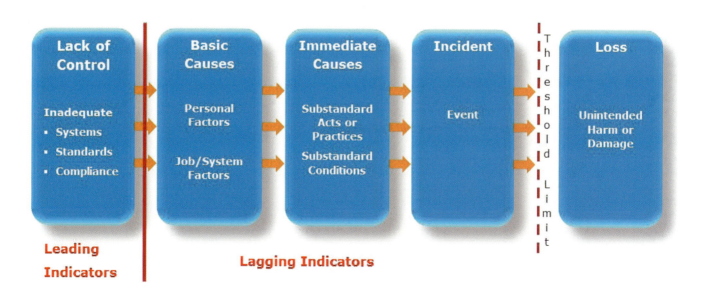

Figure 13.3: Loss Causation Model

Steps or Phases in Investigations

There are essentially eight steps or phases to a proper investigation. The quality and effectiveness of each step or phase is largely dependent on the quality and effectiveness of the previous steps or phases. Figure 13.4 outlines these steps.

Initial Response
- Quite often the success of an investigation is determined in the first few moments following an incident. A proper response is necessary to both take care of people and get a good investigation started.

Initial Walk-Through
- Take a few moments to get the big picture. Avoid the temptation to start picking up and examing evidence. To do so runs the risk of compromising the information.

Gather Evidence
- There are four sources of evidence to be considered in any investigation. Avoid the temptation to focus too much or put too much credibility on one single source.

Conduct Cause Analysis
- Effective cause analysis is not an intuitive exercise and largely depends on having gathered valuable and appropriate information.

Develop Corrective and Preventative Actions
- Development of effective and appropriate corrective and preventive actions largely depends on accurate analysis of both immediate and basic or root causes.

Complete the Investigation Report
- The report is only a report of what you found out in the investigation. It is not the investigation itself.

Distribute Lessons Learned
- Share what you have learned in the investigation process with those who may be faced with the same or similar exposures.

Complete and Assess Follow-Up Actions
- Ensure that all corrective and preventive measures have been completed and assess their effectiveness.

Figure 13.4

The Initial Response

There are several actions to be taken when an incident occurs. Not all of these actions are appropriate in every case and they may not always be taken in the same order, depending on the specific situation. The effectiveness with which these actions are taken can affect the outcome of an investigation. The critical actions include:

1. Respond promptly and positively. In some cases, there will be an active incident scene at which persons are injured and/or property is damaged. In other cases, the investigator may be acting in response to an individual's physical complaint or report of recently discovered property damage, where there is no active scene. In either case, the responsible person's visible response to the incident can affect the attitudes of employees and the culture of the organization. Care must be taken to respond in a way that doesn't place blame or demonstrate extreme frustration.

2. Take control of the scene. The responsible person, usually the immediate supervisor, should remain calm and direct all actions in orderly fashion.

3. Provide care for injured or ill employees. If the incident has resulted in injury or illness, the primary concern is immediate and appropriate care for affected persons.

4. Prevent the secondary incident. A secondary incident is one that occurs as a result of conditions created by the initial or primary incident. For example, an automobile crashes into an electrical power pole, which falls down and causes live wires to come in contact with the automobile. A well-intentioned responder immediately tries to check on passengers in the automobile and is electrocuted. Often, the secondary incident is more serious than the primary. Leaders must learn to recognize the risks present at the scene and take prompt actions to control those risks.

5. Identify and preserve sources of evidence or information. Some evidence is very fragile and can easily be lost or compromised. It is extremely important that the responsible person at the scene identify physical evidence that must be preserved and/or collected quickly. Such evidence includes the spatial relationships of equipment, materials, and persons, as well as items that should be collected for technical examination.

6. Notify appropriate persons. The organization should have developed a list or call tree of persons to be notified in case of specific types of emergencies or incidents.

7. Please note that the first four steps above are for the purpose of making the scene safe and protecting people. As soon as these steps are completed, the investigation begins immediately. Quite often, the success of an investigation is determined in the first few minutes.

In some work environments, especially where work is done remotely from defined plant perimeters by crews in the field, beginning a proper investigation immediately is a bit more difficult. Crews in those situations need to be trained and equipped to do at least a preliminary collection of information, so that ultimately the investigators can have some degree of confidence in the information with which they are working.

Conduct an Initial Walk-Through

An investigation can be negatively affected if those on scene quickly begin picking up physical evidence and rushing to judgment. Best practice is for the initial investigators to pause for a brief period, conduct a quick walk-through of the scene, and get the big picture. Investigators should look over the scene to identify any sources of evidence they will need to collect. In some instances, they need to listen for background noises and identify any smells that may be important.

As the walk-through is conducted, investigators may begin making lists of evidence. They may also begin making at least mental lists of potential causes of the incident. This is somewhat natural, and may be OK as long as they are willing to discard items on their list as evidence proves otherwise, or add items as evidence develops.

Gathering Evidence or Information

There are four sources of evidence that should be gathered and evaluated in any investigation. They are:

1. Position Evidence – Position evidence actually includes two distinct types, spatial and temporal. Spatial evidence involves the physical scene, and questions such as:
    a. Where did everything end up?
    b. How far did a specific piece of physical evidence travel from the initial point of contact?
    c. How far was the affected person from the piece of equipment?
    d. How far was the person from an appropriate escape route or place of safety?
    e. Was there any item or material present that should not have been?
    f. Was there any essential item or material that was missing from the scene?

Temporal evidence involves the construction of time-lines, and essentially asks questions such as:

   a. At what point in a series of events did the incident occur?
   b. Were there any indications of a developing problem that should have been identified?
   c. Was this a stand-alone event or the culmination of a series of events?
   d. How promptly and effectively was the incident controlled?

2. People Evidence – People evidence consists of witness information.
3. Parts Evidence – Parts evidence consists of any physical evidence that needs to be collected for a technical examination, such as hand tools that are broken, pipes that are corroded, or liquids that are spilled.
4. Paper Evidence – Paper Evidence essentially involves records that may exist in paper or electronic form. Types of potential paper or records evidence include task procedures, training records, maintenance logs, work schedules, etc.

These four sources are listed in the order in which they tend to disappear or be compromised. Attempts should be made to protect and gather this information accordingly.

One of the major mistakes commonly made by investigators is to rely too much on witness information. It is not necessarily the most reliable source, and can be either confirmed or contradicted by the other sources.

Position Evidence

Of the four sources of evidence, position evidence is the most fragile. The instinct following an incident is to clean up as soon as possible and get back in operation. People present at the scene may move or remove items that could be crucial to the investigation.

It will sometimes be necessary to move items and disturb the scene in order to rescue people. The best practice, however, is: If you don't have to move it, don't move it.

Spatial evidence is best captured by drawing sketches or maps and taking photographs of the scene. Until such methods can be employed, it is vital that the scene be protected by actions such as marking off the area with hazard tape, posting signs, stationing persons at strategic points to monitor the scene, and removing extraneous personnel from the area.

A sketch is a quick drawing of the scene. It is not drawn to scale and need not be too detailed. Sketches are not the preferred method of capturing this evidence, but may suffice in the absence of photography resources. In today's work environment, unless restricted for safety or trade secret reasons, cell phone cameras are often readily available.

A map is also a drawing, but will be more detailed than a simple sketch, and will be drawn as close to scale as possible, using precise physical measurements. Maps may supplement photographic evidence in that they provide accurate measurement of distances and dimensional relationships not readily discernible in photographs. In addition to maps of the physical scene, maps of conditions such as temperature and noise variables can be very helpful.

Photography is the preferred method for preserving spatial evidence. There are several tips for proper and effective use of photography.

1. Take photographs from all sides of the scene.
2. Take a series of three photographs from each position; long-range, medium, and close-up. Put an object of known size in the close-up to give correct perspective.
3. If there are true eyewitnesses to the incident, stand where they say they were standing and take a photograph from their perspective. This will help you interpret their statements as you conduct interviews.
4. Photograph all parts or items that will need a technical examination before they are moved to document their original condition.
5. Keep a log of all photographs. Make a note relating to each photograph: What the intended subject or focus is, when it was taken, etc.

Many organizations have internal, legal restrictions on the use of photography in the workplace. Be sure to seek the advice of legal council for how photographs of incident scenes should be handled.

People Evidence

Witnesses are people who know something related to what happened. Some people are eyewitnesses who were involved in the incident, or who were present and actually saw the incident occur. True eyewitnesses are relatively rare. The thing that most often attracts a person's attention to an incident is noise. If a pedestrian is standing on a street corner and they hear the squeal of tires and a crash, they naturally turn toward the noise looking for the source. Quite often, such persons will claim to be an eyewitness when, in fact, they did not see the event. They heard the event and saw the aftermath. It is natural for human beings to fill in the gaps and come to a quick conclusion about how things happened. These witnesses' stories are largely a product of their assessment of the situation, and not an accurate accounting of the event.

Investigators often put too much credence in eyewitness accounts. Sometimes witness statements are the only source of evidence considered. The other three sources of evidence are critical, and can either confirm or contradict information gathered from people. All four sources must be considered in any investigation.

The following are practical steps in gathering people evidence.

1. Identify all potential witnesses. A witness is anyone who knows anything about the people, equipment, materials, or work environment involved in the incident. Aside from eyewitnesses, additional witnesses may be people who designed facilities, purchased equipment, performed maintenance on the equipment, trained the operator, or operate the equipment on another shift.

2. Interview the witnesses as quickly as possible. People evidence is fragile and can easily change when people are given too much time to rationalize or analyze their information, or allowed the opportunity to talk to co-workers about the incident. People forget, and some are easily influenced to think differently about what they know.

3. Prior to the interview, spend some time thinking about the personality of the witness you are about to interview. If the investigator understands the witness's basic personality, they can adjust their approach accordingly. For example, if the investigator is about to interview a person they know is essentially an introvert, they may realize they need to be patient and encouraging, using more probing questions. Similarly, the extrovert witness will probably require some measure of control, and the information is more likely to be a product of that person's need to be heard and credible than it is an accurate accounting of what actually happened.

4. The setting for witness interviews can be important. Sometimes it is advantageous to interview at the scene of the incident. This can aid the witness in recalling critical details, and aid the interviewer in understanding the context of the information. If it is not possible or desirable to interview at the scene, the interviewer should ensure a comfortable, non-confrontational environment. Group interviews should be avoided. Witnesses can easily be intimidated in group settings. Sometimes there are natural leaders in the group who will dominate the discussion and distort information.

5. The first question in a witness interview is not really a question. It is a request. The interviewer should explain the purpose of the interview and try, as much as possible, to put the witness at ease with the process. The interviewer should then present the opportunity for the witness to talk. For example, "Can you please tell me what you know, what you heard, what you saw?" As the witness talks, the interviewer can begin developing follow-up and probing questions to explore the details. While some preparation is desirable, it is a bit dangerous to approach the interview with a pre-existing list of specific questions and simply write in the answers.

6. Learn to take good notes. Avoid using video or audio recorders. They make people uncomfortable and you run the risk of compromising information.

7. Ask the closed-end, probing questions at the right time to fill in details.

8. Use photographs, maps, etc., to prompt the witness to provide specific information and help them recall details.

9. Ask the witness for their ideas on how similar incidents could be prevented.

10. Thank the witness for their cooperation.

11. Encourage the individual to return to you if they think of anything else that may be important.

12. Evaluate the information you gather from witnesses in light of the information you have gathered from the other three sources of evidence.

Parts Evidence

Parts evidence includes any items of tangible, physical evidence that may need to be examined. Examples are broken tools, damaged equipment, corroded pipes, and spilled liquids.

These items need to be identified as quickly as possible following the incident and preserved from alteration or removal.

Some of this evidence can be evaluated rather easily. For example, a worker is using an adjustable wrench in a tight space. He has to use significant pressure to break a bolt loose. Under pressure, the wrench breaks and the worker's hand is jammed into the space, resulting in broken fingers. The wrench will need to be examined. The investigator looks at the wrench and discovers the broken tine. Along the edge of the break, part of the surface is bright and shiny, but part of the edge is discolored. This is ample evidence that there was a pre-existing crack in the wrench.

Other parts evidence will need to be sent to qualified persons, perhaps specialists, for examination. For example, a corroded pipe breaks, spraying caustic liquid on a worker. The pipe will need to be examined. A corrosion specialist or metallurgist would be able to answer such questions as how long the corrosion has taken to develop, what agent was causing the corrosion, how the potential breakage could have been detected, etc. It is best practice for the organization to identify sources for these kinds of evaluation beforehand.
Tips for handling this type of evidence include the following:

1. Identify all parts or items that should be examined.
2. Prevent those parts or items from being disturbed or altered. This can be accomplished by using hazard tape to mark an area, putting up signs, and stationing people at appropriate points to keep watch.
3. Take a photograph of the part or item before it is ever moved to record its original condition.
4. Mark the location of each part or item on a map to document the location in which it was found.
5. Preserve the part or item in its original condition. Do not clean parts or items before the evaluation can be conducted. Plastic bags, cups, and other containers should be readily available for this purpose.
6. Label or tag each part or item with information, such as where and when it was found, who found it, who has had custody of it from the date of identification until the investigation is complete, and all related issues such as legal concerns.

Paper Evidence (Records)

Paper evidence or records hold clues that indicate the basic or root causes of incidents. In a previous chapter, we introduced the concept that basic causes can be divided into two categories: personal factors and job or system factors. Included in those categories are potential causes such as inadequate physical or mental capability, lack of knowledge or skill, stress, inadequate engineering, inadequate purchasing, and inadequate work standards. The investigator will most likely find or confirm these basic or root causes in training records, work schedules, engineering, and management of change documents, purchasing records, and operating procedures.

This type of evidence is not at the scene of the incident, and it takes a special effort on the part of the investigator to identify and research them. If this is not done, the likelihood is that the underlying causes and management system deficiencies involved in the incident will not be discovered. The resulting corrective and preventive actions will not be adequate, and the goal of preventing recurrence will not be realized.

Conducting Effective Cause Analysis

Effective investigations are a process in which the effectiveness of one phase is largely dependent on previous phases or steps. If the process of gathering information is carried out properly, cause analysis becomes much easier. Conversely, if the information available for analysis is inadequate, cause analysis will also be inadequate.

Cause analysis is not an intuitive activity and investigators most often rely on robust analysis tools to guide them through the process. There are several such tools available, such as TapRoot, 5 Why's, Fishbone, Fault-Tree Analysis, and Systematic Causal Analysis Technique (SCAT), among others. As mentioned earlier in this chapter, the organization should choose one or more of these techniques that they believe are most valuable for their specific use, train investigators in their use, routinely practice and apply the tools, and continually assess their utility.

In all investigations, both immediate causes (substandard acts or practices) and basic or root causes (personal factors and job/system factors) must be identified and addressed. Otherwise, the investigation will largely be a waste of time. The information gained in effective cause analysis should eventually be used to identify management system deficiencies: That is, missing or inadequate system elements, missing or inadequate standards for managing the system, or missing or inadequate efforts to measure/monitor the work being done to control loss and use the resulting information to implement or improve management system activities.
There are two very fundamental and critical management principles to be applied in the investigation process.

1. The Principle of Multiple Causes: Seldom, if ever, are loss-producing events the result of a single cause. It is improper to ask, "What was the cause of this incident?" That question will lead to the quickest, easiest answer, which will likely be an immediate cause, not a basic or root cause. The underlying problem will not be fixed. The proper question is, "What were the causes of this incident?"
   In March of 2005, a refinery explosion resulted in the deaths of 15 persons, multiple injuries, extensive property damage, loss of production, and other losses. The simplest explanation of a cause would have been that a splitter tower was overfilled, resulting in the release of thousands of gallons of gasoline and vapor that ultimately ignited. However, when the investigation was completed, numerous additional causes were identified, including issues with training, overwork and stress, improper management of change, inadequate maintenance, and inadequate staffing. Had those causes not been identified, the person(s) responsible for overfilling the splitter tower would likely have been disciplined and/or retrained. Neither of these actions would have solved the underlying problems.

2. The Principle of Basic Causes: Solutions to problems are more effective when they address the root or basic causes. Immediate causes are sometimes described as symptoms. Basic causes are described as the reasons why the immediate causes exist. If investigation efforts stop with immediate causes or symptoms, there will most likely be numerous, additional opportunities for the organization to experience the same or similar incidents. Management system deficiencies, if not identified and corrected, will eventually manifest themselves in some type of loss.

The Role of Organizational Culture in Incident Causation

Investigators should be aware of the role that the organization's culture plays in causation. Many organizations have very robust safety and health management systems defined and implemented. These systems are based on systematic, comprehensive risk assessment, best practices, legal requirements, and the body of knowledge that exists for managing safety and health exposures. There may be few, if any, inadequacies in the design of the management system.

The causes of incidents may well have their roots in the organization's culture. In its simplest terms, culture may be described as the way people think and act about something. The safety and health management system may be fine, but the way people are thinking and acting about safety may be such that it does not allow the system to work as designed.

For example, the organization may have a very robust policy and procedure for lockout/tag-out/try-out. All appropriate persons have been trained effectively. Senior managers reinforce the need for compliance, and are confident the message is getting through. However, because front-line supervisors are primarily measured on production numbers, there is a serious temptation to suspend LO/TO/TO in favor of expediency. Most supervisors resist the temptation, but a newly hired supervisor, who came from a much different and less structured culture, incorrectly perceives that the LO/TO/TO requirement is not as important to the organization as getting the job done. As a result, he or she yields to the temptation and instructs a work crew to proceed without following the procedure. The work crew has been told they have the right to refuse work in case of a perceived safety and health issue. There is a written procedure for exercising this right. However, the refusal-to-work procedure is relatively new and not yet fully incorporated into the culture. As a result, the crew is intimidated into doing the work without LO/TO/TO. A serious injury occurs as a result. The system was in place, but it was not working because of the way in which people were thinking and acting about safety.

Following both the Challenger and Columbia space shuttle incidents, much of the discussion about causes centered on the culture in the National Aeronautics and Space Administration (NASA).

An article published in the Atlanta Journal-Constitution in April of 2005 by Associated Press journalist Marcia Dunn was titled "NASA's Safety Culture Under Siege." A similar article published in the Houston Chronicle by journalist Mark Carreau was headed "NASA Culture Still Jeopardizes Crew Safety." Both articles described decisions taken by mission management as being based more on the need for return to flight (following the Columbia disaster) and pressures to meet flight schedules than proper risk management and safety concerns.

Other incidents have been linked to similar concerns. A rail disaster just outside Paddington Station in London in October 1999 was investigated by a panel headed by Lord Cullen. The resulting public inquiry report included the phrase, "[The railway] was riddled with complacency." The organization may have had a proper safety and health management system in place, but the way in which people were thinking and acting about safety controverted the best efforts of the system.

Proper cause analysis should consider the potential impact of organizational culture on the way people think and act about safety.

Developing Corrective and Preventive Actions

The development of effective corrective and preventive actions is largely predicated on the quality of cause analysis. If causes have been thoroughly and accurately identified, corrective and preventive actions almost write themselves.

Investigators should think of corrective and preventive actions in two additional categories: short-term actions for immediate risk reduction, and long-term or permanent actions.

Short-term actions, those taken as quickly as possible to mitigate risk, typically only address immediate causes or symptoms.

As a result of an investigation, it may be identified that leaking brake seals on a piece of mobile equipment resulted in failure of those brakes and a collision with a pallet of product. It is appropriate to replace the seals. Another investigation may conclude that an individual involved was not trained in proper chemical handling procedures. It is appropriate to provide training for that person. Yet another investigation may reveal a failure to conduct proper task analysis prior to initiating a job. A proper short-term action may be to reinforce the importance of task analysis in appropriate situations. All of these actions may be necessary and proper. However, they only address immediate causes. It is tempting to stop here and assume that the situation has been controlled. To do so is easier, less time-consuming, and requires fewer resources than more comprehensive plans. It also means that the chances that the same or similar events will recur are significant, and the overriding purpose of an investigation, to prevent recurrence, is not achieved.

Long-term or permanent actions address basic or root causes and inadequacies in the management system.

Those leaking brake seals on the mobile equipment should be replaced. All such pieces of equipment should be examined to determine if they, too, have leaking seals. The investigation must determine why seals are leaking. Is it because they are old and were not replaced according to a preventive maintenance (PM) schedule? Is it because they were damaged in some way? Is it because they are not the appropriate seals for that particular equipment? When these and related questions are properly answered, more permanent corrective and preventive actions can be developed. It may be necessary to change the frequency of PM inspections, or modify the PM inspection checklist. It may be necessary to improve the purchasing process by developing specifications for brake seals and modifying purchase orders. Such actions are more permanent and result in a higher level of control.

It may be appropriate to train an individual on chemical handling procedures. However, the most effective actions would include determining why that individual missed the required training in the first place. If that individual missed the training, chances are pretty good that others may have done so. The actions taken may include conducting or updating a training needs assessment, modifying record-keeping procedures, or implementing more effective auditing of the training system.

Both short-term and long-term actions are important.

Report Writing

This section does not seek to prescribe a specific incident investigation report format. There are, however, several best practices when it comes to effective report writing.

1. Remember: The report is only a report of what you found out in the investigation. It is not the investigation itself.

2. Resist the temptation to start writing the report early on in the investigation process. Most organizations have a requirement that specifies an initial report must be completed within a certain time frame. Some require an initial report by end of shift, some within 24 hours, some within 48 hours. The purposes of the requirement are to help ensure that an investigation is started promptly, provide critical information to persons who may be involved in managing the situation, and provide prompt safety alerts to others in the organization that may face similar risks. This requirement must be met. However, beyond that initial report, adequate time must be devoted to the investigation, and unreasonable pressure to complete a report should be avoided. When we put too much emphasis on completion of the report, two things can happen, and neither is desirable. First, the mission can become to complete the report, not to complete the investigation. Second, we are tempted to confine ourselves to report only what is required by the form.

3. An effective report form (electronic, of course) should be structured such that information can be reported in a logical and consistent manner. Typically, such a form moves from a pattern of initial data (name, date, part of body, piece of equipment, etc.), to a description of the event, to an assessment of the risk in the event, to cause analysis, to corrective and preventive actions, to proper approval signatures. Be careful in the design of report forms. Some information might be nice to know, but not important to the investigation process. Inclusion of too much nice-to-know information results in frustration for the person completing the report.

4. The report form should be designed such that it allows for ease of data collection and analysis.

5. Reports should be completed in their entirety. If a specific section of the form is not applicable to the given situation, "N/A" should be entered. There should be no blank spaces on the report.

6. Personal opinions and conjecture should not be expressed in a report. Only articulated facts and supporting evidence should be cited.

7. Completed reports should be circulated to appropriate managers, according to the investigation procedure described early on in this chapter.

8. Each individual organization should seek the advice of legal counsel in the proper completion of investigation reports.

Effective Follow-Up

The organization should have a robust corrective and preventive action tracking system. This system does not have to be designed specifically for the investigation process, but must be structured in such a way as to receive and record follow-up actions, identify persons or entities responsible for follow-up actions, establish a time frame for completion of actions, provide a means of tracking progress, require a sign-off on completed actions, and facilitate ease of auditing the process.

Sharing Lessons Learned

The organization should have an effective system for sharing lessons learned following incident investigation. Failure to share these lessons can lead to, and has led to, other units, departments, or locations within the same organization suffering from the same or similar events.

The government investigation into the refinery explosion mentioned earlier in this chapter revealed that the organization had experienced numerous similar events in other locations and declared its intention to share the lessons learned throughout the organization. For various reasons, this did not happen. It may be unreasonable to state categorically that the explosion would never have happened if the information had been shared, but the likelihood of it happening could have been significantly reduced.

It is best practice that a summary of critical information, purged of names and similar finger-pointing information, be distributed to all units and locations within the organization as soon as possible. It is also important that a summary of the findings of completed investigations be similarly distributed.

Management Actions

Following major or high-potential events, as defined in the investigation procedure, senior management should conduct a timely review. This is in addition to the investigation itself, and is for the purpose of providing accurate information to persons who must manage the situation. In addition, lessons-learned summaries can be generated and approved. The review should be conducted within 24 hours of the incident.

Management should ensure that all appropriate persons are trained in investigation techniques. However, the effectiveness of this initial training fades over time, especially when individuals do not conduct investigations on a regular basis and practice their skills. The initial training should be supplemented with a coaching and development process. Management should regularly measure the quality of investigations, evaluate the strengths and opportunities of each individual investigator, and provide feedback to commend the positive points of performance and coach for improvement where necessary. An example of a measurement and feedback technique is found in Figure 5. A designated person could evaluate the quality of each investigation report using this form. The process is not completely objective or scientific, but provides an approximate measure of quality. The investigation report is broken down into its component parts, and a value factor is assigned to each part, weighted as to its importance to the worth of the whole. The designated person reviews the report part by part to determine not only how complete it is, but how accurate. Based on that review, a score is determined according to the weight of the section. A total score is determined for the report. This information is not to be used as a report card, or to determine pass or fail, and is not to be distributed or revealed to any other person. It is to be used only as a tool to assess the individual's strengths and opportunities for improvement in the investigation process. The designated person then acts as a coach, using the information to positively commend the individual's strengths and to constructively provide advice for improvement. In this way, the individual not only maintains a high level of skill, but continually improves as well.

Section	Points Possible	Points Awarded	Comments
Identifying Information	10		
Description of Incident	15		
Risk Evaluation	5		
Immediate Cause Analysis	15		
Basic Cause Analysis	15		
Remedial Actions	30		
Timely Submission	5		
Proper Signatures	5		

Figure 13.5: Measuring Report Quality

Important Information

This chapter is by no means a complete guide to proper investigations. It is intended to provide basic information for the development, implementation, and improvement of investigation processes. Effective investigation of events described as major or catastrophic will require additional expertise and resources.

Incident investigation is not a simple process. It is rather like putting together a puzzle to get a complete picture.

Learning from Successes

As mentioned earlier, the investigation process as described here, with some obvious modification, can be used to learn from positive events as well. Our Vice President of Operations provides a good example.

Henry Moves Up

Henry has been a successful plant manager for over seventeen years. Early on in his career, he was identified as having leadership potential and was pretty much groomed for that role. Henry's plant was annually among the leaders in production, financial results, and safety and health performance. For the last six years of his tenure in the plant, his unit led the organization in almost every category of measurement. He was drawing more and more attention and credibility as a leader. The one signature event that elevated Henry to the office of

Vice-President of Operations was a major ergonomic breakthrough discovered and developed in his plant.

There had been a continuing problem with repetitive motion injuries in all the organization's plants. It involved hand assembly in one production area. Henry was determined to solve that problem.

A team comprised of a production operator, a supervisor, and the safety manager was assembled. Being a hands-on manager, Henry designated himself as a team member, though the lead was the supervisor. Henry had invested in training his staff in proper investigation techniques. It paid off. The team identified the basic causes of the repetitive motion injuries and developed and implemented effective corrective and preventive actions. In a period of months, such injuries were reduced by 45%. They shared lessons learned with all other plants and they experienced similar improvement.

Henry wasn't satisfied. He decided to initiate an effort to further reduce repetitive motion injuries. A project was developed and a team consisting of three operators, the same supervisor who led the initial investigation, and the department head was formed. He engaged an ergonomic specialist to consult with his team. They were challenged to develop a program to drive improvement.

The team presented their conclusions and ideas to the plant leadership team. It was very positively received and the necessary resources were appropriated. Within three months, a further reduction in repetitive motion injuries of approximately 30% was documented. Progress was monitored and, although the pace of reduction slowed, the level of these injuries remained at the target level. Again, the lessons learned were shared with all plants and, although the results varied, the improvement was significant.

Henry's boss and his predecessor as Vice-President of Operations asked Henry why he thought the project was such a success. Henry conducted his own investigation of the project. He identified the specific successes and the events that brought those successes to light. He explored the specific actions the project team took to achieve their goals as well as what it took to make those actions possible (basic or root causes) and determined the following:

1. The repetitive motion injuries were so numerous that they had become commonplace and accepted in the culture as a natural hazard of the operation. No one thought it was an issue that could be solved until Henry had become dissatisfied with the situation. One key recommendation of the project team was that operators should not just be trained on ergonomic controls, but educated on the reasons for concerns. The culture had to be changed and, over time, it was.

2. The project was successful because:
    a. The team consisted of people with vested interest in solving the problem. They had ownership.
    b. The team consisted of people with direct knowledge of the work processes. They had technical competence.
    c. The team had been empowered to research the issue and develop recommendations. Truly empowered with necessary resources and decision-making authority.
    d. Leadership listened. They were willing to give the findings of the team due consideration.
    e. The project team actually engaged the work force in developing materials for raising awareness. Some very creative media came out of that part of the project.

Henry shared these findings with his boss.

Within a few months, the Vice-President of Operations announced his pending retirement. He then endorsed Henry to succeed him and convinced the corporate leadership team accordingly. One year after the successful project, Henry was promoted to Vice-President of Operations.

Key Point Summary

1. Incident investigation is a problem-solving process, not a blame-fixing, fault-finding process. Its ultimate purpose is to prevent recurrence or, at a minimum, reduce the risk of the event or similar events recurring.

2. The organization should have a predetermined, written procedure for proper conduct of investigations.

3. Persons with investigation responsibilities should be adequately trained in proper investigation techniques.

4. The incident investigation system should encompass the whole scope of loss and near-loss the organization may face including injuries and illnesses, property damage, process interruption, environmental events, non-conformities, etc.

5. The organization should work to continually improve the culture around reporting and investigation of incidents.

6. There are several critical steps in the investigation process. The proper completion of each of these steps is highly dependent on the quality completion of the previous step.

Personal Planning

Is our incident investigation process appropriate (according to best practices), effective, and producing the results we want? Why or why not?

Do our investigations really get to basic or root causes and system deficiencies?

Are the people who are primarily responsible for incident investigations properly trained?

Y – Model for Action Planning

Present Situation

Desired Situation

Need for Change

Present Situation

Stop Responsibility Target Date

REVIEWING PERFORMANCE

Chapter 14

REVIEWING PERFORMANCE

> **CHAPTER OBJECTIVES**
>
> 1. To describe the differences between proper and improper uses of both lagging and leading indicators.
> 2. To advance the idea that, although any organization should continue to keep incident statistics (lagging indicators), the most valuable information for health and safety process improvement is found in leading indicators.
> 3. To help the organization drive a culture change from too much reliance on lagging indicators to a more prominent use of leading indicators.

The Annual Plant Performance Review

Henry has come to Joe's plant to conduct the annual plant performance review. This is routine for all plants in the organization. It is the time when all departments and functions sit down to review the past year and set targets and

objectives for the year upcoming. Since Joe's is the largest plant in the group, there are several departments represented in the two-day meeting including human resources, finance, sales and marketing, operations, maintenance, supply chain, IT, logistics, and health and safety.

The meeting opens with the usual greetings and thanks for the past year's successes. Each department representative is then asked to make a brief presentation on their past performance, current state, and expectations for the future.

As Lisa listens to each report, she realizes that all the departments are reporting lagging indicators (sales figures, customer complaints, profits, budget status, etc.). She also realizes that, when her time comes, she will be reporting similar information in the form of incident rates. Lisa knows these numbers speak management's language and will be important; however, she also knows that these numbers are not necessarily an indicator of the level of control the organization has over its health and safety exposures.

"How can I make this group understand the fallacies of lagging health and safety indicators and how can I help them understand the need to move to consistent use of leading indicators?" She asks herself. Lisa's report is not due until the afternoon, so she spends her lunch hour revising her presentation.

She would like to share with you some of the information she used as the basis for her final report.

Introduction

Imagine you have received an invitation to represent your health and safety department in an annual performance review. You will be giving a presentation much like that which Lisa is giving to her group. You understand the concept of "plan, do, check, act," and the importance of measuring and monitoring all management systems and processes, as indicated in Figure 14.1 below. You also understand the vital differences between lagging and leading indicators, and the need to transition to more consistent use of leading health and safety indicators. What information would be important to communicate to the leadership team to convince them of this need?

The overall objective of this chapter is to provide you with the necessary information to help your organization's leadership understand proper use of both lagging and leading indicators in evaluating health and safety performance.

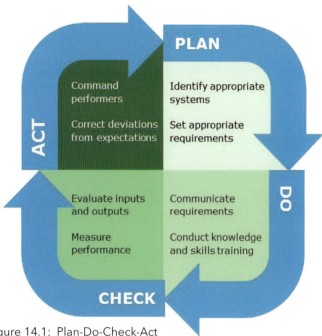

Figure 14.1: Plan-Do-Check-Act

Language of Management

The language of H&S is usually different from management's business language. Depending on the organization, the language and symbols of senior leadership are often related to tangible measurements, such as sales orders fulfilled, profits gained, consumer complaints, product returns, and financial status (balance sheet). For safety, the norm is related to expressing the lack of safety, usually through the language of lagging indicators (LTI, Severity Rates, Number of Fatalities, etc.).

Is the measurement of health and safety performance, as currently described in lagging indicators of incident rates, the correct language to express the safety conscience of the organization, the current efforts made at all levels, and the current commitment from the leaders towards their employees?

Lagging Indicators

Traditional measures of safety performance by governments and by private companies are most commonly related to the amount of loss, as defined by different levels and categories of harm to people. These formulas will include fatalities, serious injuries, minor injuries, recordable cases, first aid, medical treatment, etc. Although different organizations use different terminology, the computation of lagging indicators is essentially the same in all organizations. Figure 14.2 below illustrates the standard formulas used in the USA to measure safety performance of an organization.

> Lost-Time Incident (LTI) Rate
>
> #LTI x 200,000 ÷ Hours Worked
>
> Recordable Incident (RI) Rate (Sometimes called Total Recordable Incident Rate or TRIR)
>
> #RI x 200,000 ÷ Hours Worked
>
> Severity Rate
>
> #Days Lost x 200,000 ÷ Hours Worked

Figure 14.2: S & H Incident Rate Formulas in US

A lost-time injury is incurred when a person is injured, or suffers a job-related illness, to the extent that they are not medically available to work the following day at their usual job, even if they are not scheduled to work.

The simplest definition of a recordable or reportable injury is any injury or illness that requires medical treatment above basic first aid. There are numerous exceptions to this rule, and all organizations should study the regulatory requirements in their jurisdictions.

The "hours worked" term used in the formula represents the total hours worked in the unit over whatever period of time is being measured (month, quarter, year).

The 200,000 hour standard represents a unit of 100 people working one standard year (40 hours a week, 50 weeks a year, allowing 2 weeks for vacation). This allows the organization to understand how many of a specific type of injury occurred per 100 employees. For example, if the organization's lost-time injury (LTI) rate is .5, that means that for every 100 employees, one-half person was injured so seriously they were not medically available to work the following day. Since it makes no sense to say that one-half person was injured, a better way to understand this statistic is to say that any number other than zero resulting from this formula means someone incurred a lost-time injury or illness. It should be noted that these formulas are used in many parts of the world, but not all. Some countries use formulas that index incidents to 1,000,000 hours.

Benefits of Lagging Indicators for H & S

Lagging indicators simply answer the question, "How many injuries/illnesses did we have, and how bad were they?" Properly used, they are the scoreboard at the end of the game. We use them to measure ourselves against ourselves over a period of time. They help us know whether we are winning or losing. Are we getting better?

Lagging indicators measure results or output. Loss indices themselves do not provide any indication of why the incidents occurred or what to do about them. However, the information gained from looking back over incidents that have happened can be used in a very positive way. If the organization has a robust and properly functioning incident investigation and analysis process (see the chapter Learning from Events), they have access to information that can be leveraged for improvement. Figure 14.3 illustrates how this can be done.

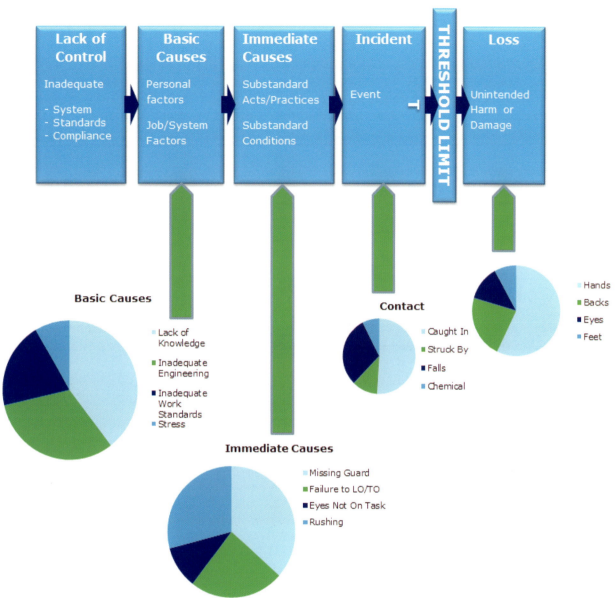

Figure 14.3: Analysis of Lagging Indicators

Cautions on Over-Reliance on Lagging Indicators

Beyond the uses described above, lagging indicators are not very useful for determining how well an organization manages health and safety. Low loss indices are great, but they are not necessarily an indicator of the level of control the organization exercises. For example, an organization might be able to demonstrate lower than industry average injury frequency rates, but at the same time, be experiencing numerous property damage, process interruption, and environmental incidents. Many of these types of incidents have the potential to hurt people, but haven't yet. There are numerous instances in which organizations became too comfortable with their positive trending on loss indices, and then experienced a rather rude awakening or epiphany when a major event occurred.

Frequency and severity rates do not measure the total loss and near-loss picture. Figure 14.4 below illustrates the relatively small percentage of incidents that are actually measured by these rates.

Figure 14.4: Incidents Measured by Frequency and Severity Rates

Lagging indicators can only be used after the fact. An undesired event has to happen in order to be counted.

The S & H results from one period to the next may not be directly related to the effort expended in that same period. Loss indices are not a very sensitive indicator of improvement in the short term. Investment in S & H activities may not yield results for quite some time after implementation.

Another caution regarding over-reliance on lagging indicators is that leaders often misinterpret them. Most organizational leaders get periodic reports on their frequency and severity rates, but do not know where the numbers come from or what they mean. As a result, they may tend to get a bit too comfortable when the numbers go down or get overly concerned when they go up a bit. There will be natural peaks and valleys in the incident rates from month-to-month, quarter-to-quarter, for no obvious or even discernable reason. Trends are more important than raw data.

Some organizations use lagging indicators to make comparisons and decisions about safety strategy and budget. They benchmark themselves against industry at large or other organizations in their own industry. They compare performance from plant-to-plant or department-to-department. There are too many variables that affect these numbers and can make them unsuitable for such comparisons. For example:

- The risk levels from one industry to another make benchmarking a pre-packaged food production operation with an underground mine a false comparison. A specific injury frequency rate might be very good for the mining operation, but over the top for the food operation. Lagging indicators do not take risk levels into consideration.

- Organizations within the same industry may well have different risk levels. And, although reporting standards are supposed to be the same for all, in reality some organizations spend a lot of energy trying to manage their numbers, not managing safety. Intentional or unintentional actions can affect the numbers.

- Even plants within the same organization may have different risk levels and it isn't necessarily appropriate to compare them using only incident rates.

- Departments within the same plant have differing risk levels.

- The decisions a doctor makes can affect the numbers. In some instances, a doctor may clear a worker to return immediately. In other cases, a different doctor, looking at the same exact injury, may err on the side of caution and prescribe a day or two away from work.

Using lagging indicators to measure and make decisions about safety and health systems is a bit like driving your car by constantly looking in the rear-view mirror. It lets you know where you have been, but not what's ahead. We want to check the rear-view once in a while – we can learn from experience, but focusing on the past is more than a bit dangerous.

Leading Indicators

Developing a sustainable safety and health management system largely depends on how well the organization uses leading indicators.

If lagging indicators are considered "after-the-fact" or outputs resulting from undesired events, then we could say that leading indicators will always be measured before the undesired event. We can describe these leading indicators as measurements of input or measurements of efforts made. In other words, leading indicators help answer the question, "How well are we doing the work we said we would do to correct the causes and change the consequences?"

Figure 14.5 below illustrates that lagging indicators focus on the last four blocks in the causation model, while leading indicators focus on the first block. They measure how well the organization is defining its S & H system, setting expectations or responsibilities, and managing conformance to those responsibilities.

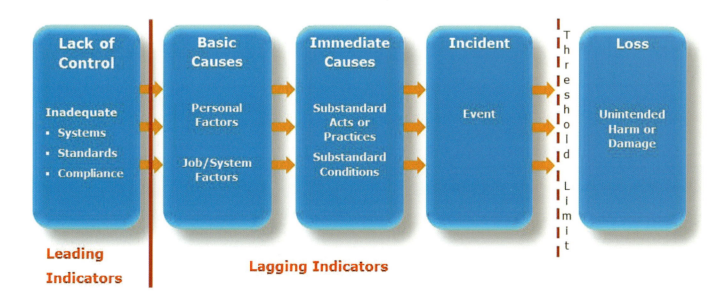

Figure 14.5: Indicators Relating to the Loss Causation Model

Forms of Leading Indicators

There are two forms of leading indicators that can be used effectively by any organization.

Periodic/Comprehensive Measures

Every organization should employ a comprehensive health and safety audit protocol. With some degree of frequency, there should be a complete assessment of the entire H&S management system. Best practice is that this should be done annually. In this case, persons who are knowledgeable of both H&S management systems and proper auditing techniques use a standard checklist to assess performance in all aspects of the organization's system. They employ interviews, checks of documentation and records, and physical observations to determine the level of conformance to both internal standards and best practices.

This application is quite like the individual who has an annual physical checkup at the doctor. Everything is checked thoroughly. However, it is only once a year. This means that there is a rather long period of time during which problems could begin to develop, but would not be detected until the next audit.

Regular/Representative Measures

In order to detect developing problems within the system, it is best practice for the organization to identify some key performance indicators (KPI's) that could be measured on a regular basis, perhaps monthly or quarterly. The organization should select indicators that they consider to be the most sensitive and important for their specific system. Among potential indicators are:

1. Number of risk assessments performed compared to the number required.
2. Quality of risk assessment reports.
3. Number of employees trained in evacuation procedures versus number of employees requiring training.
4. Number of safety observations performed by the supervisors versus required.
5. Number and quality of incident investigation reports.
6. Quality of group safety meetings performed by the supervisors.
7. Number of pre-use inspections of packaging equipment performed versus required.
8. Number and quality of job safety analyses performed.

Any activity in the health and safety management system could be similarly measured.

If the analogy of the health and safety audit to an individual's annual physical is valid, then the representative/regular measures would be analogous to taking your vital signs once in a while. Checking your blood pressure, blood sugar, and cholesterol periodically would be considered prudent and would help catch developing problems at an early stage. These types of measures would allow the organization to keep a finger on the pulse of the system and identify developing problems before they manifest themselves in incidents.

A second analogy was made in the paragraphs above. Dependence on the use of lagging indicators alone to manage your health and safety system would be like trying to drive your car by only looking in the rearview mirror. If one accepts that premise, then the following analogy may also be valid. Using leading indicators to manage your health and safety system would be like driving by looking ahead, through the windshield, and using the dashboard monitoring devices to alert you to potential problems. There is a reason why we have rear-view mirrors in our automobiles. Periodically, we need to see what's behind us. However, what's behind us is not a reliable indicator of what may lie before us. By the same token, where we have been in our past health and safety performance is not necessarily a reliable indicator of what lies ahead.

Benefits of Using Leading Indicators

Those organizations that have decided to include the reporting of leading indicators within the periodic updates to management will describe the benefits of these measurements as follows:

1. The tone of the presentation and communication is usually positive. Therefore, management also reacts positively to the results and gets the team inspired.
2. The measures will produce a tangible improvement before the accident or incident occurs.
3. Employees will be more willing to report positive efforts made, especially if they believe that these efforts are now measured by management, and if such measures provide a true validation of a safer workplace (meaning safe acts and safe conditions readily visible at the workplace).
4. The topics presented will give an opportunity for management to be engaged in active coaching and mentoring.
5. They promote a more proactive decision making process.
6. There is more validity between the efforts made and the specific root causes that the organization wants to eliminate or significantly reduce.

Cautions on Using Leading Indicators

There are some perceived concerns with using only leading indicators for health and safety monitoring.

1. Local regulatory agencies, governments, or corporate departments within most organizations still do not request or require organizations to document these types of indicators. Therefore, management may not want to continue to measure these indicators if they do not receive feedback or comments from these external stakeholders and groups.
2. In some instances, the quantity of leading indicators needed may be too much for the H&S department to collect on a periodic basis. It will be a resource-based decision by management, in order to validate improvements made over time, understanding that external stakeholders and groups will still be more interested in the lagging indicators. Focus your collection of leading indicators on your top issues—what are the critical few, if the above is an issue?
3. Having additional leading indicators does not mean that the lagging indicators will be deleted. It certainly means additional reporting and additional documentation.
4. Although many managers may conceptually agree with the improved use of leading indicators, it will be a major culture change for them to come to rely on those measures for decision-making. They will most likely continue to rely, at least for a while, on the more familiar and comfortable lagging indicators.

Conclusion

The authors do not intend to promote the sole use one of form of health and safety system measures over others. In fact, the organization should use a combination of these measures in order to get an accurate picture of both results and effort. Many organizations have developed balance scorecards or safety dashboards that combine these measures in some meaningful way.

Tool Box: Measuring Quality

The following method could be used to measure the quality of any activity in the health and safety management system. The illustration is an example of how the method could be used to measure the quality of an incident investigation.

Method:

1. Determine the specific activity you want to measure.
2. Determine the critical factors or parts that comprise the whole of the activity.
3. Apply a value factor to each factor or part that reflects the relative value of that factor or part to the worth of the whole. These factors should total 100 for ease of interpretation.
4. Review the activity and ask critical questions to make a value judgment and score each factor or part.
5. Total the scores for the various factors or parts to get an overall quantitative evaluation

Illustration:

You want to measure the quality of incident investigations. You may begin with the fairly safe assumption that there is a high degree of correlation between the quality of the investigation and the quality of the investigation itself. In other words, if you have a good report, it represents a good investigation. A poor report represents a poor investigation. Indirectly, by measuring the quality of the report, you are measuring the quality of the investigation.

You might identify seven critical factors or parts of a comprehensive and proper investigation report, as illustrated below. Then you will decide the relative value of each part and assign point values as illustrated. By reviewing a report in detail and asking questions related to the content of each part, you could make a value judgment of its completeness and accuracy. You then total the scores to get a score for the report.

CAUTION: There are but two reasons for measuring the quality of investigations.

1. **To get an idea of whether investigations are being carried out in an effective and beneficial manner.**
2. **To enable you to identify the strengths of each investigator as well as their opportunities for improvement. This allows you to be a more effective coach and continually improve the quality of investigations.**
   Should you choose to use this tool, please be aware that this approach is not for the purpose of giving report cards or pass/fail scores to investigators! In fact, neither investigators nor anyone else ever need know these scores! They are not meant for publication and should not be made public. Their primary use is to help you provide both proper commendation and constructive correction and motivate improvement.

The following is only an example of how this approach could be applied.

Measurement of Carlos' Investigation Report

Critical Factor	Points Possible	Points Awarded	Coaching Points
Accuracy and Completeness of Basic Incident Data All identifying information such as name, time of incident, part of body, piece of equipment, age, shift, department, etc. should be filled in accurately.	10	9	This section of the report was very complete and accurate with one small exception. The time and date of the incident recorded in the report was 24 hours off. It seems to be an honest mistake.
Risk Assessment The investigator should make an assessment of the potential of the incident to recur and the severity potential. The extent of the investigation is based on its potential, not its actual outcome.	5	5	The risk assessment was done as prescribed and, based on current information, it was accurate.
Description A complete description should allow the reviewer to get an accurate picture of the scene and the event.	15	10	Carlos needs a little help in writing complete descriptions. This one was not written in chronological order and it was a bit difficult to follow. I will provide some examples for him to follow.
Analysis of Immediate Causes All immediate causes (substandard acts, practices, and conditions) should be identified and described in detail.	15	12	Immediate causes were treated very well. One identified cause was listed as "inadequate guard" without any detailed explanation. I will remind him of the need to be more thorough in describing causes.

Critical Factor	Points Possible	Points Awarded	Coaching Points
Analysis of Basic Causes All basic causes (personal factors and job/system factors should be identified and described in detail.	20	10	Carlos has been trained on basic causes; however, he missed two contributing factors: inadequate risk assessment and inadequate procedures. A scheduled risk assessment on the piece of equipment involved was never completed, and the task procedure had not been updated in three years.
Corrective and Preventive Action Plan A plan to correct issues related to both immediate and basic causes, as well as prevent recurrence of this type of event should be detailed, with responsibility for completion assigned and target dates.	30	15	Because of the failure to identify two significant basic causes, the corrective action plan was incomplete. I will review basic causes and the need to address all of them with Carlos. He is a conscientious guy and I expect him to respond positively to coaching.
Signatures of Appropriate Persons This is to ensure the report has been properly distributed as prescribed in the procedure.	5	5	The report had been signed by all appropriate persons.
Total Points	**100**	**66**	My target is to review and coach Carlos by Friday, 6 December. If we can get the issue with basic causes improved, the resulting corrective action plan should follow suit.

You should never expect perfection, but continual improvement. The philosophy is that the more and better work the organization does to manage the system, the less likely it is to experience incidents.

Key Point Summary

1. Lagging indicators such as frequency and severity rates have value and should be used as the ultimate measure of the effectiveness of health and safety efforts. Are we hurting fewer people? Are the injuries and illnesses less severe?

2. Lagging indicators and related information can be used to identify repetitive causes, both immediate and basic, and recurring system deficiencies. This information, when properly used, can help the organization develop more effective corrective and preventive actions.

3. Lagging indicators are not the most suitable for driving improvement plans. Lower frequency and severity rates are everyone's goal, but in themselves, they are not necessarily an indicator of the level of control the organization has over its exposures.

4. Leading indicators measure input or effort. Results are inextricably linked to effort. Leading indicators measure how well the organization is doing the work it said it would do to correct the causes of incidents and change the consequences.

5. Leading indicators tell leadership where strengths and opportunities for improvement exist in the health and safety management system.

6. Both types of measurement are important; however, all organizations would benefit from an increased understanding and focus on leading indicators for continual improvement.

7. Leading indicators are all about sustainability.

Personal Planning

1. Does my organization use lagging indicator information effectively? How could we improve?

2. Do we understand the meaning and proper use of both lagging and leading indicators?

3. Do we use leading indicators effectively? How could we improve?

Y – Model for Action Planning

Present Situation

Desired Situation

Need for Change

Present Situation

Stop　　　　　　　　　Responsibility　　　　　　　　　Target Date

CLOSING THE CIRCLE: ACHIEVING SUSTAINABILITY

Chapter 15

CLOSING THE CIRCLE: ACHIEVING SUSTAINABILITY

CHAPTER OBJECTIVES

1. To provide ideas, tools, and techniques by which an organization can drive sustainable business development.
2. To help answer the question, "Where do we go from here?"

Learning the Organization

As our friends Carlos, Lisa, Joe, and Henry have learned from their experiences, Henry has diligently ensured that those lessons learned have been shared with other plants in his organization. The results have been somewhat mixed. Most plants have taken the lessons to heart, developed their own health and safety improvement plans, and shown marked performance improvement.

A couple of plants, where leadership did not readily accept their responsibility for health and safety, have lagged behind. Now, having seen the improvement demonstrated in the majority of plants, leadership in the struggling planet is beginning to come around.

Henry believes he has everyone's attention and he is ready for the next step: to ensure that a strategic plan for health and safety improvement exists for the overall operation, and that it is sustainable.

Henry decides to focus his next plant leadership meeting on health and safety. He engages Joe to present his plant's experience and to focus on how the health and safety initiatives have contributed to production and quality goals as well as the overall financial health of the operation. He enlists Lisa to present her plant's health and safety successes and to focus on how they moved from dependence on lagging Health and Safety indicators to an understanding and effective use of leading indicators. He also invites Carlos to present, from a supervisor's perspective, how Health and Safety initiatives have contributed to improvement in employee morale, communications, teamwork, and individual competence.

The team's presentations are well received, and create and even greater level of enthusiasm for moving forward.

Henry also engages a professional facilitator to conduct a strategic planning session for the group. Henry's challenge to his group is simple. **What do we need to do to drive an overall Health and Safety improvement strategy for the organization, and most importantly, how do we ensure it is sustainable?** The facilitator uses various methods to first collect myriad ideas from the group, and then to lead the participants to prioritize their ideas. The top five ideas were chosen for more immediate focus, small groups were formed, and each group was assigned one of the five ideas to develop.

The five top ideas to meet the overall goal of sustainability were:

- Focus on regulatory compliance.
- Include health and safety at the business planning table.
- Adopt lean manufacturing principles.
- Implement a robust internal auditing process.
- Employ periodic, third party scored assessments as a means of developing meaningful improvement plans for each plant.

The small groups spent a full day on their respective assignments and made comprehensive reports to their colleagues. Although there was a lot of discussion following the reports, and a number of changes made, the group ultimately and unanimously adopted the plans.

The group then spent time identifying persons with responsibilities related to the plan, writing performance expectations, setting deadlines, and formalizing the project plan. They also determined that they would meet in three months to audit their own plan.

Obviously, the scenario you have just read is fictitious, though based on real-life situations. We could speculate on what the results of this initiative were for our fictitious organization, but such speculation would only be for fun.

DNV GL has significant experience working with organizations much like the one in our story. We can state, with a high degree of confidence, that organizations that are open to learning, that demonstrate a real concern for the health and safety of their stakeholders, that are committed to continual improvement, and that understand and employ sustainability thinking, are those that ultimately lead the way.

Do you want to lead the way?

Oh, by the way, here are the small group reports that came out of Henry's meeting and formed the basis of the organization's sustainable business development planning.

Idea 1: Regulatory Compliance and Systems Engineering

Introduction

Organizational leadership must understand a simple truth. Regulatory compliance is the minimum standard to which an organization must comply just to exist. However, just being in compliance with regulations in no way assures the organization that it is providing a healthy and safe working environment for its people. A proper health and safety process must be based on a thorough understanding of the organization's risk profile, not the regulations under which the organization operates.

Still and yet, regulatory compliance is a major concern for all organizations. In today's regulatory and competitive environments, all organizations need a disciplined approach to identifying all current and pending regulations and implementing robust means to ensure compliance.

Organizations are held accountable for their compliance behavior and non-compliance carries heavy risks. Leadership needs assurance that their organization is in compliance. Proper compliance with legislation and regulations is a precondition for operating a sustainable and socially responsible business. An organization's leadership can only state with conviction that it has control of its compliance when it is working on it systematically.

In addition, compliance with legislation and regulations is one of the basic requirements of both the ISO 14001 and OHSAS 18001 standards. Various elements of both the ISO 14001 and OHSAS 18001 standards contain direct or indirect references to compliance with legislation and regulations. Together these elements constitute the compliance management system.

Managing regulatory compliance is increasingly challenging and costly for organizations worldwide. While such efforts are often supported by information technology (IT) and information systems (IS) tools, there is evidence that the current solutions are inadequate and do not fully address the needs of organizations.

Henry's team identified systems engineering as a reasonable approach to achieving and maintaining regulatory compliance.

Systems Engineering

Systems engineering is an interdisciplinary field of engineering that focuses on how to design and manage complex engineering projects over their life cycles.

Issues such as reliability, logistics, coordination of various teams, requirements of management, evaluation measurements, and other disciplines like compliance assurance become more difficult when dealing with large, complex projects. Systems engineering deals with work processes, optimization methods, and risk management tools in such projects.

With the increase in complexity of systems and projects, especially regarding compliance issues, the need for systems engineering arose. Systems engineering is an interdisciplinary engineering management process that evolves and verifies an integrated, life cycle balanced set of system solutions that satisfy customer needs and that helps identifying legislation and regulations for regulatory compliance.

Organizational leadership must first identify the regulatory requirements that apply to its operations. Systematic, comprehensive identification of health and safety exposures are a good starting point. Information on how such identification is properly carried out, including the use of a risk register, is found in the chapter on Risk Management. Subject matter experts should review the organization's risk register to identify issues covered by existing and pending or anticipated regulations. If an organization has operations in multiple countries, it must also identify the applicable legal requirements for all. Identifying the relevant legislation and regulations is more and more done with a systems engineering approach.

As illustrated by Figure 15.1, systems engineering management is accomplished by integrating three major activities:

- Development phasing that controls the design process and provides baselines that coordinate design efforts.
- A systems engineering process that provides a structure for solving design problems and tracking requirements flow through the design effort.
- Life cycle integration that involves customers in the design process and ensures that the system is viable throughout its life.

- Subsystem/component level, which produces first a set of subsystem and component product performance descriptions, then a set of corresponding detailed descriptions of the products' characteristics, essential for their production.
-

Consideration of each one of these activities is necessary to achieve a complete and comprehensive understanding of the regulatory requirements that apply to each phase.

Development Phasing

Development usually progresses through distinct levels or stages:

- Concept level, which produces a system concept description (usually described in a concept study).
- System level, which produces a system description in performance requirement terms.

Consideration of regulatory requirements should begin at the concept level. This is a major reason why health and safety professionals should be involved in projects from their beginning. All too often, projects are well underway before the health and safety function is even informed of them. It is then often necessary to revisit and restructure project plans and specifications in order to meet regulatory requirements. This rework negatively affects both budget and deadline objectives.

Because it produces a system description in performance requirement terms, the system level of development phasing must include health and safety performance requirements. If it does not, such requirements may not become apparent until the operational phase of the project, which

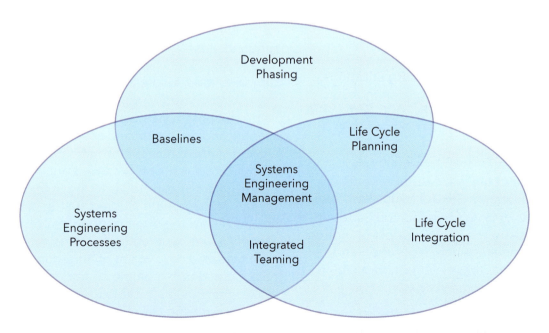

Figure 15.1: The Activities of Systems Engineering

again requires retrofitting. When health and safety requirements are not included, the attitude that health and safety are something separate and apart from operations is reinforced. These performance requirements are commonly called configuration baselines.

The subsystem or component level of development phasing requires that all requirements, including health and safety, be refined and detailed. Significant development at any given level in the system hierarchy should not occur until the configuration baselines at the higher levels are considered complete, stable, and controlled. Reviews and audits are used to ensure that the baselines are ready for the next level of development. The effective consideration and inclusion of health and safety requirements should be audited at each stage of the project.

Life Cycle Model and Integration

Every system has a life cycle. A life cycle can be described using an abstract functional model that represents the conceptualization of a need for the system and its realization, utilization, evolution and disposal. A system progresses through its life cycle as the result of actions, performed and managed by people in organizations, using processes for execution of these actions. The detail in the life cycle model is expressed in terms of these processes and their outcomes, relationships and sequence.

Consideration must be given to health and safety regulations at each stage of the system's life cycle. There are health and safety regulations that apply to:

- Research and development activities
- Construction
- Contractor and supplier management
- Operations and maintenance training
- Development and implementation of procedures
- Startup of equipment
- Mechanical integrity
- Management of change
- Shutdown, dismantling, and disposal, etc.

Planning for compliance should be included for all stages from the day of conception.

The Systems Engineering Process

The systems engineering process is a top-down, comprehensive, iterative and recursive problem-solving process, applied sequentially through all stages of development, that is used to:

- Transform needs and requirements into a set of system product and process descriptions (adding value and more detail with each level of development).
- Generate information for decision-makers.
- Provide input for the next level of development.

When health and safety regulatory requirements are properly integrated into the systems engineering process, the organization can have a high degree of confidence that all such requirements have been identified and compliance properly integrated into the process.

Since systems engineering can be applied to all aspects of an organization's delivery of products and services, we believe it would be a good way to help integrate health and safety into the total business. We also believe such integration is essential for our future.

More detailed information on systems engineering and how it can be used to help achieve regulatory compliance can be found in the ISO/IEC TR 19760.

Idea 2: Health and Safety at the Business Planning Table

A corporate health and safety professional was called to a meeting where she was told of a recent acquisition. The organization had bought one manufacturing plant from a competitor and leadership was already in the transitioning process. A new plant manager had been assigned and had visited the new location. He was concerned about several issues, including the state of health and safety in the operation. The corporate H & S professional was assigned to go to the new plant, make a first-hand assessment of the situation, and submit plans to corporate leadership to bring the plant up-to-speed. This was not the first time this professional had been surprised by new initiatives and given the assignment to retrofit health and safety into the system and culture. She resigned her position one month later.

The two examples on this page are real-life. Most organizations today understand the absolute need for due diligence of health and safety issues in both acquisitions and management of change. Unfortunately, that understanding is not universal nor is it always routinely practiced.

As mentioned in the previous section of this report, health and safety must be involved in the life-cycle of the organization. This is true not only to ensure compliance with regulations, but compliance with industry best practices and effective management of specific exposures. It is critical to achieve sustainability goals and objectives.

A business case can be made for sustainable business development and the role health and safety can play in achieving that development. Not only can well-managed health and safety processes protect the lives and well-being of employees and other stakeholders, but they can contribute to the overall health (read financial performance) of the organization as well.

The only way an organization can leverage health and safety processes for improved business performance is to include H & S as an equal partner in the strategic planning process. Health and safety professionals must sit at the table with operations, R & D, sales and marketing, legal, public relations, and other entities and have input to new initiatives. Budgets must be developed with a health and safety component based, not on initial cost concerns alone, but on a substantial understanding of the organization's risk profile.

A major mining company experienced a catastrophic incident when a roof collapse killed 9 miners and injured 15 others. The investigation into the incident revealed that a new roof control technique had been implemented without any formal safety and health risk assessment or input. No new written procedures were in place and there was no record of formal training for operators.

Leadership determined this would not happen again and began to include safety and health staff in all operations and maintenance planning activities. Even considering complaints from some operations managers that safety and health were slowing down their work, leadership pursued the initiative. They were so satisfied with the ultimate result, they resolved to begin including safety and health staff in strategic business planning.

This particular organization is currently among the leaders in the mining industry both in terms of financial and safety and health performance. They have redefined the role of the corporate safety and health staff to include a significant business component and intentionally recruit S & H professionals who have operations background and business acumen.

Our team recommends all leadership reads the book: Practical Leadership for Sustainable Business: Health and Safety Management, especially the chapter on The Sustainable Organization. It strongly advocates and justifies our position that health and safety, well managed, can contribute to a healthy future for our business.

Idea 3: Adopt LEAN Manufacturing Thinking

Lean Management: When the organization improves on quality and efficiency, it will have a positive effect on safety. True or False?

Lean management is about eliminating waste, reducing complexity, improving process flow, and improving work planning. The original focus of lean management was about improving quality and efficiency, but the links to health and safety improvement are obvious.

Recognizing the Impacts of Waste on Health and Safety

Consider these eight wastes and their impact on health and safety hazards:

- **Defects** when defects in products or service exist, the result is the need for rework. Rework requires increased exposure to health and safety hazards such as those present in production equipment, chemical substances, hand tools, mobile equipment, the work environment, etc.

  A large part of the US recently experienced unusually cold and life-threatening temperatures. Electrical and gas supplies were interrupted and emergency repairs had to be made quickly. A crew servicing an electrical supply grid rushed their work and did not complete repairs properly. Consequently, the grid failed a second time and crews had to be dispatched a second time to work in a very hazardous environment. Defects often lead to increased health and safety exposures, but minimization of defects through lean methods can have the corresponding effect of reducing those exposures.

- **Overproduction** brought on by poor planning, can increase health and safety exposures in much the same way as defects. Workers spend unnecessary time exposed to hazards, providing more opportunity for incidents.

  An organization that manufactures children's toys overestimated seasonal demand for some of its products. The result was the overfilling of warehousing and shipping facilities, such that every available space was stacked with boxes of product. Additional space was acquired within a few days, but for a while it was very difficult for mobile equipment to operate in the facility, traffic patterns were altered, the field of vision for mobile equipment operators was severely limited, and the potential for boxes to fall was increased. An incident occurred when a forklift struck a stack of boxes, knocking them over. Although the boxes did not fall on a person, there was damage to the product and the obvious potential for someone to have been seriously injured.

- **Waiting** due to poor planning, allows for workers to be left in the presence of exposures for longer periods, thereby increasing the risk. It also may result in frustration and boredom on the part of workers, factors that in themselves can contribute to incidents.

  A plant that manufactures insulation materials had two identical production lines running side by side a few feet apart. One of the lines had to be shut down for several minutes while waiting for some routine maintenance to be completed. There was no thought of what to do with the five people who normally worked on the down line during the wait time. As a result, the five workers decided to have some fun and play soccer on the concrete pad at the warehouse docks. One of the workers produced a soccer ball from his car and the game was on. Unfortunately, there was a collision between two of the participants, resulting in one of them receiving a broken jaw and a couple of missing teeth.

- **Not using employee ideas** people at the front line have a great deal of knowledge of health and safety exposures and should be an integral part of risk identification and assessment activities. These employees often have very good ideas for effective means of dealing with exposures. Ask them. Their insight can be very helpful, and providing them with the opportunity for meaningful participation goes a long way toward getting their ownership of health and safety efforts. A paper manufacturing facility recently developed and implemented an intentional, systematic effort to engage all employees. For years, the culture in the facility had been one of command and control, with little or no employee engagement. The result was a negative work environment featuring a blame culture. Employees would not report substandard conditions or near misses. They would not cooperate in incident investigations. Meetings became very unpleasant. The initiative is still ongoing and, although significant progress has been made, there are still pockets of resistance to leadership efforts. In this scenario, health and safety became a tool for beating up the other side.

- **Transportation** activities involve significant health and safety exposures. These exposures can be increased when transportation activities are not well planned or coordinated. Loading operations can be rushed. Materials handling equipment may be improperly operated in an effort to catch up to the schedule. Additional personnel may crowd an area, adding risk. An independent long-haul truck driver arrived at his destination to pick up a large container scheduled for quick delivery a good distance away. The facility shipping the container was not prepared, and loading was delayed by several hours. The driver, under pressure to deliver the load at the promised time, decided to drive late into the night to try to make up lost time. Although he was within the legal limits of his active driving time, he was seriously fatigued. He went to sleep at the wheel, lost control of the vehicle, and left the roadway. He was killed in the incident.

- **Inventory** Excess inventory can produce health and safety exposures. In addition to the example in the over-production situation above, excess inventory can result in alteration of production schedules, downtime, and frustration.

- **Motion** Wasted motion due to poor ergonomic design results in health and safety exposures. Excessive motion can strain muscles. It can weaken the capacity of the body to withstand contacts. It can cause repetitive motion injuries such as carpal tunnel syndrome. Proper planning and design can not only reduce the potential for injury, but also time exposed to hazards, providing more opportunity for incidents.

- **Extra Processing u**nnecessary steps and poorly conceived procedures can increase time of exposure to health and safety issues.

By carefully planning processes to improve efficiency and quality, we simultaneously minimize safety risks, work can be less hazardous and we can reduce this form of "waste" in terms of reduced accidents and injuries.

Steps for Improving Processes

There are some steps you can use in improving processes—and thus improving efficiency and safety—in your organization:

Map and measure the process. We need to look at the process and see what is being done, why it is being done, and how well is it being done. We need to determine the impact of each process step on costs, safety, and customer satisfaction. Processes can involve anything in the company, not just manufacturing, maintenance, or procedures used in accounting. We have processes in safety such as accident investigations, hazard identification, and risk assessment. We need to map and measure each of these processes as a step in improving things.

Identify the problems experienced by staff, managers, suppliers and customers with the current process. These can be internal and external. Determine what causes frustration, and what issues people have with the current process. When it comes to health and safety, your employees are your customers. Look at health and safety issues from their point of view. Perception is reality, particularly to the perceiver, and if a person perceives an H&S problem, then it's a problem and should be treated as such.

Identify all waste in the current process. Look at waste from an H&S standpoint. For each waste, ask why it occurs and what could be done to prevent it. The best way to do this is with a group or a team, engaging the workforce in the process.

Apply the principles of good process design. What would the process look like if it were perfect? Ask yourself how things would be done if we were not constrained by the process in place now. Ask what would happen if an attempt was made to eliminate every element of waste from the process.

Re-introduce reality into what you've come up with as the perfect process. By forcing people to move from perfection back to the best they can do in the real world, you make people think differently. They challenge preconceptions more and end up with a better solution. Keep introducing realism into your perfect process, until you arrive at a process that can be implemented now.

Involve staff in planning the change process, and ensure the resources are in place to move from the current process to the improved process. Do what you say you are going to do, and don't allow critics to derail your process.

Put in place effective process measures.
Make it the responsibility of the team and line management to monitor the new or modified process, and continue to make changes to the process based on the performance observed in terms of safety metrics, or other appropriate metrics, in terms of efficiency.
Following these steps will lead you to more efficient, safer processes. Better for employees, and better for your bottom line.

A Natural Partnership

Judging by the name alone, lean principles might seem to conflict with the demands of safety. Take a closer look, however, and you'll see that the disciplines actually support each other in at least three important ways:

1. The focus of lean management is standardized work. Standardized work defines process stability. If standardized work cannot be completed as defined, it signals instability. When there is instability, exposure is likely to increase. If work is unable to be performed in the designed time, it signals a problem. Whether assembling a part, mining coal, or drilling for oil, completing it without rushing, by doing the steps specified (no more and no less), in the order they were expected to be done, should mean it is done at a level of exposure the organization accepts. All of the steps cannot be completed? They are unable to be done in the designed order? In both cases, exposure increases and instability triggers problem-solving that can address both.

2. Elimination of waste. Lean defines the elements of waste as over-production, inventory, motion, transportation, defects, and over-processing. An increase in waste can lead to increased exposure. Consequently, leaders make the connection that working on eliminating waste also improves safety.

3. Engagement of people. In addition, respect and care for people is the essence of safety—doing everything you as a leader can do to ensure that anyone who contacts your business experiences no harm. Respect for people is also a central theme in the true application of lean, with its emphasis on having people enabled to contribute to their fullest. For success, both require engagement. They recognize those

doing the work as the content experts for that work. If a change is needed to improve efficiency, the best person to ask is someone who does the work. Similarly, if an exposure or at-risk behavior is to be mitigated, those best able to help identify barriers and potential solutions are those involved in doing the activity or behavior each day.

A leader's role is to make a connection between what the organization undertakes and safety. There is no trade-off. We believe lean management principles and thinking are an effective means to achieve our health and safety goals.

Idea 4: Internal Auditing

Organizations are increasingly under pressure to show how they can create value while meeting the world's economic, social and environmental needs. With increasing complexity and risks due to the overall financial situation, globalization, and demands for business to operate sustainably, companies are challenged to demonstrate that they are responsible and trustworthy.

A mature management system should contribute to the achievement of an organization's goals in all areas of concern, including health and safety. It should also serve to demonstrate due diligence in meeting the demands of all stakeholders. In order to demonstrate that the management system is mature, internal auditing protocols should be routinely and rigorously applied. Accordingly, the results of internal audits and other measures are discussed within a strategic internal analysis of the company, and are a primary resource for implementation of sustainable development initiatives.

During internal audits, the organization itself determines how the parts of its management system are working. The question is also whether the management system is good enough to achieve its objectives.

The internal audit is done to test the effectiveness of the management system. During the audit, an assessment will be made about the extent to which everyone keeps the agreements. Performance requirements will be laid down regarding the management system (the performance assessment), or how the requirements of the system are being met (the system assessment), as well as how the system or procedures can be improved. This is done with the end goal of improving the organization's performance.

The health and safety aspects of the management system should be audited just as rigorously as other aspects.

We recommend development and implementation of a systematic, comprehensive internal audit protocol for our health and safety process. The ISO 19011 standard will be a good resource for us to use to help establish a proper internal audit process. That standard was written specifically for environmental and quality auditing, but the structure is perfectly valid for us in the health and safety arena.

We also believe we can use a tool called risk-based certification to help make our internal audit process most practical. We may or may not seek any external certification for our health and safety management system, but the thinking behind risk-based certification can help us make sure we are paying attention to the right things and using our resources wisely.

Risk Based Certification (RBC)

Risk Based Certification™ is a useful method for focusing the management system audit on issues of greater importance.

Risk Based Certification™ is a structured approach to focus the audit on the effectiveness of a management system capability, in order to mitigate the most important risks and enable the organization to reach its goals. It is based on an understanding of the principle of the critical/vital few, or Pareto's Law. All organizations face myriad health and safety exposures. Not all of these exposures present the same level of risk. Many would be considered trivial and require little or no attention. However, the critical/vital few of these exposures (according to Pareto, approximately 20 percent) have the potential to produce the vast majority of negative effects and, therefore, demand adequate attention.

The RBC internal audit approach will serve as basis for our management decision-making process, and will provide us with the right information regarding the status of critical health and safety issues.

The Framework

The framework is based on the following considerations:

- All organizations have established management systems to reach their business targets.
- Health and safety are key business targets.
- Depending on the relevant business target, some parts of the management system are more critical than others, and there are greater expectations as to how they shall be managed.
- By connecting the internal auditing scope and the agreed-upon focus areas to the critical parts of the management system, internal auditors are able to add a tangible value to the auditing activity: that is, more efficient and effective use of audit resources.
- In the execution of the internal audit, the internal audit team evaluates and reports the existing gaps between the current and targeted levels of the agreed-upon focus areas.
- The results are presented to the senior leadership so that they can plan and implement the necessary improvements.
- The follow-up of the results, and the verification of the established management system status, are part of a continuous process enabling the organization to identify new needs for improvements, either by using the same focus areas for more internal audits, or by following up the findings during the next internal auditing activities.

The framework includes the internal audit as an integral part of the whole improvement process. The framework can work with whatever business goals/targets and target levels are set. We believe this approach can work efficiently and effectively to drive our health and safety management system.
Similar approaches are being used to drive the environmental and economic dimensions of sustainability. It is possible, and desirable, that we develop and implement one such internal auditing process that meets the needs of all our sustainable business development efforts.

DNV GL has developed a model for Risk Based Certification™ that is currently being applied around the world.

Idea 5: Scored Assessments

Organizations measure production by the numbers. If a plant manager asks his or her operations manager, "What was our production today?" he or she will not be satisfied with an answer like "pretty good" or "not great." That plant manager wants numbers: number of units, gallons of throughput, trucks loaded, orders filled, etc. If a corporate executive asks his or her quality manager, "How is our quality running?" he or she will not be happy with a response like, "We're doing just fine!" Again, that executive wants numbers: amount of rework, percentage of spec and off-spec product, number of customer complaints, etc. Even though these numbers are important, most organizations have come to realize they are lagging indicators. As such, they do not provide sufficient information about the actual performance of production and quality processes for reasonable decisions to be made regarding how to improve. Leading indicators have been developed and implemented to provide more specific and meaningful information.

There are commonly accepted, internationally recognized standards that provide process measures: For example, ISO standards for quality and environmental management systems and the OHSAS 18001 standard for health and safety systems. These standards require close scrutiny of the input to management systems, not the output. They are leading indicators. We may well benefit from conformance to these standards, if not certification.

However, when it comes to assessing the level of health and safety performance, many organizations have not made the vital transition from dependence on lagging indicators to more appropriate use of leading indicators. This transition is a must if our organization is to move confidently into the future. No longer can we define our health and safety performance as "improving" or "not bad." Although we need to keep our incident statistics as before, we need to realize that these are lagging indicators and, as such, do not provide sufficient information about the performance of our health and safety system to enable proper improvement decisions.

We would like to propose a slightly different approach, one that enables us to use numbers to measure leading health and safety indicators.

We would like to develop a *thermometer* to measure our health and safety system. Thermometers use numbers to measure the health of an individual. We would like to use numbers to measure the health of our health and safety management system. We propose the implementation of scored assessments.

Scored Assessments, Benchmarking and Business Excellence

During the past thirty years, thousands of organizations across the world have begun using rating systems in various industry sectors. A rating system evaluates an organization's management performance through an effective assessment system that provides a road map towards sustainable business development. And they use numbers to do so. It would be much more useful to organizational leadership to know that performance in a specific element of their health and safety system was at 85 percent of expectation, than to simply know whether or not an expectation had been achieved. A scored assessment allows the organization to more precisely identify strengths and opportunities in their processes.

Figure 15.2 below illustrates the kind of precise information a scored assessment of our health and safety system can provide.

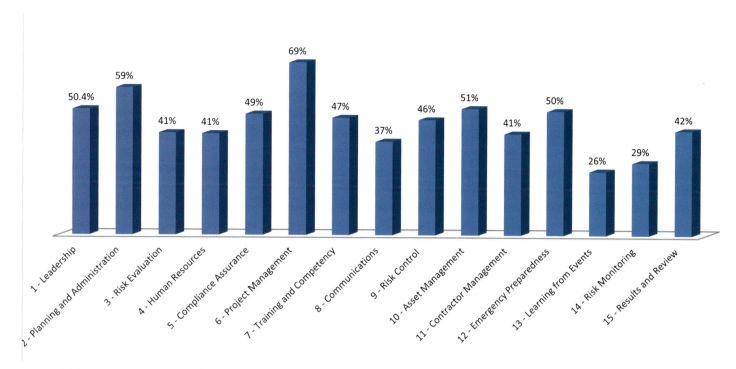

Figure 15.2: Scored Assessment Results

Such an assessment can help an organization achieve operational efficiency, provide assurance of management control and create confidence among stakeholders. It also drives business results and helps organizations establish a competitive advantage.

Based on internationally accepted schemes and best practices, a scored assessment allows leadership to focus on issues of high importance and track their effectiveness throughout the organization. It facilitates setting of quantifiable targets and monitoring of status on both an overall and a detailed level. It is flexible and extend-able to cover all types of organization and stakeholder requirements and it can be customized to cover the preferences of each individual customer.

A rating system can be used either as an assessment tool or as a development tool. As an assessment tool it can produce an evaluation of the overall organizational performance, give an appraisal of individual or group performance, rate degree of compliance with chosen references, such as various ISO standards, the Baldridge criteria and the EFQM criteria, and finally, benchmark organizations, functions, processes. Scores can be presented on a facility level and consolidated on country level; regional level and corporate level and best practice can effectively be established across the organization.

As a development tool, a scored assessment can be a facilitator of synergy, harmonization and standardization in an organization, as well as a means for identifying challenges and threats, an indicator of management commitment and organizational discipline, a strong motivator, and finally, a road-map towards excellence.

A rating system can effectively be used as a baseline for supplier evaluation and monitoring, and also as a tool within a supplier development program. It can help suppliers move from chaos, through structure based on recognized standards, into simplification, and continuous improvement towards the goal of business excellence.

The use of a scored assessment can help us track our health and safety improvement efforts more precisely and lead to more efficient use of resources. We believe that the continuous and proper use of a health and safety management system scored assessment will be a major factor in driving sustainable development.

Conclusion

We started this book with the premise that sustainability or sustainable business development is a primary objective of business today. Although there are three primary dimensions of sustainability, environmental, economic, and social, we determined to focus on one area – health and safety. We firmly believe that the ideas, tools, and techniques we have presented are not only valid and vital for health and safety, but properly applied, can improve an organization's performance in all dimensions of sustainability.

While the information in the book can be very helpful to any organization, the primary and overriding issue is leadership commitment. We are defining leadership in the broadest sense of the word. Everyone in an organization is a leader, whether or not they carry a title. Each stakeholder's words and actions convey their understanding of and commitment to health and safety. And each one must demonstrate their commitment to sustainability by continually answering the question, **"What must we do to ensure we meet our objectives today while preserving the opportunity for future generations to do the same?"**

Key Point Summary

1. In order to ensure regulatory compliance now and in the future, such compliance must be systematically and pro-actively considered in each phase of an operation. A systems engineering approach can help ensure your organization's compliance efforts are sustainable.

2. Health and safety must have a role in strategic business planning. It is both frustrating and inefficient to try to retrofit health and safety controls after business decisions are taken. The prudent organization will include health and safety staff at the planning table and consider related issues on par with all other dimensions of business concern.

3. LEAN manufacturing thinking and principles can provide an appropriate and viable platform for building health and safety into the organization. While LEAN focuses on quality and efficiency, its principles for success are much the same as those for health and safety. Integration of the two reinforces the concept that health and safety are not something separate and apart from running the business and ensures that health and safety become a vital part of an organization's culture.

4. Internal auditing is a critical activity to drive continual improvement. All organizations set goals and objectives, develop incremental plans to achieve them, and assign responsibilities around those plans. Failure to measure progress, identify strengths and opportunities for improvement, and take corrective actions would be irresponsible.

5. Scored assessments provide distinct advantages over non-quantified measures. Numbers speak leadership's language. Organizations measure production and quality performance with numbers. Health and safety should be no different. While lagging indicators are important, scored assessments allow quantification of leading indicators and are much more precise measures than whether a specific activity meets or does not meet a standard.

6. Taken individually, none of the ideas presented in this chapter will be sufficient to drive sustainability. The organization must develop a multi-faceted approach. Above all, leadership from the CEO's office to the front-line must be committed to the future. They must continually pursue their own answer to the question, "What must we do to ensure we meet our objectives today while preserving the opportunity for future generations to do the same?"

Personal Planning

1. What is my organization doing to drive sustainability in our health and safety system?

2. Considering the information in this chapter, what two areas can we implement or improve?

3. What role can I play in driving these system improvements?

Action Plan

Steps	Target Date	Completion Date	Notes

Y – Model for Action Planning

Present Situation

Desired Situation

Need for Change

Present Situation

Stop Responsibility Target Date

THE FUTURE

Chapter 16

THE FUTURE

Let's move ahead a couple years and see what has happened to our friends Henry, Joe, Lisa, and Carlos.

As expected, Henry did retire. He and his wife have moved to their new log home in the mountains. They spend their spare time golfing and traveling. However, Henry has also taken his interest in health and safety to a volunteer position on his local hospital advisory board. He spends a lot of his time helping the hospital improve its risk management plan.

Joe was not promoted to VP of Operations. He has been able to leverage his knowledge of health and safety management and expand his knowledge of the concept of sustainability to the point where a new corporate position was created for him as Corporate Director of Sustainable Business Development. He is now working with all the organization's plants, as well as its support functions, to drive the mission to build a sustainable future.

Lisa is still the H&S manager at the plant. Within the last few months, and at the request of her old friend Joe, she has taken on a dual role as Corporate Health and Safety Consultant. Resources were allocated for Lisa to hire an assistant for the plant so that she could commit more time to her new role. In that role, she spends half her time working with all the organization's plant locations to share the lessons learned from her in-plant experiences and help them improve their systems. Joe's intent is to have Lisa gradually move to a full-time corporate position.

Carlos has been promoted to department superintendent. He remains a champion of health and safety, and has begun classes at a nearby college to become a degreed professional.

None of these things happened solely because of our friends' efforts in health and safety. They happened because of a combination of factors around their work ethic, personal ambition, intellectual curiosity, and ability to take advantage of opportunity when presented. However, if you had the opportunity to ask them, it would be a good bet that every one of them would credit their experiences in health and safety for a large part of their success. They would also likely tell you that, in the drive toward sustainable business development, health and safety is not a bad place to start.

BIBLIOGRAPHY

- A Short History of Nuclear Regulation, 1946-2009 by J. Samuel Walker and Thomas R. Wellock. History Staff, Office of the Secretary, U.S. Nuclear Regulatory Commission
- AccountAbility, United Nations Environment Programme et al, (2005) Stakeholder Engagement Manual Volume 2: The Practitioner's Handbook
- Anderson G. M., (2006). Safety 24/7 Building an Incident-Free Culture. Results in Learning
- Bird F. E., Germain G. L., (2007). Practical Loss Control Leadership. Det Norske Veritas (U.S.A.), Inc
- Bird F. E., (1999). Profits are in Order, Det Norske Veritas (USA), Inc
- Clark M. D., (2001). Your Optimal R Integrating Risk into a Successful Business Strategy. Det Norske Veritas (U. S. A.) Inc.
- Center for Chemical Process Safety (CCPS) of the American Institute of Chemical Engineers, Guidelines for Chemical Process Quantitative Risk Analysis, Second Edition
- Cunningham, T. R., Galloway-Williams, N., & Geller, E. S. (2012, Dec. 14) Protecting the planet and its people: How do interventions to promote environmental sustainability and occupational safety and health overlap?, Journal of Safety Research, 41(5), 407-416
- Department of Chemical Engineering, Texas A&M University, Lee's Loss Prevention in the Process Industries: Hazard Identification, Assessment, and Control, (3 Volumes). Fourth Edition. Edited by Sam Mannan
- Flin, R., Mearns, K., Fleming, M., & Gordon, R.(1996). Risk perception and safety in the offshore oil and gas Industry. Health and safety executive books. Aberdeen: HMSO
- Geller E. S., (2013). Actively Caring for People. Make-A-Difference
- Goleman, D. (1998). What Makes a Leader? Harvard Business Review
- Hudson, P.T.W (1998) Safety Culture - The Way Ahead? Theory and Practical Principles. In L. Hartley, E. Derricks, S. Nathan & D. MacLeod (Eds.)
- http://www.accountability.org/standards/aa1000ses/index.html
- http://www.nestle.com
- ICMM, International Finance Corporation (IFC) and Brunswick, (2013) Changing the Game, Communications & sustainability in the mining industry, ICMM
- Ismail, N. (2012). Environment, Health and Safety: Going Beyond Compliance. Boston, MA. Seabrook, K. A. PS Asks, Professional Safety (Vol. 58, pp. 38-42): American Society of Safety Engineers
- Johnson, B.B. (1993). Advancing understanding of knowledge's role in lay risk perception. RISK: Issues in Health and Safety
- Ket de Vries, M F R. (2005). Global Executive Leadership Inventory.John Wiley and Sons
- Kotter J. (1995). Leading Change: Why Transformation Efforts Fail, Harvard Business Review
- Kotter J. (2001). What Leaders Really Do, Harvard Business Review
- Kouzes M, Posner Z. (2002). The Leadership Challenge. John Wiley & Sons
- National Safety Council.(2013). Injury Facts
- Risk Competences and Safety Engagement Process (1997), Urwin C
- Senge, P. (1990). The Fifth Discipline. Century Press
- Shell Safety Committee (1984) Principles of Enhanced Safety Management. Shell International, The Hague
- The Tomorrows Value Rating (2012, 2013), http://www.twotomorrows.com, DNV GL
- Wordcloud tick from http://www.tagxedo.com/app.html